W9-DGH-743

The author and editor sharing a convivial glass.

S A N S C U L O T T E

A NONKNICKERBOCKER HISTORY

of the

COLLEGE ENGLISH ASSOCIATION

(1938 - 1975)

in seven fyttes, *sive lustra*

By
JOE D. THOMAS
(late of Rice University)
Historicus CEAE primus
Sometime Director and National Coordinator of Affiliates, CEA

Editor: Donald E. Morse
Sometime Executive Secretary and President (etc.), CEA

PUBLISHED BY THE COLLEGE ENGLISH ASSOCIATION FOUNDATION

CUM PRIVILEGIO

ad

IMPRIMENDUM SOLUM

L'histoire

        est

             un roman

                  qui

                    a

                    été . . .

                            —les Goncourt

Absque

HELENA

foret

nihil

CONTENTS

PORTRAITS

A NOTE OF ORIENTATION

This volume was preceded by platform addresses on College English Association history delivered by the Author at two successive annual conventions of CEA: "Reading between the Lines" (unpublished) at Savannah, Georgia, on March 22, 1979; and "À la Recherche du Temps Perdu: The College English Association's **History** in the Making" (privately published, Houston, Texas 1980) at Dearborn, Michigan, on April 11, 1980. Hearing neither was needful as preparation for reading this History, though anyone with access to the second (widely distributed but unfortunately no longer "in print" for new requests) might like to glance through it. The former, never printed, is gone with the wind of speech; luckily, having been composed when little research had been done, it was largely anecdotal and, withal, little more than a twinkle in the hopeful Author's eye.

A word must be said about the organization into *lustra*, or periods of approximately five years. As serious research proceeded, the Author soon discovered that events marking significant change for the College English Association tended to happen in years ending with zero or "5." Because the beginning did not occur in such a year, LUSTRUM ONE (1938-1945) is more like seven years than five. Also, the 1950's and 1960's constituted two fairly solid blocks of CEActivity; but, in order to avoid a brace of chapters monstrously long, the Author refused to hobble his little mind with a foolish consistency and did a hatchet job by boldly splitting each decade down the middle. His own appointment in 1965 as Regional Coordinator gives some cloak of legitimacy to the second of those splits. The *terminus ad quem*, 1975, extends one year beyond his term as National Coordinator of Affiliates (the later form of the title).

Gentle Readers, you have happily now heard the last of "the Author" as abstraction; henceforth, he will reveal himself in his proper person, the grammatical first. Welcome to his parley. *Lasciate ogni paura, voi ch'entrate.*

Early PATRONS – SPONSORS – FRIENDS
(*to mid-February, 1985*)

Patrons

J. Randolph Fisher

Frances Hernández

John H. Hicks

Donald E. Morse

Sponsors

Howard O. Brogan

Marion Folsom, Jr.

Robert E. L. Hacke

Elizabeth and Edward Huberman

Alex B. McFadden

Laurence Perrine

Friends

Cortland P. Auser
Wendell Aycock
Lee Ball, Jr.
W. John Bauer
David S. Berkeley
Dollie Black
Martha L. Brunson
Truman W. Camp
The Culley Clyde Carson family
L. Arlen Collier
James L. Colwell
James W. Culp
John S. Davenport
Angela G. Dorenkamp
Clyde H. Dornbusch
The Drinnan - Webster family

Lavon B. Fulwiler
Harrison E. Hierth
Lee E. Holt
John N. Igo, Jr.
John J. Joyce
Earle Labor
Charles E. Linck, Jr.
The Frances Morton family
T. M. Pearce
Earle Leighton Rudolph
Jo C. Searles
Rosemary and Ira Shepard
Michael F. Shugrue
Helen S. Thomas (*amie de coeur*)
Frederick von Ende
Melvin G. Williams
Peyton W. Williams, Jr.

IN THAT DAWN TO BE ALIVE

being

LUSTRUM ONE (1938 - 1945)

of

S A N S C U L O T T E

A NONKNICKERBOCKER HISTORY

of the

COLLEGE ENGLISH ASSOCIATION

Burges Johnson (1944)

After a painting by Joseph Cummings Chase

LUSTRUM ONE (1938 - 1945)

In That Dawn To Be Alive

The origins of the College English Association[1] have been so much addled and obfuscated that I dare believe I am the first person in the past third century to tell the story straight. I do not mean to suggest that I am the sole extant witness of those primordial events. As a matter of fact, though old enough and to spare, I was not personally present to attest them. As designated Historian, I have had to grub out neglected and sometimes well-hidden truths that often appeared perversely reluctant.

Before unrolling the scroll,[2] I must scatter a few sibylline leaves of pre-history. The teleological if, self-evidently, not the proximate causes of the creation of the College English Association were the birth of Johns Hopkins University in 1876, of the Modern Language Association of America in 1883, of Teachers College (New York) in 1888, of the National Council of Teachers of English in 1911, and (brace yourselves) of the Third Reich in 1933.

In our degenerate later times, we have become so mesmerized by the word "university" that almost every former normal school or agricultural college now boldy wears the diadem. In my own state, for instance, not only do we have a Texas A&M University and a Texas Tech University (these are official names, not short forms); nay, professors at what they still regard as THE University of Texas must now, like medieval scholars adding "de Eblana" or "à Kempis" after their names, identify themselves as "at Austin." We forget that although never officially defined, the magniloquent ten-letter word was once comparatively rare in America, signifying an institution of varied professional as well as liberal education, usually including either a school of law or a medical school, or both.[3] The heart of higher education in the humanities, or liberal arts (not excluding but usually not strongly emphasizing the exact sciences), used to be the college. Even universities commonly had core colleges (Harvard College, Yale

College, the College of the University of Chicago). Once upon a time "college" was a very proud name in the United States, and our colleges and college professors expected to live happily ever after.

Meantime, at German universities and those modeled after them in central and eastern Europe, *Kultur* had been given so thorough an infusion of the spirit of exact science that research even in humane literature had been diverted into quasi-scientific paths. Their influence was strongly transmitted transatlanticly through Johns Hopkins University, which set a beat for the most advanced movement in American higher education. To a great extent, though not wholly, the Modern Language Association was a consequence of that intensified devotion to rigorous research. At first (as again at present), MLA also paid more than mere lip-service to the importance and problems of teaching. A Constitution adopted in 1903 defined the Association's purpose as advancement of the study of modern languages and literatures. In 1928 and 1929, on first and second reading at the annual conventions in Toronto and Cleveland, some amendments were passed by the membership, along with an entirely new set of By-Laws. Possibly as one of the "slight verbal changes" in the committee draft that were made by the Executive Council before the business meeting at Toronto, MLA's purpose was restated in the Constitution as follows: "The object of the Association shall be the advancement of research in the modern languages and their literatures." Substitution of "research" for "study" was a distinction not without a ponderable difference.

The preparation of primary and secondary teachers, meanwhile, was taking on a socially "progressive" character in place of the old indoctrination, on the model of French écoles normales, in supposedly immutable norms for various grades. (The normal idea is being revived of late by movements demanding "accountability" of teachers and proficiency tests for students—to the dismay of progressives suddenly presented with tabulated evidence that for years they have been making rapid retrograde progress.) For the English-teaching profession, NCTE spread the idea of Teachers College and its scions at least as earnestly as MLA spread the German gospel of research.

Professors of English in the colleges, who gladly learned, gladly taught, and often gladly published[4] (a few much, others occasionally, some seldom or not at all), must have had a growing if ill-defined sense of malaise in the world they never made which showed some menace of unmaking them, or of radically remaking those able to roll with a punch. Devotees of liberal college education attending the yearly Thanksgiving-tide conventions of the National Council of Teachers of English were jostled by infinitely larger groups whose interests were centered in teaching pupils of nonage, or in the newfangled training of such teachers. If they then went on to MLA at Christmastide, they found themselves at a convention divided by multiple disciplines, foreign and domestic, but united in seemingly single-minded commitment to rigorous, supposedly scientific research that to some lovers of old-fashioned good teaching must have seemed like rigor mortis. Mark Hopkins and his log would have been heaved out of MLA, though he might just have qualified at NCTE as an administrator.

A subsidiary cause of the malaise that I have postulated arose imperceptibly, but in the long run importantly, from dis-affection with things Teutonic—a note sounded in CEA's early *News Letter* with particular force by the Association's third President, Norman Foerster. German research had contributed to German efficiency, and German efficiency was beginning its disturbing demolition of a world of relative geographical, social, and political stability.[5] I do not know what the still-practicing remnants of the aging New Critics will think of the idea, but I am constrained to attribute, in some considerable part, the Anglo-British revolt against "scientific" literary study to the same anti-Germanism that precipitated French Existen-tialism. I hope no one will infer from that outlandish sugges-tion that I am unaware that both movements had important (and widely different) antecedents which not even a paranoid anti-Fascist could impute to the National Socialist Party. Just the same, Adolf Schicklgruber's Third Reich had branching consequences that only the imagination as understood by Coleridge can trace to their extremities.

Two professors of college English among the older generation in the 1930's, who suffered unsatisfactory experiences
at large national conventions, were first Robert Malcolm Gay
of Simmons College (Boston) and then Burges Johnson of
Union College (Schenectady). They had long been carrying
on a correspondence about their interests and activities. In
1938 neither was listed as a member of MLA, but Johnson
contributed a poem to the June issue of the *English Journal*
(College Edition) of that year and from time to time was active
in the National Council of Teachers of English in various ways.
Presently (I should imagine sometime after the NCTE convention of 1937 at Buffalo in his own upstate New York), he
came round to Gay's view that "it was time college English
teachers had an organization and publication of their own."

As has been generally understood though usually misdated,
the emergence of the College English Association (tentatively
and only briefly named the College English Teachers Association) occurred during an annual convention of the Modern
Language Association of America. The place was New York
City, under sponsorship of Columbia University; the time,
December of 1938—*not 1939*, as long believed and even proclaimed in official CEA documents.[6] The specific occasion,
however, was one of the "associated meetings" that are given
welcome (of late somewhat grudgingly) by MLA because they
tend to swell general attendance and cannot, in any event,
be forbidden. In 1938 the College Section of the National
Council of Teachers of English, presumably at the instigation
of its chairman, O. J. Campbell of Columbia University, decided
to hold such a meeting in connection with the MLA convention in New York. I have not been able to ascertain the precise
date, but believe it most probably was the next-to-last day
of the convention, Thursday, December 29. The place was
the then Pennsylvania Hotel.

How much Burges Johnson and Robert Gay may have had
to do at the start with the calling of such a meeting is not
perfectly clear. They certainly took advantage of it to promote
their pet project of an organization "of their own" for the college
English teachers of America. Johnson, in particular, is known
on much good evidence to have been a very persuasive, though

not unpleasantly "pushy," person. Somehow he, or he and
Gay, contrived to enlist the support or at least tolerance of
Chairman Campbell, who at some point during the associated
meeting yielded the floor of the National Council session to
the separatists. It is clear that not all attendants were agreed
on the necessity or desirability of a new academic society concerned exclusively with English beyond the secondary school
level.[7] One of them, George B. Parks (afterward himself a
chairman of the NCTE College Section), remembered the
episode as follows:

> ...Professor Oscar James Campbell...turned the
> meeting over to Professors Burges Johnson and R. M.
> Gay. These gentlemen announced their intention to found
> a society of college teachers of English, and motions to
> that effect were made and passed. . . .
> I have always thought that Professor Campbell was
> somewhat too generous in abandoning our meeting to
> provide a forum for our severest critics. For several years
> they had been complaining, as I recall, that the NCTE
> was much too teacher's-college-oriented,[8] and their prov-
> ocation may well have led to our separate periodical
> *College English*, and to our separate College Section.
> I am frank to say, however, that the complaints had
> annoyed many of us who had no teacher's college
> connection, and had rallied our support of the NCTE....
> When then Professor Campbell abandoned the chair
> to these outsiders,[9] who proceeded not merely to con-
> duct a forum but to organize a rival society, I thought
> that our hospitality had gone too far. When a motion was
> entertained to form a college English society, I moved
> a facetious amendment to make it read "another English
> society." Professor Johnson was not amused, and it took
> some parliamentary finagling to take out the word
> "another." That is all the opposition I remember, and
> it was not serious. Does the cuckoo expect not even
> token opposition when it takes over another's nest?

Parks went on to say: "I hasten to add that it was probably not the NCTE which had drawn the large attendance at the meeting."[10] He could have meant merely that hordes of English teachers are automatically available for special meetings during any MLA convention, but I fancy that he alluded to some industrious press-agentry that turned out a covey of covenanters. In a helpful letter to me of June 8, 1980, Robert Fitzhugh spoke of mimeographed sheets distributed in advance by Burges Johnson and Robert Gay to advertise their intentions, and insisted that the turn of events at New York "was not something sprung by Jim Campbell on an unsuspecting audience."

From Fitzhugh's letter, I also draw the conclusion that George Bruner Parks considerably understated the amount of opposition to the foundation of a new Association. Burges Johnson once remarked that the birth of CEA had been "brought about by Caesarian section." Robert Gay, who presided during the break-away and therefore was in control of the "parliamentary finagling" mentioned by Parks, recalled that "organized groups were apparently trying to keep a vote o[n] organization from ever reaching the floor; and I had finally to rule that I would recognize no more speakers unless they spoke definitely on the motion to organize." Clearly, George Parks was not without support. Still, following the cited ruling Gay says that "it took only a few minutes, and we adjourned, having accomplished about everything necessary." In his first *News Letter*, issued six month later, Editor Johnson recorded that the assemblage had voted "by a large majority" for a new organization while at the same time they "carefully avoided" the term "independent organization." That reservation is easily understood. Like Archimedes, the founders of CEA needed a platform from which to move their world, and so in order to placate potential future hosts, including NCTE and MLA, they had to walk softly and try to make their long lever look like a little stick.

By the time, however, when the record just quoted from Johnson was printed (June, 1939), the issue had already been effectively settled by an accommodation that was to continue for three decades. Burges Johnson, with the perseverance of a long-time journalist as he had been before becoming a college professor, first softened up the Modern Language Association with a letter dated April 18, 1939, drafted by him and co-signed by twenty-eight other adherents of CEA (or C.E.T.A., the abbreviation first actually used for the Association's tentatively chosen longer name including the word "Teachers"); and then insinuated himself into the Spring meeting of the MLA Executive Council as dinner guest on April 29, where he persuaded his hosts to "exchange courtesies" by arranging an associated meeting for the College English Teachers Association at the December convention. Comity was confirmed by a letter to Johnson signed by MLA Secretary Percy W. Long on May 5 and printed in the first *News Letter* the next month. The arrangement was ratified more fully a year later, when MLA's Council instructed Secretary Long "to sanction public notice" that the College English Association (so renamed even before the convention of 1939) "meets annually with the Modern Language Association." Johnson also saw to it that CEA's original Constitution (adopted, as will be narrated more fully later, at New Orleans following two publications in the *News Letter*) contained a reciprocal provision for his Association to meet yearly with MLA unless for cause the directors should explicitly vote to the contrary, with due notice to the membership. The custom of associated meetings continued, except for interruption by war, through December of 1969; and, on a different scale, was revived in 1978 by inauguration of a CEA miniprogram and cash bar during Modern Language Association conventions—not in any way supplanting the yearly Meeting and Conference conducted each Spring (in cooperation with one or more regional affiliates) that had become the College English Association's official annual convention, New Style, beginning at Notre Dame (with Indiana CEA) in April of 1970.

Designation of the New Orleans meeting in 1939 as the First *Annual* Meeting of CEA, although technically correct (since nothing "annual" had happened at New York), became the source of endless confusion about the year of origin. For instance, delegates attending the final regular associated meeting with MLA at Denver in December of 1969 were issued crimson lapel pennons imprinted in silver: *CEA 30th*

ANNIVERSARY 1939. [11] At the outset, there may have been some feeling that the break-away from NCTE did not properly constitute a meeting, despite the calling of a separate session the next day that Gay considered "in some ways more interesting than the first." We know from his report in the October, 1939, *News Letter* that voices were then and there raised against the conversion of English studies into "social study," but the report also concedes that "very few were able to attend" (because, I speculate, the time may have been late during the proceedings of MLA). When I elsewhere called that follow-up session "in effect. . .the first real meeting of the fledgling College English Teachers Association," a colleague in retirement who had been present (though, not being a member of the National Council of Teachers of English, he had not sat with its College Section the day before where the fireworks began) demurred that it could "by no means be considered the first meeting of the C.E.A." [12] He also remembered planning for the New Orleans convention of the next year as the principal topic, rather than the reported discussion about the proper nature of English studies. Having entangled myself, and with it this modest History, in a semantic problem of when a meeting is or is not a meeting, I fall back (limply) on a Solomonic pronouncement by George Parks, who was an attendant and vigorous participant at the National Council session: "The CEA was founded. . .in 1938,. . .and held its first regular meeting in New Orleans in 1939."

Robert Gay, after the act of secession which he instigated and directed, became less and less active in CEAffairs. He himself generously admitted uncertainty why he, rather than Johnson (who was a little over a year his senior), was chosen to preside at New York: "Perhaps we tossed up a coin.[13] . . . But there is no doubt that Burges, more than anyone else, was responsible for the organization and even the survival of C. E. A. during the first years. [After m]y year as president. . .I could give little work to C. E. A. because I became involved in the establishment of the School of English at Simmons, and that was all I could handle."

Burges Johnson, who was born in Vermont on November 9, 1877, and died at Schenectady on February 25, 1963, was a useful combination of maverick (or—as Robert Fitzhugh, his successor as Executive Secretary and Editor, called him—"academic sport") and go-getter. Before going into teaching he had been a newspaper reporter, an editor, a friend and literary adviser of writers, an editorial administrator for publishing houses, and a man about Midtown Manhattan. In the *Directory of American Scholars* he stated his field as WRITING. As first Editor of CEA's *News Letter* he pretended just to throw together whatever came to him; but communications from people like Ray Stannard Baker, George Ade, Joseph Hergesheimer, Willa Cather, Walter Lippmann, Pearl Buck, and H. L. Mencken—some, including Mencken, writing repeatedly[14]—were not brought by the stork.

Lee Holt, who as a neophyte Ph.D. taught under Johnson at Union College, refers to "Burgy" as "the enemy of pedantry and solemn scholarship," and amusingly mentions "an untidy office guarded by a cigar-store Indian."[15] More formally, he calls him Dr. Johnson in recognition of the degree of Litt.D. conferred in 1924 by Amherst College on the twenty-fifth anniversary of alumnus Burges Johnson's graduation as Bachelor of Arts. Robert Fitzhugh said of his predecessor that "happily and improbably, he became a professor of English, and eventually a head of department, without graduate training or [academic] 'administrative experience.'" I myself, to my misfortune, knew Johnson only through his whimsical column "Jibberings of an Old Ghost," published in the *CEA Critic* beginning a decade after his term of office ended, from 1955 to 1958. At our future communal feasts, whether we enjoyed acquaintance with the original Mr. CEA in the flesh or are only haunted by his genial ghostly presence in the cellerage, I propose that each of us turn down an empty glass—or, better still, that we raise our steins and fling our nightcaps into the air.[16]

Johnson, not President *pro tem.* Gay, presided at the business meeting in 1939 at New Orleans. A "helpful letter" of Robert Fitzhugh not long before his death, from which I have previously quoted in relation to the New York meeting the year before, confirms a suspicion I had developed from strong but inconclusive evidence that Robert Gay chose not to leave the comfort of his Yule log in Boston for an arduous journey across half a continent *in persona praesidentis*. A generous, and indeed plausible, explanation could be that having had his own hour of glory at New York, he felt that Burges Johnson (who was never President, *pro tem.* or otherwise, of CEA) also deserved one.[17]

Indications are clear that the New Orleans meeting, including dinner in the French Quarter at Arnaud's Restaurant (with 190 diners), where the Old Guard of MLA were also whooping it up on the same night, was a roaring success. The price of the banquet, $1.50 a plate (which remained standard for the next several years), shows how far the Quarter could go in the olden daze, when a dollar was still money and even looked like a dollar instead of an American 25¢ piece laid over an English 50p.[18] The one contretemps was something less than a disaster. About sixty more CEAers came to dinner than had been expected, and so a longer interval than planned had to be given to preprandial socializing; in consequence, some speeches were carried over to the already-scheduled "adjourned meeting" of the next morning. Dean William Clyde DeVane,[19] however, who was then a councilor of the Modern Language Association (he had been present at its Executive Council dinner in New York City on April 29, where the associated meeting of CEA was arranged), had time to convey Mother MLA's welcome to the fledgling tucked under her wing. Tactfully, he was elected President of the College English Association for the coming year. Herbert Drennon of Mississippi State College (now University) served as program chairman and as toastmaster for the dinner. In the morning session of Friday, December 29, at which Clifford P. Lyons presided, both Cleanth Brooks and John Crowe Ransom were speakers.

During the New Orleans MLA of 1939, the College Section of the National Council of Teachers of English also held an associated meeting, at which both Burges Johnson and Robert Fitzhugh spoke—as members rather than guests, but still signifying a certain comity between CEA, in which both were prominent, and NCTE. The March, 1940, issue of *College English*, seeming to hint at a lower-than-expected attendance of its own group, stated: "The new College English Association, which professes aims very similar to those of the College Section of the National Council but whose leaders think they can work better independently of the older organization, held two sessions . . . It was announced that the association now has four hundred members . . ." I think it is evident that someone was eying that strayed multitude for possible enticement back to the fold of NCTE. Other evidence, in fact, suggests that efforts of that kind continued for several years. The two organizations have, however, gone their separate ways to the present time, though of course with considerable overlapping of membership. Lately, also, CEA presents an associated program at NCTE's as well as at MLA's annual convention.

Clearly, the College English Association was already thriving by the time of its so-called First Annual Meeting. It had a journal of four to six pages that had been issued in June, October, and December of 1939 and was thereafter to become monthly during the academic year.[20] It had a name as well as a local habitation, guarded by a wooden Indian, for its editorial and executive business. By Burges Johnson's count, the Association represented more than a hundred campuses six months before the meeting in New Orleans, where as was just mentioned a roster of four hundred members was reported. It had, beginning there, a regular time and place for annual conventions in symbiotic relationship with the Modern Language Association. After the business meeting at New Orleans, it also had a formally adopted Constitution.

The vote for that original Constitution of the College English Association (revised in the mid-50's, again at the turn of the '60's to '70's, and most recently at the turn of the '70's to '80's) did not settle all general issues confronting the new society. Drafted by a committee from several parts of the country, it was accepted essentially intact except for one monstrous excision. Article II (Purpose) sounds innocuous enough as printed in advance by the *News Letter*:[21]

> The objects are: the establishment and maintenance of high standards in the teaching of English literature and oral and written composition; the furtherance of cooperation and mutual understanding among teachers of those

subjects; and collaboration with other organizations of teachers seeking similar objectives within their own field of activity.

Nevertheless, the clause was subjected to "vigorous" debate from the floor, and in the end its adoption was "postponed"; by a strict construction, therefore, the new Association left the Vieux Carré without any fixed purpose. Actually, that seemingly serious lack was filled by a tacit understanding among the membership of what they were essentially about.

It may have been a foreshadowing of the Old Ghost that Burges Johnson was later to call himself, when a statement of the College English Association's original stance, concise and unequivocal, appeared in his first *News Letter* (June, 1939) as a bibliographic "ghost." Along with a letter to Johnson signed by MLA Secretary Percy W. Long and dated May 5, 1939, was printed a notice about the new Association—"primarily for teachers of undergraduate courses in English literature and composition, who are not concerned chiefly with research on the one hand, or teacher training on the other"—purportedly quoted from a May issue of *PMLA*. To the best of my knowledge, *PMLA* had no May issue in those times, and I have not found the notice in any other.[22] Whatever the provenience, that phrasing crisply conveyed the way the founders saw themselves and their new organization. What a pity some ghost could not have risen through a trap door to chant it just before a vote was taken on Article II. I fancy that with a little reshaping it could have been accepted as a hasty amendment, and thereafter might well have endured as a short-title statement of CEA's place in the spectrum of academic societies. ("Teacher training" of *college* teachers was, however, another matter that would become important for CEA, especially in the 1950's.)

Two years later, the *News Letter* of November, 1941, printed a "Statement of Purpose" for CEA drawn up by a committee headed by immediate Past President DeVane. It is as much an account of unfulfilled needs that brought forth the Association as a detailing of positive aims. (Incidentally, if any holdouts still believe the myth I have tried to demythologize about CEA's arising at New York in 1939 [cf. fn. 6], I call their attention to the fact that in this article the date of founding is given several times as 1938.) A somewhat stiff and not particularly remarkable statement of purpose for the College English Association, apparently drafted by a single member (whom I have not been able to identify) on his own initiative, but "approved by the directors" at least for comment by the membership, may be found in the editorial columns (p. 2) of the October, 1947, *News Letter.*

The official statement of purpose in the Preamble of the present Constitution of the College English Association is adapted from a corresponding statement in the By-Laws drafted and adopted in the middle 1950's during the Executive Directorship of Maxwell Goldberg. The current text reads:

> Purposes of the Association are (1) to provide opportunities for discussion of the preparation and professional improvement of college teachers of English through annual and special national meetings, regional meetings, serial and occasional publications, and conferences with representatives of other professional organizations; (2) to encourage the humane as well as the immediately practical study of language and literature; (3) to maintain and develop the functions of English studies as a major element in American higher education; (4) to promote fruitful interrelationships among English and other disciplines; (5) to interpret the relationships of the study and teaching of English to society at large; and (6) to receive and administer gifts, donations, and bequests for these purposes.

It is good to have all our intentions spelled out so fully and clearly in stately numbers, and particularly gratifying to see the grounds laid in legal form for the acceptance and administration by the corporation of benefactions. For daily use, I should like to revive a declaration that appeared in the most casual possible way. An "Extra" issue of the *News Letter* in August, 1943, which has already been mentioned in an especially arid bibliographical footnote, contained a fold-out map to show the far-flung stations of American armed forces. Carto-graphic projection of the globe left spaces or "ears" at the upper left and right, which were filled by brief general state-ments about CEA and about its *Newsletter* (irregularly so spelled). The former is worth quoting, for it is an epitome of the tacit early—and, on the whole, abiding—consensus about the aims of the Association that I have postulated:

> The College English Association is a society of teachers interested primarily in the problems of teaching, who believe that literature is something more than a social study and that written composition may be a fine art as well as an essential tool. By closer acquaintance and exchange of ideas they hope they may be able to deter-mine more wisely both immediate procedures and the ultimate goal.

If sound ought to echo good sense, what a credit that ephemeral, throw-away passage was to a society of college teachers of English!

One point of early dispute was really serious and—more serious still—was for the nonce settled in a wrong-headed way. The draft Constitution proposed in 1939 basically provided for limitation of membership to teachers of undergraduate English in **four-year** institutions "of recognized standing," together with minor other categories including retirees and professors who had played truant to the classroom for careers of critical or creative writing. The limiting phrase that I have blackened at once became a bone of contention, but following debate was by vote allowed to stand. Not subsiding after the business meeting at New Orleans, the controversy broke out in the *News Letter*: for instance, an insistent communication (printed in November, 1940) by a teacher in Pasadena Junior College pointed out the high repute in California of two-year institutions. In view of the struggles of CEA in the 1950's, 1960's, and subsequently—partly mine own, especially in the later '60's—to attract junior and community colleges into our field of gravity, the exclusionary attitude appears unthinkable until we remember that the founders had a sort of Platonic

Idea of the college of liberal and humane studies as occupying a discrete locus on their CEA-charts of higher education.

I am pleased to report that within a year and a half the snobbish restriction sickened and died of galloping lunacy. From the beginning, Burges Johnson (who editorially defended the limitation) held that desirable exceptions could be made by committee rulings or if necessary by amendment of the Constitution. Though no early membership list before 1946 is known to me, I have a shrewd suspicion that from the start any two-year people who may have innocently or impertinently sent in annual dues ($2.00) were placed on the rolls. In the *News Letter* of February, 1941, a box on p. 3 concerning eligibility for membership suddenly leaves out the "four-year" phrasing and briefly prescribes "a 'recognized' college." Three months later, on p. 1 of the May issue, membership is explicitly declared to be open to teachers of English in junior colleges, with the rather offensive proviso that they "may by action of the Association be placed in a special class."[23] Snobbery died hard; for decency's sake, I pray that the insulting addendum was never invoked.

Later, as will come out several *lustra* hereafter, an Association of English Teachers at Two-Year Colleges was our "affiliate organization" in the 1960's, and indeed in a Pickwickian sense our creation, but it suffered a premature demise—bequeathing to CEA as parent what was left of its treasury, in accordance with the final clause about "Purposes of the Association" (essentially unchanged from the By-Laws of 1955-56) quoted a few pages back. Today, members of the College English Association from two-year, three-year,[24] and any-number-of-years colleges and universities are as perfectly homogenized as the lacteal strains blended at a creamery. My successors in the office of National Coordinator of Affiliates have included an extremely able professor at a two-year county college in New Jersey, Edward ("Regenschirm") Cifelli. In some matters, luckily not many, our sainted founders were sopho-mores.[25]

Still another point of controversy, or at any rate protracted discussion, was the nature of publication which the College English Association ought to undertake. Burges Johnson regarded his own *News Letter* as a makeshift or interim production until that question could be settled. As might have been anticipated, some members desired and others opposed a conventional scholarly or critical quarterly. Some felt that a magazine would be desirable. As also was to be expected, the question of the meaning of "magazine" (a term Johnson rejected for his *News Letter*) was raised but never answered to general agreement. John Erskine, who I am sure must have been drawn into the budding organization through personal solicitation by Johnson and who signed the petition to MLA of April 18, 1939, suggested—with Johnson's concurrence—that the Association publish and offer for sale brief monographs, pamphlets, or brochures at irregular intervals as suitable authors and topics presented themselves.

In the long run, all those ideas came to fruition. During most of our history, the *CEA Critic* was a combined magazine and news letter, with an increasing infusion of "learned" as well as critical articles and reviews amid its pedagogical papers and its news of the Association. In 1970 it underwent karyokinesis, yielding our present *Forum* and new-born *Critic*—the latter (and to a degree the former, also) now richly deserving the name of scholarly-critical quarterly.

In the short run, the *News Letter* and the—by title—supplanting *CEA Critic* (the interesting reasons for the CEA-change of name will be revealed "in our next": see LUSTRUM TWO) persisted as pretty much the kind of readable miscellany that Burges Johnson founded. Early-on (I trust the refined Briticism will be admired by Commonwealth readers of this eclectic History), the Erskine - Johnson idea had borne seed fruit when a pamphlet by I. A. Richards, *A Certain Sort of Interest in Language*, was mailed with the October, 1941, *News Letter*. It was the first of the Chap Books[26] that for decades would give our Association a peculiar distinction. The new *Critic* (reborn November, 1970) deliberately borrowed the format of the Chap Books and to some degree, *mutatis mutandis*, has continued their function. The format of the old *Critic* survives, *mutatis etiam mutandis*, in the *CEA Forum* that began publication in October of 1970.

I suppose that the gentle reader, after having persisted thus far, will not fall down amazed if I now generalize that the hallmark of the periodical edited for the College English Association by Burges Johnson was controversy, almost unfailingly good-tempered and generally, in reflection of his own temperament, good-humored as well. Among the topics that drew protracted debate—now, with a pair of writers dueling: thrust, parry, and riposte; now with wider melee— were the inevitable questions of the content and conduct of Freshman English (in those benighted times no one had yet learned to say Freshperson English); the related question of a college professor's obligation to semi-illiterate matriculants;[27] the legitimacy of courses in contemporary literature (both Henry Seidel Canby and Willa Cather wrote on the negative of that issue), in creative writing, and in semantics; and, with growing urgency, the role of English professors and English curricula in the "war effort"—a battle of paper bullets that began long before the bombing of Pearl Harbor, running from sword rattling (by Norman Foerster and Harry Warfel, among others) to denunciation of propaganda within the classroom whatever its cause or form. Letters (or extracts from letters) signed by the Secretaries of War and Navy, printed in the *News Letter* of May, 1942, and reprinted in a September "Extra" issue, replied to an inquiry from Johnson about college English in wartime with ringing affirmations of the importance of mustering into both services personnel who had been taught to use the language clearly—with no mention by either of literary study.[28] More and more the question of relevance, supposedly a later fetish not reverenced before the waning 1960's, began to be bruited as a criterion for the choice of reading assigned in college English courses.

About one matter which might have been controversial, harmony was manifested from the start: the importance, or rather necessity, of regional CEActivity. Deplorable cynic that I am, I will begin by mentioning an ambitious early project, not exactly "regional" yet of that ilk, that evidently came to naught with considerable style. The first issue of the *News Letter* reported that a member traveling abroad was about to propose affiliation with the English Society (not further identified). If the intended reference was to the English Association (London), the emissary was pretty badly snubbed.

The January *News Letter* of 1941 quotes a communication from Vice-President Frederick S. Boas, for the English Association, reiterating that society's refusal of an offer by CEA "to become responsible" for the 1941 volume of *Essays and Studies*, which he says the Oxford University Press thank-you-very-much is quite capable of handling on a continuing basis. He adds that for "a financial contribution of a satisfactory kind" the English Association's magazine, *English*, would be willing "to insert articles by your members," provided the quality was adequate to editorial acceptance. A subvention of, but emphatically **not** contributions to, *The Year's Work in English Studies* (which Boas was then editing) would also be entertained. Surely the pachydermic Burges Johnson must have cringed at least slightly under that douche of ice, for which the British notoriously have better use than in beverages. (You will even more admire the aplomb of the English Association spokesperson when I tell you that he had recently been bombed out of his London home by what England at war unflappably called "enemy action.")

The original Constitution of the College English Association directed: "Regional meetings shall be encouraged..." Even before formal adoption of the compact during the national gathering at New Orleans designated as the First Annual Meeting, President *pro tem*. Robert Gay had a New England CEA going in the Autumn of 1939. Afterward, looking back at a distance of time upon the beginnings, he was to give public witness of his devotion to the regional idea: "My year as president I spent largely in trying to promote the organization of local sections;[29] for the only hope of sustaining a national association seemed to lie in the formation of such groups." Experience of nine *lustra* has reinforced the wisdom of that "only" but never forlorn hope, even if a few national leaders have occasionally (fortunately, only momentarily) lost clear sight of it.

The New England College English Association was formed during the convention of the New England Association of Teachers of English at Worcester on November 3-4, 1939, and has since normally met (except for interruption by war in the 1940's and an unexplained spell of inactivity in the early '80's) twice a year. A Mid-Atlantic (or Middle Atlantic) CEA was organized by Robert Fitzhugh on February 10, 1940; it, too, still exists. A regional group for Virginia, West Virginia, and North Carolina, which first met in Richmond on October 26, 1940, is the ancestor of a surviving North Carolina - Virginia CEA. (West Virginia has gone partly astray in ways to be brought out later.)

Indiana CEA is a special case. The June, 1939, issue of the *News Letter* contains a message from President Henry F. Staunton of an existent Indiana College English Association, already so named and antedating by some four or five years the "new national organization" he begins by mentioning. This Indiana CEA affiliated twice with the national Association: first on May 11, 1940, "retaining its complete autonomy," for what was called a "trial year"; again, presumably permanently, on May 1 of 1948. An Indianapolis convention (1941) was a fruit of the first mating.

In both the New England and the Indiana affiliates, non-members of the national College English Association were explicitly declared eligible. The New England regional constitution, however, drew a distinction between "active" members belonging also to the national body and "associate members" merely attending "sectional conferences." Both categories carried entitlement to vote and hold office.

Another long-time affiliate has been variously denominated through the years: Upstate New York CEA; Western New York State CEA; of late, after a former Greater New York CEA became New Jersey CEA, simply New York CEA—though it still admits members from neighboring states (nowadays, I presume, exclusive of New Jersey). It seems to have had a beginning, though not the name College English Association, long before CEA itself was formed. As I read the shadows on the cavern wall of a microfilm room where for a term of years I lived and tried to breathe and have my being, sometime probably early in the 1930's college teachers of English had two unstructured Springtime gatherings at Cazenovia Lake, about midway of the Buffalo - Syracuse - Schenectady area. Some Jungian memory among oldsters of the region produced a revival of the practice in the Autumn (October 19-20) of 1940, this time rescheduled, because of a large registration from eleven colleges, to Syracuse. Since few stayed for the second day (a Sunday), the next year a one-day meeting— described as "still in the experimental stage"—was arranged at the Linklaen House, Cazenovia, for Saturday, October 18, 1941. Two notable facts are recorded: thirteen campuses sent representatives, and Burges Johnson read a paper. The November *News Letter* refers to that meeting as the annual Conference of College Teachers of Up-State New York, but does not report affiliation with CEA—which, nevertheless, I can hardly imagine Johnson not attempting. Possibly certain unpacific events in the Pacific Ocean less than two months later dissuaded the experimenters of Cazenovia from any immediate new experiments with tighter organization.[30]

When I became Regional Coordinator, at the end of 1965, the mast of the *CEA Critic* listed— besides the Association of English Teachers at Two-Year Colleges as an AFFILIATE ORGANIZATION—sixteen regional affiliates.[31] At the end of the 1970's there were twenty-two. National membership has never been compulsory; instead, as I urged (unpersuasively, though others had supported the idea before me) in my daze as Coordinator, it is now encouraged by a rebate system of joint national - regional memberships at reduced combined cost. Time has confirmed my strongly expressed judgment that CEA draws at least as much strength from affiliates, which are its seedbeds of growth, as regionals take from the national Association. In the wise words of the Constitution (Article XII): "Organizational affiliates...shall retain their autonomy as members of a federation, and shall not be considered as provinces of the national organization." For "federation," if you are sentimental, you may prefer to read "family."

During the immediate pre-war and war years of our earliest history, the real question was not how much regional activity was desirable but how much national activity was appropriate. The second and third CEA Presidents, William DeVane and Norman Foerster, as successive members of the Modern Language Association's Executive Council, could not have been unaware that some other members of the MLA hierarchy did not look with perfect favor upon the new and somewhat bumptious College English Association that was enjoying their yearly hospitality.[32] In December of 1940 the *News Letter* reported that President DeVane had proposed to the directors of the College English Association that CEA become mainly regional in its activities. Two delegates from each affiliate would sit with the Board of Directors (which included the officers, ex officio) at the annual meeting, composing a kind of senate. Otherwise, most of the Association's "important work as a group interested in teaching" would be "conducted in regional meetings." Accompanying testimonials showed the individual directors to be largely favorable to the proposal. At the annual meeting that year, it was referred to the membership for vote by ballot, but I haved failed to find any final tally or plain statement of the outcome in subsequent issues of the journal. In the fullness of time, no such formal decision proved necessary, for conditions of war meant that within a year or two almost all academic meetings tended to become effectively regional. CEA met with MLA at Boston in December of 1940, and again at Indianapolis in December of 1941 despite declaration of total engagement early in the month; after that, for the duration, Association meetings if held at all were mainly attended by members in the local area.

Perhaps partly in continuing consequence of dislocation by war and rumors of war, when I belatedly came on the CEAn in the early 1950's—and continuing through the 1960's—conventions of the College English Association were generally a rather small and chummy sideshow within the larger circus of MLA, though I do recall one jumbo CEAssemblage at Chicago (to be reviewed later, in due course) with auditors thronged up and down passageways of the Palmer House. Any idea of an annual three-ring, full-length performance of our own had to wait for Notre Dame in 1970. Nowadays we have our separate big-top, which one or more regional affiliates synergistically join in setting up. What Association operates the greatest show on earth in the 1980's, I leave to the candor of the Republic of Letters to judge.

A banquet in the French Quarter of New Orleans having been the centerpiece of CEA's 1939 convention, a dinner was

again announced for the Second Annual Meeting, at Boston,
the next year. It turned out, however, to be a luncheon served
on Saturday, December 28, which by some amazing interven-
tion of gremlins conflicted with the luncheon of the College
Section of the National Council of Teachers of English.
Seemingly, Robert Gay of Simmons College, local arranger
for the College English Association, had neglected liaison with
his opposed number in the rival, as it were parental, organization of college English teachers. Reporting the fouled-up
situation (after the fact), CEA's *News Letter* shed what I refuse
the temptation to suspect were crocodile tears, calling it "unin-
tentional and undesirable." How attendance divided between
the simultaneous luncheons, or how many persons with dual
membership attempted to look in upon or even eat both, Clio
declines to declare. Those faithful to CEA heard Cleanth
Brooks break New Critical ground by reading an explication
of Ernest Hemingway's "The Killers" jointly composed by
himself and (three guesses) Robert Penn Warren.

At the business meeting of the 1940 Boston convention,
Treasurer William Rittenhouse Richardson (College of William
and Mary) reported the College English Association's accounts
to be comfortably in the black—along with a tidbit of information volunteered by Secretary Johnson that "money advanced
at the launching of the new Association from a small Carnegie
grant was more than covered by the treasury balance; so that
if return of the advance ever seemed advisable the CEA would
still be solvent." Robert Fitzhugh explained that Johnson had
obtained leave to use "a little money left over from a foundation grant." What relation, if any, that permission bore to "an
unexpected Santa Claus who scorned fixed categories" is not
clear to me. Johnson mentioned the mysterious stranger, as
having financed the early *News Letter*, while responding—over
a decade later, during another Association convention in
Boston—with some "un-Proustian reminiscences of things
past" to his nomination and election as "CEA's Younger [*sic*]
Statesman of 1952." As a pensioner of TIAA, I trust that the
debt to the Carnegie Foundation, if debt it indeed was, has
long ago been repaid in full with 3% interest compounded

semiannually, which would have been about right for the paradoxical daze of small but comparatively easy money.[33]

For the coming year, 1941, "A Presidential Message" by
Norman Foerster, who had been elected at Boston, was
printed in the February *News Letter*. It set a keynote for stren-
uous times, and for the annual meeting at the end of the year,
by calling on the Association to find appropriate ways of "serving the national welfare," especially in the first two years of
college English. The next month, parallel and opposed articles
by Foerster and Robert M. Smith of Lehigh University set
off a debate, some of it atypically acrimonious, about "slanting"
the teaching of literature for propaganda. The United States,
still technically at peace, was already loining for war and to
a degree militarizing even such organizations as the College
English Association. One interesting contribution to the debate
came from outside. When Burges Johnson invited Walter Lippmann to say something about "teaching for democracy," Lippmann allowed him to reprint (in the *News Letter* of May, 1941)
a newspaper column headed "On Being Too Current" that,
in substance, recommended an old-fashioned liberal education in place of "current issues."

In October, 1941, Editor Johnson welcomed with playful
humor an equally (un)salaried Associate Editor: Cornell M.
Dowlin, Assistant Professor of English at the University of
Pennsylvania; and announced transfer of publication from Union
College to the University of Pennsylvania Press, which is
known to have volunteered for that function. Although the
arrangement did not last long, Dowlin was the first of a pro-
cession of Associate, Assistant, Managing, Consulting, Guest,
and Interim Editors through whose services CEA has pieced
out whatever imperfections of time, energy, or ability might
otherwise have handicapped the incumbent Editors. It is not
at all evident how much or what kinds of service Associate
Editor Dowlin actually rendered, or even for how long. From
his academic situation at the newly designated publications
office, I should assume that he was in effect Managing Editor.
In the February, 1942, *News Letter*, at least stop-press notices
are seemingly directed to be sent to him in Philadelphia

(though, frankly, I do not find the intent absolutely clear: it could be that they were to be in the Editor's hands at Schenectady in time for him to forward them to Philadelphia before the stated deadline). When an "Extra" was issued in September of that year, Union College replaced the University of Pennsylvania Press as publisher or place of publication, and the short-lived Philadelphia imprint was never restored to the *News Letter.* Dowlin's name remained on the mast through November, 1942; the next month, Robert T. Fitzhugh of the University of Maryland replaced him, with the title of Assistant (not Associate) Editor.

When in the Spring of 1943 Assistant Editor Fitzhugh departed for service as Lieutenant (jg), United States Naval Reserve, the name of John Abbot Clark showed up in replacement, purportedly "for the balance of the current year," but remained on the mast only one month. Beginning in January, 1944, J. Gordon Eaker (then Professor of English at Kansas State Teachers College, Pittsburg; now Professor Emeritus, University of Houston) assumed the function of Assistant Editor without portfolio. I use that expression because until the September issue of 1944 no title accompanied his name on the mast. A curt "Asst. Editor" was inserted in that one issue; then both name and title were dropped, until both were restored (with the title more politely spelled out) in an August issue of the next year.[34] Gordon Eaker, who had participated in CEAffairs since 1939, contributed a principal article (on instruction in English under the Navy V-12 program) to the same issue of the *News Letter* where his name (sans title) first flew from the editorial mast. The gap in his term of service, during the academic year 1944-45, can be explained by his becoming head of the Department of Language and Literature at his college. I shall speak of him again in LUSTRUM TWO, for he continued and intensified his service to the journal under the Editorship of Robert Fitzhugh that began toward the end of 1945.

CEA's Third Annual Meeting was held at Indianapolis on December 28-29, 1941, with a surprising wartime attendance of 141—indicated as about 20% of the membership, which thus may be estimated at around 700. At the dinner, delegates heard readings from the works of James Whitcomb Riley, and two addresses by President-Elect Howard Foster Lowry. His own was an attack on what later would be known as the publish-or-perish syndrome. The other was the Presidential address, read by Lowry because of President Norman Foerster's "enforced absence." Titled "Have We Kept the Faith?" it was a plea for "belief in man" and for educational emphasis of "the dignity of the individual man." The over-all theme of the meeting, planned prior to but following hard upon Pearl Harbor, was: What Can Teachers of English Do to Help Preserve the Democratic Tradition in America (with particular reference to Freshman and Sophomore courses)? A committee was appointed to consult with George F. Reynolds about a proposed collection of literature embodying democratic ideas.[35] Manifestly, there was now a far bigger war to wage than the lost skirmish against "slanting."

As could be anticipated, one question overrode all other thinking of the College English Association in 1942: The Undergraduate English Classroom during This War, and After. Accordingly, that was announced in October as a general theme for the annual meeting projected for New York on December 28-29. Dinner would be served at an inflated cost of $1.75 instead of the customary $1.50. In a sobering vein, the October *News Letter* also quoted a radio speech by the U.S. Commissioner of Education ominously suggesting that some literature had become an expendable luxury. Plain handwriting was now on walls for those with eyes to see.

MLA's Secretary Percy Waldron Long, who also served as its program chairgentleman, alas proved no sharp-eyed Daniel. Optimistically, the Modern Language Association continued planning its usual December convention, for which he prepared the usual Long program; in it, the usual associated meetings of the College English Association and the College Section of NCTE were as usual announced. Business was not, to be sure, proceeding altogether as usual. MLA moved the site of the convention from Washington, D.C., where it had originally been scheduled, to New York City. The small Advisory Committee was prudently empowered by the full Council to modify arrangements in an emergency. When, in

late November, Uncle Sam's transportation-snarled bureaucracy snarled that travel during holiday periods for attendance
of large conventions must be abated, Percy Long plausibly
pleaded that a meeting in Manhattan really would require
almost no travel at all, for it would be to all intents and purposes "localized." A printer's fist on the cover of his printed
program pointed to the legend: "Primarily for members in and
near New York, N.Y." The beleaguered functionaries of government lent him, however, only a part of one ear. While he was
frantically trying to flap it with a somewhat one-sided correspondence, on December 5 the Advisory Committee sprang
a trap under the yet declaiming Secretary by totally canceling
the MLA convention of 1942.

Never was the resourcefulness of Burges Johnson more
brilliantly exhibited. He performed a quick editorial overhaul,
in particular of the forme for his December *News Letter's* front
page, announcing that the meeting advertised for December
28-29 had been deferred to a one-day stand in New York on
January 23, 1943. The formerly somewhat clumsily phrased
theme was streamlined to read: College English in Peace and
War. Luncheon would be served instead of dinner, with the
hallowed price of $1.50 restored. Howard Lowry would give
a Presidential address. Christopher Morley would speak, by
no means on haunted bookshops or on the Trojan horse but
(with predictable whimsy) on "Accelerated English," and John
Erskine on "What Should Teachers of English Teach?"[36] In
addition to the luncheon addresses, there would be a morning panel on the relative importance of the classics and contemporary literature, and in the afternoon a report by Harry
Warfel on government plans for English departments. A highly
respectable emergency arrangement!

With a few deviations, the irregular "annual" meeting of
January 23, 1943 (*for 1942*—if we may borrow the style of year-
books), proceeded as planned. The topic that had been
announced for the morning panel was shaped up to the times
by an added question: "Propaganda for Democracy?" Besides
guests, 126 members attended the luncheon, where despite
a sprained wrist John Erskine patriotically rendered, on a
valetudinarian hotel piano, a one-handed national anthem.

Howard Lowry being obliged to leave early (he quaintly asked permission of the Secretary) for the funeral of a colleague, the President's Message on the theme of this-war-too-will-pass was read for him by Harry Warfel, doing double duty as Lowry himself had done thirteen months before at Indianapolis. Henry Seidel Canby, whose connection with the College English Association went back to his signing of the petition to MLA of April 18, 1939, was elected President for 1943 (and prospectively, as things were to work out, for 1944).

In the spirit of the late Wilkins Micawber, the Modern Language Association incredibly again planned a full December convention for 1943; and, when it was inevitably canceled, rather pathetically printed and "issued for the record" a program with abstracts (the accidental ancestors of a present useful custom in *PMLA's* table-of-contents) of the papers that would or could or should have been delivered. The College English Association, with better perception of realities at a time when the decisive actions of a total, global war were in preparation, decided that one general meeting in a calendar year was enough.[37] Instead, turning with doubtful validity to a provision in the Constitution of 1939 for polling of the membership by mail under certain circumstances, the Board of Directors ruled that ballots to be sent out late in 1943 and to be returned by February 1, 1944, would be *quantum sufficit* for the normal annual meeting.[38]

Those ballots distributed at the end of 1943 and tallied early in 1944 were founded, more firmly, on still another clause in the Constitution, to the effect that officials of CEA could succeed themselves once but (with exemption of the Secretary and the Treasurer) once only. The slate called for re-election of all incumbents for another term; the reported division was 94% aye and 6% nay. Accordingly, Henry Seidel Canby was for two years (1943, 1944) President of an organization in which he presided at no real annual meeting.

Again in 1944 MLA bravely planned, still for New York as in 1942 and 1943 (three's the charm), a December convention—which, despite the Battle of the Bulge, was actually permitted to proceed. (The program was based on the one aborted in 1943.) The NCTE College Section went along, with a dollar-and-a-half dinner meeting; but once more the College English Association passed,[39] and so was not to have any participation at a Modern Language Association convention before December of 1945. Readers of the *News Letter* of that year could have known only by hearsay, for in a strange misprint the date was announced as *January 29*, as if the irregular meeting in January of 1943 (for 1942) were about to be imitated in 1946 (for 1945). No wonder that only about fifty members assembled at a Chicago tea room for a cheap ($1.35) lunch and "a discussion of the Association's future plans." They included three directors, Executive Secretary Robert Fitzhugh (who earned his new-filed spurs by presiding), and Assistant Editor J. Gordon Eaker. One of the two resolutions passed lauded Burges Johnson for meritorious service to CEA and awarded him an honorary life membership.[40]

Mark Van Doren, elected as President for 1945 by ballots mailed out once again in December of 1944, was re-elected for a second term by the same process a year later. It is true that CEA members attending their quasi-national meeting (which MLA did not even acknowledge in its program as an associated meeting) in Chicago on December 29, 1945, as subsequently those attending the more exactly advertised gathering at Washington, D.C., the following December, were told that they could bring instead of mailing their ballots if they so chose. No statement was made of how many did so choose; I should guess comparatively few. Willy-nilly, the mail system of balloting for officers was by then permanently established. In the new era of Spring conventions, results of elections, wholly conducted by mail, were at first announced at the annual "meeting and conference." By a recent amendment to the Constitution, elections are once more conducted in the Autumn, as they were for long years when the outcome was revealed at the yearly associated meeting with MLA in December; results are thus now available for publication in the *CEA Forum* in advance of the yearly convention.

That in the mid-1940's members of CEA got together at least twice in New York City, typically at Mark Van Doren's Columbia University, can be regarded as the consequence partially of a relative lack of opportunity to attend traditional national meetings; partially of a general policy in the College English Association—even more than in the Modern Language Association—of actively promoting regional and metropolitan organization, action, and responsibility. Readers of this winding History with long memories may recall that in 1940 President William DeVane had broached a plan for decentralizing the Association's "important work as a group interested in teaching" into dispersed regional meetings. Response to a questionnaire circulated among the membership in 1943 showed overwhelming support for holding such meetings (at least for the time being: the question was framed rather open-endedly, as was natural during the uncertainties of war) in place of a national convention, and also for allowing non-members as well as members of national CEA to attend. (Cf.—or review—fn. 37.) On the question of merging the College English Association with either MLA or NCTE, the vote was negative.

As national CEActivity declined, the October, 1943, *News Letter* announced the humble birth of a war baby that was to grow up into one of our most persistently active affiliates, Ohio CEA: "A group of C.E.A. members and their associates, from six institutions in central Ohio, met June 17 on the campus of Capital University, Columbus, to discuss the teaching of English to Army and Navy units." In March of the next year, Burges Johnson offered to promote "small meetings wherever two or more colleges are conveniently adjacent"; in October he renewed the offer, suggesting Saturday sessions, not specifically limited to members of the national Association, on post-war problems of college English. War had its blessings, if less than peace. I am fain to believe that World War II gave another timely turn of the screw that, from the beginning to the present day, has always held fast the federation or family of national and regional College English Associations.[41]

I close the chapter of CEA's beginnings with a fact that deserves mention among the other notabilia. After steady sturdy service almost as long as Johnson's in essential tasks largely unsung, Treasurer William R. Richardson asked to be relieved and, in 1944, was succeeded by his department head at the College of William and Mary.[42] The opening act of our Association's dramatic appearance on the stage of the English-teaching profession was approaching its curtain; a new CEAn was about to be set for a second, to be laid in the uncertain but hopeful post-war era. An impressive and illustrious *lustrum*, despite difficulties and disturbances, presaged the dawn of an even brighter day when the lights of the world could once more shine.[43]

I deem LUSTRUM ONE to terminate in the Autumn of 1945, with the voluntarily relinquished tenure of our most authentic Founding Father, Burges Johnson, as younger capable hands bravely took up the onerous-honorable burdens he had so long carried. For nearly four more *lustra* the Old Man of the CEA continued to watch and cautiously counsel the society of teacher-scholars he had nurtured and shaped. As humorously self-proclaimed Old Ghost of our gatherings, he remains for always the College English Association's tutelary spirit and guardian angel against snares, delusions—and pomposities.

(Here endeth the reading of LUSTRUM ONE.)

Notae pedales for

LUSTRUM ONE

[1]Legally, since 1954, The College English Association, Inc.

[2]Let me say at once that I shall disappoint the lemon-squeezers of historical records by neglecting to furnish tightly footnoted citations of sources. (In my footnotes, I usually have altogether other fish to fry.) Concerning the earlier periods, most though not all information came out of a slightly coupé microfilm of CEA's *News Letter* and subsequent *CEA Critic.* For those who do not have time to peruse the journals serially (no pun intended), they have been well indexed, with the indexes also microfilmed: to the end of December, 1958, wholly by Lee Holt; thereafter, until annual indexing was instituted, laboriously by Earle and Betty Labor. Thus anyone who runs to Xerox University Microfilms can run down whatever (s)he specially wishes to read.

[3]For nearly fifty years, Rice University, having (as it still has) neither, modestly denominated itself the Rice Institute.

[4]An analogy could be drawn to publication by teachers at present-day two-year colleges.

[5]That supposedly stable world was of course not very old, largely going back only to 1919. Germanicism had also taken a hard drubbing in the original World War. (Someone ought to record for a wondering posterity the fact, symptomatic of attitudes in 1918, that patriotic dime-stores at least in Kansas City sold toilet tissues imprinted with the spike-helmeted likeness of Kaiser Bill, as Wilhelm II was known in America.) Without Hitler, Germany would nevertheless almost certainly have regained its full prestige—much as Japan has done following World War II.

[6]The By-Laws drafted in the 1950's, at about the time I was becoming a member, declared in the opening sentence of the Preamble (and I accordingly long believed): "The College English Association was founded in 1939 at New York. . ." The letterhead furnished to high officers for official correspondence of the Association used to carry the following bottom line: "College English Association / Established 1939." It is readily CEAn that a revisionist Historian of the Association has his work cut out for him.

[7]CEA remains to the present the only such society in the United States. I do not say "in America," for in 1957 Canadians founded a counterpart with the initials *ACUTE* (Association of Canadian University Teachers of English). When I once pronounced the seeming acronym like the adjective it spells, the member I was addressing (a visitor on my campus) almost broke his spectacles by violently raising his eyebrows nearly an inch. He informed me with gravity that one says A - C - U - T - E, pronouncing each letter or full word rather than uh-CYOOT. You will not be surprised to learn that as Regional Coordinator for the College English Association I never succeeded in persuading ACUTE to accept Comity Affiliation. (See, hereafter, LUSTRUM SIX.)

[8]A more recent view of their complaint, independent of Parks' letter but complementary to it, can be found on p. 123 of J. N. Hook's lively "personal view" of NCTE history (*A Long Way Together*, Urbana, ©1979), where he speaks of "the secession of a few college-level CCTE members who felt that the Council was insufficiently attentive to college interests and who founded the College English Association." See, however, the footnote (9) immediately below for a suggestion of the problem of ascertaining how many were actual renegades from the National Council, and how many "outsiders" from the start.

[9]As I have previously indicated, at least Burges Johnson was not an "outsider" to NCTE; I am not so certain about Robert M. Gay, who despite his early leadership of CEA does not appear to have been markedly an "organization man."

[10]That "large attendance" can be estimated at around 325, for in entirely separate accounts Gay later spoke of "between three and four hundred being present" and Johnson (writing at a time close to the event) mentioned "approximately 300."

[11]Until recently one of the Association's two periodicals routinely carried a slightly ambiguous circled legend on the front cover, reading "THE CEA CRITIC / An Official Journal / of the / College English Association / founded in 1939 / Vol. No. /..." (with the date of issue printed as the bottom line). It could, if one chose, be read as correctly indicating that not the Association but its journal was founded in 1939.

[12] (A trivial note:) As will be mentioned in LUSTRUM TWO, some uncertainty was evident in the early daze about whether to treat the Association's initial letters as a solid block or as three abbreviations, with or without periods and spaces. I CEA them as an acronym or quasi-acronym.

[13]I have a different theory: that they counted honorary degrees. Gay held two diplomas of Litterarum Doctor; Johnson, but one.

[14]Mencken ends one of his notes with the hope that Johnson is "in the best of health, and full of sin." Bliss was it in that dawn to be alive; **being there** must have been very Heaven!

[15]The wooden Indian is still remembered at Union College, but my informant there had not discovered its present habitat. I do not know whether "Burgy" conferred a name upon the graven image, but if he did I am willing to wager that it was "Lo."

[16]An anthology could be made of Johnson's dry humor to which we should be wetting our lips. Usually some context would be needed to do it justice. I give as a more or less self-contained quickie sample his suggestion (*News Letter*, March, 1942) that "some technical men might learn English and substitute it for whatever it is they now use when they write." A ghost of rare esprit!

[17]Johnson, like Gay, at first intended to serve only briefly and insisted on the title of Secretary *pro tem.*, to match his collaborator's title of President *pro tem*. As his term kept being extended, he shed the temporal qualifier and tinkered with the title in two stages, first as bare Secretary, then as Executive Secretary.

¹⁸ To avoid generation shock to young professors brought up to believe that only persons bearing credit cards could possibly carry enough clout to attend a national convention, I decline to quote the modest (ought I say shy?) rates in those innocent times at MLA's official hostelries and CEA's sometimes subsidiary ones.

¹⁹Orthography has yet to solve the riddle of the spelling of his last name. CEA publications usually printed it solid, as I shall continue to do, but sometimes spaced before the "V." As author, DeVane or De Vane apparently gave his editors and publishers carte blanche. I have never seen his holograph signature, but will bet a Susan B. Anthony dollar to a doughnut (or vice versa, as dictated by the state of inflation) that he left a little room but not a full space between the two parts of the name, in much the same impartial spirit by which students put an apostrophe directly above the "s" of a possessive noun.

²⁰Inexplicably, the front cover of the Index of the *News Letter* and *CEA Critic* for the period from June of 1939 through December of 1958 (published November, 1968) states that the journal "appeared nine times a year from 1940...and five times in 1939." (Equally inexplicably, it also spells *News Letter* as a solid word with only one initial capital letter.) If there were more than three issues in 1939 or more than eight in either 1940 or 1941 (or in 1945, a special case on which we shall soon break our bibliographic shins), I wish I could find copies of those omitted from the microfilm. Somewhere in the early *News Letter*, Burges Johnson alludes to the possibility of his sending out multigraphed bulletins in Summer months; did he actually do so, without numbering them like regular issues of the journal?

Half-accidentally, the *News Letter* did settle down to a frequency of nine times per year. There were "Extra" issues in September of 1942 and August of 1943. The December issue of 1942, although the ninth of that year, was designated as Vol. IV, No. 8, because the September "Extra" had borne no number. Neither did the August issue of 1943 when it too appeared as an "Extra"; however, in October it was retrospectively treated as having been No. 6 of Vol. V: the October, 1943, issue was designated as No. 7, and the mast now restated the frequency (formerly given as eight issues per year) as "Nine Times a Year." The volume for 1944 included a September issue as No. 6, making December again officially No. 9 as in 1943. In 1945, as will be explained later (see fn. 34), only eight issues appeared but some extraordinary anomalies of numbering still allowed the December *News Letter* to be shown as No. 9. After that, publication of the journal was regularized to the months of January through May and September through December.

Much later (1962) the volume year of the *CEA Critic* became October through June (the June issue being No. 9). Finally, in 1970, alchemists in an unsmoky den at Notre Dame dissolved the journal into separate but qual quarterlies: the *CEA Forum* and a new *CEA Critic* which, neglecting to avail itself of the useful bibliographic device of "n.s.," perhaps inadvisedly continued the volume numbering from a displaced journal of identical name but radically different format and scope. The story of that thaumaturgy must simmer in the cauldron before being ladled out at a chronologically appropriate time of this gourmets' History.

[21]In June, 1939; again, slightly revised (but with no changes of Article II), in December, 1939.

[22]Invoking something a little more than guesswork, I have a suspicion that the notice may (no pun) have been printed on the inside back cover of the June, 1939, number. Librarians routinely cut away back covers of journals when binding annual volumes; some ruthlessly cut away the front covers, too, even ones that carry the table-of-contents—instead of binding them in at the back for permanent reference. (It is all part of library economy.)

[23]This seemingly grudging liberalization was connected with a multiple-question ballot mailed to the membership on February 15, 1941, with the *News Letter* of that month. The whole episode remains something of a mystery to me, for I have not discovered any record of a final tally of the voting. (I shall recur to this matter in text.)

[24]I cannot affirm that literally "today" we have any members from three-year colleges (a mid-stage sometimes occurring while junior colleges are working their way up to senior status), but it has happened in the past. On the other corridor, I am certain that applicants from universities with graduate divisions were never at any time refused membership by narrow construction of the "four-year" provision in the original Constitution.

[25]A footnote originally inserted here was determined to be libelous, scandalous, defamatory, indecorous, and offensive to faith and morals. Copies engrossed on asbestos-coated parchment will be deposited in the Library of Congress and the Department of Manuscripts of the British Library, with instructions that they shall remain sealed until the year 2085 and then opened by deconstructionists.

[26]Every conceivable form of the name was experimented with before the capitalized form in two words without a hyphen was adopted. At first, CEA Chap Books came out rather frequently: the second, *Short Words Are Words of Might* by Gelett Burgess (do not try to discriminate his name from that of Burges Johnson, for it cannot be done successfully), was distributed with the December, 1941, *News Letter* and offered to outsiders at the hardly

exorbitant price of 10¢ a copy—the cost of a taxi-dance, as also of a certain type of lurid novel that had pioneered in paperbound publication and could still be purchased in some dime-stores.

Since the Editorship of Donald Sears, which ended with the mitosis of the journals in the Fall of 1970, CEA Chap Books have been issued only rarely. An extremely useful bibliography of all those published through April of 1970 (numbering twenty-six) can be found on p. 15 of the April, 1970, *CEA Critic*.

[27]In an article of December, 1942 (titled, with ironical ingenuity, "The Humanities—Yes!"), Robert T. Fitzhugh brings his argument round to the conclusion: "But literacy first, and then the Humanities as something more than a playground for scholarship." The note of back-to-basics, by no means exclusively a recent tune, was often heard in the early years of CEA.

[28]Johnson appears to have been shaken by those pointedly functional evaluations of English teaching, predictable as they surely were. In rebuttal, he editorially quoted a statement by President Franklin Roosevelt (made well before Pearl Harbor) to the effect that students should continue "the normal course of their education until and unless they are called...for other patriotic services."

[29]During the early daze after emergence of CEA from NCTE's College Section, the word "section" was understandably often used in referring to regional affiliates. "Group" was sometimes applied in the same way.

In this unpedantic History, I shall ordinarily ignore such minutiae of nomenclature. What's in a name? While serving time (for my sins) in a Registrar's Office, I learned I could safely look away from the stray majuscules and ungallic accent marks written into many student signatures.

[30]Mention, even full reporting, of local or regional meetings in the early journal was not apodeictic of CEAffiliation. I should be tempted to claim that the successful "start for the new regional group of Tennessee English teachers" reported by the *News Letter* to have occurred at Knoxville on April 17-18, 1942, inaugurated the present Tennessee CEA (or Tenne-CEA, as I have never been able to persuade its officials to rename their affiliate), except that close reading shows that the meeting was not limited to college and university teachers; it appears more likely to have been inspired by NCTE than by CEA.

[31]In candor, I have to add that sometimes one finds "ghosts" in lists of purportedly extant academic societies, just as one encounters non-existent books or articles in the bibliographies that some professors (and many students) compile. On that topic, I could a tale unfold, of manifests and men.

[32]To the account of hostility which I have previously given in another publication, and which I shall not repeat here, I add Max Goldberg's testimony that "the CEA was called 'that crack-pot outfit' and 'troublemaker'" and "suffered the slings and arrows of outraged Establishments." Goldberg makes clear that the bone of contention with MLA, or at least with some of its officials, was CEA's valuation of teaching as the major concern proper to college English professors, secondary in importance to research as then rather narrowly conceived.

[33]Readers who cannot believe what I have just said should ask their grandsires and granddames for confirmation. In the 1940's certificates of the (since abandoned) Postal Savings System paid only 2% interest, as was reasonable in view of the printed declaration that "The faith of the United States is solemnly pledged to the payment of the deposits made in postal savings depositories." Those principal sums were not compounded at all, and of course no one had even dreamed of daily compounding by electronic bookkeeping. (On the other hand, bankers still knew how to figure interest with a pencil, and so did not have to plead that "the computer is down.")

[34]The issues for 1945 show several anomalies. (No wonder: Burges Johnson, already Professor Emeritus at Union College, was in transition from seven years of CEAmanship to fresh turf and canters new.) The January *News Letter* was amusingly misnumbered as Vol. VI, No. 10 (instead of VII, 1). A single issue dated February - March, 1945, was (correctly) shown as Vol. VII, No. 2; and April as No. 3. May (in most years, then, the month of the fifth issue) was erroneously designated as Vol. VII, No. 5. An August issue (abnormal, but not unprecedented) was shown as No. 6, October as No. 7, November as No. 8, and December as No. 9. (The month of September, when transfer of authority to a new Editor was being arranged, had no *News Letter.*) Thus, the issues actually published in 1945 totaled only eight, despite the designation of the last as No. 9. If you are lost, you are in good company: so were the Editors.

[35]The resultant volume, *Freedom Speaks* (1943), ultimately paid royalties of several hundred dollars into a CEA fund for benevolent purposes at least partly connected with the war. Hope being a cardinal virtue, I devoutly hope that this patriotic anthology helped English professors help their students help win the war and peace.

[36]Erskine's address (more compactly titled *What Should English Teachers Teach?*) was published as the fifth CEA Chap Book in March, 1943.

[37]I say "better perception" and yet wonder at a proposal announced in the October, 1943, *News Letter* to hold an ersatz annual meeting chopped up into regional gatherings at several selected cities. Given a widely dispersed membership from CEA to shining CEA, the notion of conducting

a binding national election in that manner was a brainstorm that seems quickly to have blown over.

[38]Declaring the ballot taken in lieu of a December meeting to **be** the annual meeting (as the *News Letter* boldly did) was a slick trick. The Association may have done well to start polling its members before somebody with a legal head cried foul about recent elections. Constitutional provision—hardly pre-vision—required that actions taken by fewer than a quorum, then defined as "more than one-fourth" of the membership, must be ratified by a mail ballot. On that basis, my best combination of fact, deduction, speculation, and intuition leads me to infer that those taken at New Orleans (1939) were almost certainly canonical, at Boston (1940) very probably so, at Indianapolis (1941) evidently not, and at New York (January, 1943, for 1942) clearly not unless there been a severe dropping-out of members at war, as was implicitly denied in the August *News Letter* of 1943: "...our membership is not falling off..."

Present members who have not read the current Constitution (which has never, to my knowledge, been printed except in Xerox or multilith and so is not easily accessible) may be interested to know that seventy-five personal or "authenticated and qualified" proxy votes "shall constitute a quorum at any annual or special meeting." In the failure of that number (and I always neglect to count heads when I attend a business meeting, not believing in borrowed trouble), a follow-up poll by mail is still technically obligatory.

[39]The *News Letter* of November, 1944, contains a small back-page notice reading (in full): "In response to a renewed and most earnest request from the Office of War Transportation, the CEA will not hold its meeting in New York until after March 1st." The reference presumably is to a local meeting that took place on April 21, 1945, at Columbia University in conjunction with the New York Council of Teachers of English.

In point of fact, the distinction between national and regional meetings became, partly by intention, blurred during the war years. MLA's surprisingly accomplished convention of December 27-29, 1944, for example, was (like one previously aborted) tactfully announced as "Primarily for members in and near New York, N.Y." At the time when annual meetings became impossible, difficult, or inadvisable for the College English Association, I judge that apart from the executive/editorial office the greatest center of CEActivity may well have been Columbia University.

[40]For the inauguration of CEA's Appointment Bureau during the convention of 1945 at Chicago, see LUSTRUM TWO.

[41]I do wish that Henry James had titled his *amusette* "The Turning Bolt," for a screw suggests more tightness than I intend to intimate. The fact is that CEA is almost free of defined lines of authority between the national

and the regional Associations, and yet something strongly holds the system together. It could be psychic forces still emanating from the Old Ghost. If that be so, may the cock never crow to call Burges Johnson's blithe spirit away from us earthlings still at CEA.

[42]Jess H. Jackson, who herewith achieves a footnote in history.

[43]The mixed metaphors in my peroration are supplied for use, by members still happily in teaching service, on worksheets or tests of faulty sentences. All claims to residual royalties are waived.

DAZE OF RECONSTRUCTION

being

LUSTRUM TWO (1945 - 1950)

of

SANSCULOTTE

A NONKNICKERBOCKER HISTORY

of the

COLLEGE ENGLISH ASSOCIATION

Robert Tyson Fitzhugh (*aetat. ca.* 70)

LUSTRUM TWO (1945 - 1950)

Daze of Reconstruction

The first illustrious *lustrum* of College English Association history was an age of finders and makers, led and dominated (without domineering) by Burges Johnson. In December of 1938, young of heart and vigorous of invention despite having already celebrated his sixty-first birthday, Johnson had gone from New York State to New York City to help a slightly improper Bostonian, Robert Malcolm Gay, pry dissenting colleagues free, at least partially, from the National Council of Teachers of English. Thereafter for nearly seven years, mostly during a difficult time of war, he was the effective shaper and principal public presenter of a unique society of college professors of English.

In retrospect, the Second World War seems to have driven as relentlessly and logically as *Oidipous Tyrannos* straight to termination. Hitler's hordes collapsed in northern Africa, then in Russia; in Italy the Axis was broken asunder. Doomed from D-Day despite a rain of rockets and a bulge into Belgium, the Third Reich—now humbled to Deutschland unter Allen—swallowed rancid dregs of defeat at Rheims. In Japan, the catastrophe of Hiroshima and Nagasaki brought tragedy to final curtain by the second day of September, 1945. For contemporaries enduring the war through immediate experience, however, whether in armed or civilian services, there had been no sense of ineluctable scenario, no absolute certainty of victory or even of any end at all. When news was broadcast of the first atomic strike, I remember exclaiming with exultant relief: "It will be over in six months," which I apprehended (never dreaming that in about a week the tenacious Japanese would cry "Hold, enough!") as a prediction of incredible brevity.

A veteran of foreign service in an earlier World War, Burges Johnson heroically bore the domestic burden of CEA for the

duration of the second—even for a year beyond his retirement
from the classroom—until the longed-for moment when, all
passion spent, peace began reconstruction of a shaken and,
abroad, a shattered world. In a tinier but not unimportant
theater, the time had arrived also for rebuilding of the College
English Association as a *force majeure* in the changed and
changing educational environment of America.

September of 1945, when hostilities were formally declared
ended in Tokyo Bay, was a month in which Burges Johnson
published no *News Letter* for the Association, while winding
up to fling the torch into more youthful outstretched hands.
The election lit on a comparative youngling nearly thirty years
Johnson's junior yet a veteran both of the war and of CEA's
journal, on which he had served as Assistant Editor before
donning uniform as an officer in the Naval Reserve. The
transfer of the Executive Secretariat and Editorship to Robert
Tyson Fitzhugh, announced in the October issue of the *News
Letter*, was completed when he edited that of November.
Fitzhugh, who was to manage CEAffairs during the coming
lustrum, 1945 - 1950,[1] had been prominent among the founders
from what he afterward called the "exploratory meeting" at
New York where his motion from the floor, leading to creation of a provisional College English Teachers Association, may
have saved the proposed organization from being parlia-
mentary-maneuvered to death.

I should like to say, in speaking of the termination of
Johnson's invaluable service, that the torch had never sput-
tered nor the candle guttered in his firm hands. Alas, the
closing triumphant years of World War II, which may look
today like the best of wartimes, were the worst of times for
an Editor and Executive Secretary of a non-military society.
Apart from merely logistic troubles about supplies and printing,[2] the somber thoughts occupying every mind were a trifle
dispiriting for the production of a light journal—"not so much
a magazine as a gossip sheet about our guild," as Editor
Johnson called his *News Letter*. Only a limited number of
weightier articles were possible about "accelerated education"
or about programs for cadets, for active personnel temporarily
billeted to campuses, and for civilian students of engineering

(usually deferred to take a speeded-up degree, although I saw engineering Seniors ruthlessly called up for combat training during the supposedly desperate Battle of the Bulge); and a smudged crystal-ball beclouded speculations on the favorite topic of post-war English.[3]

Special topics connected directly or indirectly with the war did, of course, frequently present themselves. In the August "Extra"issue of 1943, Johnson published an Open Letter to the Secretary of the Treasury, calling sharp attention to economic disadvantages afflicting college professors in an inflationary period,[4] and warning that neglect of their problem "will drive out of the profession" those flexible enough to leave it. Presumably he was intimating a need for some kind of differential tax relief, or perhaps for relaxation of the tight restraints on wages and salaries; he never quite got around to outlining a concrete proposal for the United States Treasury Department to consider. In another editorial (December, 1944), Johnson opposed universal military training—which, though paradoxically impossible in time of war when limited facilities had to be concentrated on enlistees actually at arms, was much under discussion for possible future use—but did almost come to proposing something like a universal service program.

All in all, as the war went on, CEA's *News Letter* became even more what it had been from the beginning: a reflection of the mind and temperament of Burges Johnson. At the same time, while contributed substantial articles tended to fall off, he gave increasing space to short letters from the membership airing views on a wide range of topics, light or heavy, whether related to war or not. Evidently to him the "Letter" of the journal's name was a signifying word: he was always calling upon readers, particularly newer members who had not written previously, to send in their ideas. Now, whether communications came in more abundantly or he became less selective, they filled as much as whole pages of the *News Letter*, at least those spaces not occupied by the Editor's own miscellaneous musings[5]—as, for instance, his defense of the right of a younger generation of poets (e.g., Dylan Thomas) to their own peculiar modes of expression. Inevitably, the hoary and apocryphal quotation of comic letters to wartime bureaucracy (probably dating back to the War of Jenkins's Ear, if not to the campaigns of Alexander or Julius Caesar) sneaked in: "Please send my wife's form to fill out"; "You changed my little boy to a girl, does this make any difference" (with full stop, not interrogation point); and all that familiar ilk. Boners of any kind seem to have tickled Burges Johnson.

When Robert Fitzhugh received the *News Letter* of the College English Association out of the probably tired but not failing hands of Johnson,[6] he was given something like a tabula rasa on which to write change. Although the Editor Emeritus kept in touch with him and occasionally contributed a piece to the journal or a suggestion for the Secretariat, I read between the lines that he had the tact not to irritate his successor by repining against novelty.[7] In his humorous way, Johnson warned Fitzhugh: "If you make CEA into just another Educational Organization, I'll haunt you." The latter, who (in a memorial notice after the Old Ghost's transit from the earthly CEAn) was to refer to his predecessor as a "man of infinite zest," did not forget the admonition and passed it on to his own successor, Max Goldberg. It was the Incomparable Max who made me conscious of what he defined as a Zany Element in the traditions of our Association; I have never forgotten, either, or let others forget. If we shadows have offended . . .

Right away in the new Editorship, innovations began to appear, though not to any jarring degree that might have unnerved old-timers. One was a "Personals" column (nearly aways a good idea for a house organ, yet never really established as a regular feature until early during the Max Goldberg regime, after which it again lapsed), in which news and notes of the membership could be briefly bruited. Under the title "As Others See Us," Fitzhugh ran a number of articles of substantial length presenting the point of view on English studies of ex-service men and executives. Later, he introduced a column headed "Bulletin Board" for general notices of interest.

Another seeming invention, which had enormous ultimate consequences, was as a matter of record a harking-back to a practice early adopted but, for seeming lack of interest among the membership, quickly dropped by Burges Johnson: announcement of situations wanted. A few such notices (headed, in point of fact, "Personal") were inserted in 1940 and 1941. Bob Fitzhugh[8] revived the custom in the first number he edited, offering (in a box at the top of p. 2 in the issue for November, 1945, headed "For Members Only") to "print keyed notices of availability and [to] put interested parties in touch with one another," and also "to print for any administrative officer the notice of a vacancy or of a prospective opening in English"—adding: "For the time being, at least, there will be no charge." Under this box appeared a solitary notice, keyed as A1, of a "Teacher Available."

Then, almost instantly revising and enlarging the plan— remember that Editor and Executive Secretary of the Association were still one and the same person—Fitzhugh announced in the next *News Letter* (December, 1945) creation of an Appointment Bureau to be operated with the assistance of Joyce Louise Kellogg, whom he credited with having suggested the idea, and supported by "a small fee . . . charged members who register." This issue carried one notice each of a "Teacher Available" and of a "Vacancy Reported" (the latter in public speaking and debating). Based on a continually updated roster, columns listing candidates available, together with an occasional reported vacancy, appeared in the journal under the aegis of the new Bureau, and from time to time catalogues of registrants were also sent to English departments. In addition, long before the Modern Language Association borrowed the patent, a face-to-face placement operation was set up at the yearly conventions.

For decades, this complex enterprise devised by Robert Fitzhugh was carried on successively by him, by Albert Madeira, by Donald Sears, by Edward Huberman, and by Edward Harris. In 1973, however, for reasons partly connected with revised placement procedures of MLA, the College English Association's Bureau of Appointments (the name had varied) was dropped deeper than did ever plummet sound into the Slough of Lost Enterprise. Through long previous years, many a seeking professor, department head, even dean (and for all I know veep or prexy) had gained happy employment by registering with our service, and contrariwise many a harried administrator had found exactly the kind of candidates sought, because of a literally personalized and continuous twelve-months-a-year operation of the Bureau.

Executive Secretary Fitzhugh lost no time in taking his new placement show on the road. Readers who started this plodding narrative at the beginning and are not trying to hop-skip-and-jump about among the goodies will remember that from 1942, when (*faute de transport*) the Modern Language Association was obliged to cancel its hallowed rite of convenery, until 1945, CEA—whether meeting separately in January, 1943, or refraining from meeting in December of that and the next year—interrupted its sequence of conjoint conventions. In 1945 the College English Association managed a sort of reduced national meeting at Chicago while MLA was there. What has not been recounted in the opening chapter is that Fitzhugh and "an attractive young woman member," as he pleasantly called Joyce Kellogg, arrived on December 26, a day ahead of the official assembling of the Modern Language Association, set up their Appointment Bureau in the appointed MLA hostelry, and proceeded to enroll applicants—the first two being refugees from academic warfare in Texas—at three dollars a head. According to Fitzhugh's account, this modest fee proved adequate to expenses (and indeed some time thereafter it was reduced by a third, to two dollars, before being still later raised to as much as five because of increasing complexity and cost of operations). With hindsight we perceive, incunable, a bouncing infant that was to grow into a great and thriving child of CEA and yet to perish in vigorous maturity, aged twenty-seven years and four months, of success and influence. Requiescat in pace. Resurgat cum gloria. Amen.

"Reconstruction" is perhaps not too strong a term for a complex of subtle differences, from the start, in Editor Fitzhugh's *News Letter*. I am reminded of eighteenth-century controversy about the aesthetics of ornamental gardening: Johnson's journal gave an impression of pleasing disorder; Fitzhugh's, of pleasing order. Where editorial or printshop disorder did occur in the latter, as in a misdated announcement about the Chicago meeting of 1945 and in occasional typographic anomalies, it was accidental and of a certainty regretted—sometimes with formal printed apology. Johnson had affected to throw together whatever came to hand, a disingenuous pretense that enfolded some grains of truth. Both Bob Fitzhugh's *News Letter* and (in two senses) succeeding *Critic* bore the clear impress of a methodical editorial hand, far from the pastepot of a mere compiler, but happily without sacrifice of the enlivening wit and humor that Burges Johnson had permanently infused into Association tradition.

In ways that I might have trouble in analyzing and that, if analyzed, might seem more absolute than I intend to suggest, form and continuity of the journal shaped up. Editorials sounded like meditated short essays, not half-extempore ruminations. Other editorial practices, always frankly experimental when not casual with Johnson, were more nearly stabilized. As already indicated, new departments were introduced. In one directly attributable to Assistant Editor J. (conservatively standing for Jay) Gordon Eaker, columns headed "I've Been Reading" brought reviews, by Eaker or other members, of books significant for the profession. Book notices had been sporadic and not especially common in Johnson's *News Letter.* One issue, the "Extra" of September, 1942, did cluster what many years later would have been called minireviews of ten "English Textbooks to Meet the Wartime Emergency" (including two respectively co-edited by Robert M. Gay and by Burges Johnson)—intriguingly confessed, however, to be "paid advertising."

Under Fitzhugh, Gordon Eaker continued as Assistant Editor (which he had been also during parts of Burges Johnson's tenure) through February, 1946, and then in March was promoted to Associate Editor.[9] From September of 1949 through Fitzhugh's last *CEA Critic* in December of that year, Eaker's title—recognizing the important function that clearly had come to engage his greatest effort—became Book Review Editor. With the March, 1950, issue of the *Critic*, his title was further modified to Literary Editor. And to think that during all the years when I was National Coordinator of Affiliates and his frequent professional associate in sundry ways, he never mentioned a word of quondam glory in the organization that I was so pushily personating! Modesty, thy name is Eaker. (To invoke it, be sure to pronounce **ACRE**, as in land measure—*not* **"EEKer,"** as in screeches of Victorian ladies reacting to mice.)

Description for publication of instructional wrinkles that work in the classroom, encouraged by Editor Fitzhugh, has continued off and on as one of the helpful features of CEA publications. Reports of regional meetings—with much more such activity available to be reported in the peaceable aftermath of war—were to a degree regularized during his Editorship, a process that would be continued and intensified by Max Goldberg and several later Editors. Fitzhugh published the first known roster of the College English Association (possibly the only one ever printed except by Addressograph plates or computer printout) in the *News Letter* of November, 1946, with names of members arranged alphabetically by state and, within states, by academic institution. He also went beyond Johnson's usually rather bland typographic style, experimenting with bigger, bolder, and broader headlines that were not uniform aesthetic triumphs, as he tacitly acknowledged by continued tinkering.

The change of name to *CEA Critic*, to be explained a page or two hereafter, had a certain psycho-editorial effect in further making the journal more serious, as Editor Fitzhugh's temperament would in any event have caused it to become. In candor, I have to admit that, as usually happens, a Law of Compensation intervened to prevent everything from being gain and nothing loss. There had been a certain comfortableness about the casual Johnsonian habits—similar to what we feel in old shoes, keg beer, and *Pickwick Papers*—that of a surety was not lost, but still was modified. An analogous shift (though entirely different and also seen as more extreme) occurred in the late 1960's, when in the opinion of a high officer of the Association, expressed to me with pointed emphasis, the *CEA Critic* was drifting in the direction of a magazine of college humor. A new surrogate Editor having abruptly taken over, there were "some changes made." (Of all that, including why I said the remark was made to me with pointed emphasis, more anon in an appropriate chapter, where mayhap and *mea culpa* the luster of our sixth *lustrum* could appear slightly dimmed.)

Concurrently with the removal of CEA's administrative and editorial office from the sign of the wooden Indian at Johnson's Union College in Schenectady, the place of publication was also transferred to the University of Maryland, at which Robert Tyson Fitzhugh had been a member of the English faculty (with leave-of-absence, 1943-44, for naval duty) since 1929. In the Autumn of 1946, a year after his assumption of the Executive Secretariat and Editorship, he moved from College Park to Lehigh University at Bethlehem (USA), again changing the imprint of the *News Letter* as well as bringing editorial and administrative operations to his new academic home. Once more in the Autumn of 1947, he transferred himself, his CEA functions, and the journal's imprint to Brooklyn College, where he stayed for the long remainder of his teaching career. [10] In the third journal and final *News Letter* published from there (December, 1947), [11] he inserted a short article headed "Brooklyn College - What's That?" in which (with an assist from a colleague who he said "doubled in brass" as the department of public relations) he explained the history and relationships of his new collegiate home in the then nearly mint condition of what would later expand into the vast CUNY system, commenting on its degree programs and division into Day and Evening Sessions. In that brief account, a reader today can sense post-war American higher education on the rapid move.

Change of the title of the *News Letter* to *CEA Critic*, which occurred a little beyond midway of the Fitzhugh period, beginning with the January issue of 1948, was connected with the acquisition of a second-class mailing permit. That privilege, valuable in mitigating the cost of distribution, is subject to rigid postal regulations. By no means available for occasional publications, it requires a definite subscription price with a specified minimum frequency at stipulated intervals. Connection with a particular post office does not permit floating journals, although re-entry at another is possible when the place of publication legitimately changes. In addition, before the College English Association ever sought the privilege, a ukase had been promulgated by some mighty Third Assistant Postmaster General to the effect that no more second-class mailing permits would be issued to publications having in their title the word "Letter." [12]

From October of 1944 through May of 1945, the mast of the *News Letter* carried a pro-forma notice that application for a second-class mailing privilege was pending at the post office in Schenectady, New York. Manifestly, a wholly different name would be requisite, and likely also registration at another post office with a change of Editor. As early as the issue of November, 1944, Johnson invited confidential application from persons willing to "understudy" his position; surely, having undoubtedly combed his own Schenectady area for any suitable successor likely to mail from there, he must have realized that the whole problem would devolve upon someone based elsewhere. And thus, of course, it happened.

The new Editor early opened the *News Letter's* columns to suggestions for another name, which came in abundantly. (Prophetically, they included "Forum," thus planting a seed that would germinate a quarter century later.) Somehow "Critic" emerged as front runner, but it carried with it a subsidiary question of whether, if adopted, it would be "CEA Critic" or just plain "Critic." In the *News Letter* of May, 1946, under the heading "New Name Proposed," appeared the following statement and request: "It is proposed at a convenient future time to change the title to THE CEA CRITIC. Comment invited." The comment so laconically provoked must have been surprising, for in January, 1947, Fitzhugh editorially declared: "CRITIC is dead, done in by democratic process. CEA in the title offends many members . . ." (He suggested substitution of THE SCRIBE.)

Presently, as a matter of fact, Burges Johnson wrote in from his travels to settle all issues with a penstroke. His letter, editorially headlined "CRITIC Redivivus" when printed in the *News Letter* of March, 1947, averred that since the journal was a medium for mutual and professional criticism, both constructive and negative, by members of the College English Association, therefore the title ought of right to include "CEA" along with "Critic." The naked word "Critic" simply would not do: the exact name must be THE CEA CRITIC (though as a second choice he would have approved the formula "English Teachers' Critic"). The quasi-acronymic initials have never been dropped, [13] even if generations of members have supposed the significantly operative term to be "Critic." (Recently, however, they have been demoted to a smaller point size of type.)

From January through April, 1948, the mast of the new *CEA Critic* [14] carried a notice that entry as second-class matter was pending at the post office of Brooklyn, New York—changed for the remainder of the year to Mineola (where the journal was now published, though still edited at Brooklyn College). Beginning with January, 1949 (Vol. XI, No. 1), the mast stated: "Entered as second-class matter August 11, 1948, at the post office, at Mineola; New York, under the Act of August 24, 1912." (Whether the eccentric punctuation was prescribed by some arcane or archaic postal regulation, I wot not.) Until 1983 the fiscally valuable privilege was enjoyed continuously by all CEA journals, with their varying imprints, names, and frequencies—though certain recent restrictions rendered it something less than an unmixed blessing in a time of transition.

Bob Fitzhugh's editorial philosophy reflected his general view of the College English Association: "From the beginning, I have always felt that CEA was the best instrument to encourage humane teaching of literature, to make it what it should be, an enrichment of the spirit." Soliciting, like Burges Johnson before him, articles in literary criticism as well as the news notes and pedagogical and general comment that continued to predominate, he expressed regret that (apart from reviews) so few critical articles were submitted. He was, however, no especial friend of criticism-for-art's sake such as the New Criticism then attempting to put to CEA with a full head of steam. [15]

Symptomatic was an editorial headed "Even, and Particularly, Mr. Eliot" in the December *Critic* of 1948, which aroused more controversy than any other Fitzhugh ever contributed. An no wonder, for it was a slashing attack beginning: "Let Mr. Eliot's Nobel Prize be his monument"; continuing:

"Whatever his absolute merit, and there is question enough about that, his cult of the erudite, the exquisite, the pale thought deliberately obscured, the haughty disdain, the determination to be different . . . seem esoteric or merely quaint to all but a handful in America. . . ."; and going on to attack Eliot's critical "construct" from—one could say—a blended viewpoint of democracy, the New Humanism (never named), and Horace's *lectorem delectando pariterque monendo*: "Literary study that is not finally and explicitly moral is dilettante, sterile, and unworthy consideration in publicly supported college education. . . . The end of literary study in the program is to reach all students in some level, and in some way to make them feel the delight and the moral value of the literature studied."

Answers began to arrive almost instantly. In the usual editorial slot of the January, 1949, issue, a letter from T. C. Hoepfner (followed by a reprint of the most pertinent paragraph of the December column) attacked the editorial as "silly." In March three letters, including one by a director of the Association (unidentified), rebuked Hoepfner and defended the editorial. In the next issue several more letters, pro and con, offered a commendation by former President R. M. Gay for the *Critic's* stimulation of controversy marked by "a certain amount of militance and plain speaking"; the judgment of a member that "The 'New Critics' have certainly helped all of us to be better readers of poetry . . ."; of another that the Hoepfner letter had been "perfectly absurd"; and an expression of dismay by Willard Thorp: "I am shocked, yes, that's the word, by the silly editorial 'Even, and Particularly, Mr. Eliot.' . . . Your . . . synopsis of Mr. Eliot's critical method is a caricature." In reply to Thorp, Fitzhugh renewed his view of the responsibility of English teachers to make "their new, vastly enlarged, public feel the humanizing values which they know are in their subject matter." A month later, two more letters opposed the Editor's position—one of which, attacking the *Critic* somewhat in general, opined: "The T. S. Elliot editorial was perhaps the all-time low."

Clearly evident from the foregoing summary must be the remarkable openness with which Bob Fitzhugh as Editor not only tolerated, but positively welcomed, strong expressions of points of view opposed to his own. In that connection, it is interesting that at the height of the storm stirred by the Eliot flap, the leading article in the March, 1949, *CEA Critic* was a long and characteristically persuasive essay by Bruce Dearing, ironically titled "On the Wickedness of Analysis," written to defend metaphorical emphasis in literary interpretation against the imputation of "Brooks-and-Warren-ism," and to urge the preferability of the new methods of close analysis over "the pant and palpitation method" of encouraging student appreciation of literature.

Of all his contributions to his own journal, Fitzhugh was proudest of an article teasingly titled "Mammouth" (consistently so spelled) that was given lead position in the November, 1948, *Critic*. Intending no more deception than Dean Swift, he signed it Herbert Huson—the patronymic being transparently "son of Hugh," or Fitzhugh, and the given name having the same rhythm and second syllable as Robert. When asked the address of Mammouth College, he gave it as the Utopia School District of Laputa County (post office Swiftville), Kentucky, but broadly hinted that correspondence had best be sent "in care of the editor."

With sober mien, Herbert Huson presents a full account, humorously designated as merely "preliminary," of "a Program in Composition and Literature in operation at the recently organized Mammouth Cave College," indicated to be the academic address of the putative author. From an "Announcement, just issued," he quotes: "Mammouth Cave College feels that the most valuable tool a graduate can have is the ability to use his language fluently, precisely, and forcefully." The first principle at Mammouth is that "the instructor is the heart of the program" and so shall receive "a basic minimum salary of $7500." Besides presenting the degree of Doctor of Philosophy, a candidate for appointment "must have earned his living as an author or editor or both, and must have published" (in several forms and fields). "Moreover, he must have had experience as a public lecturer." [16] Ideal class size and "load," with relief from chores and distractions, are prescribed. "To keep everyone from being burdened with too much administration, the department chairmanship rotates every three weeks."

Students take English courses through all their college years. Except in special advanced sections, a classroom mixture of varied aptitudes is deliberately contrived. Grammar is treated as a prime essential; logic is also emphasized: "Since Mammouth believes effective writing to be merely a verbalization of clear thinking, it requires that all students learn to think right." A full, four-year utopian curriculum of integrated instruction in composition and literature is set forth in considerable detail, even down to the naming of textbooks and literary selections. The article ends with an amusing account of a riot "in a dormitory on the lower level of the cave" occasioned by a dispute among students about the second book of *The Faerie Queene*.

Robert Fitzhugh, alias Herbert Huson, obligingly informed me that the piece "was widely taken seriously, and I even got an inquiry from a publisher's man asking the address of Mammouth." (Seemingly, that query is not to be identified with a letter soliciting the address of the college purportedly from an otherwise unidentified "C.E.A. member" that was printed in both the February and March *Critics* of 1949—and editorially answered, tongue-in-cheek, in the latter issue.) Today's college teachers may be unacquainted with the quaint custom of visitation by publishers' agents, those seldom brief chroniclers of gossip, bounteous dispensers of "examination copies," who have all but disappeared from the circuits in recent decades. It would be interesting to discover whether one of them went on a wild-goose chase after a mare's nest in Kentucky! They were a pleasant breed, characteristically youngish and beamish, often would-be English teachers *manqués*.

Grammar—clearly in the sense of basic "standard" grammar— is not only, as mentioned, a foundation course of Mammouth College but is repeated until mastered, indicating Fitzhugh's personal attitude toward the growing question of its suitability as subject matter for higher education. That question which was to rock, rack, and almost wreck the English-teaching profession, particularly in the 1960's, was not especially acute during his *lustrum* as Editor. Nevertheless, the coming battles were anticipated in a cluster of articles and replies about the place of grammar (including the question, not yet prominent, of which grammar) toward the end of his tenure. In December, 1948, Bertha M. Watts published "The Place for Grammar" (pro). In March, 1949, William G. Leary followed with "Another Place for Grammar" (despite the title, con—with something of the tone of invective that was to become common in discussions of linguistics a decade or two later). Then in May came both Wilson O. Clough's "Grammar Commented on" (pro) and excerpts from a sweet-tempered follow-up communication by the initiator of the exchange, Bertha Watts, "In Reply to Mr. Leary." Finally, Fitzhugh's next-to-last-issue (November, 1949) carried an untitled letter-to-the-editor by George P. Winship, Jr., whose attitude was, with reservations, humorously pro-grammar for Freshman English.

Executive Secretary Fitzhugh, no less than Editor Fitzhugh, was a vigorous and efficient administrator of CEAffairs. He recalled that when he took office the Association's treasury contained "several hundred dollars," and with no tone of braggadocio alluded to a "hard-headed concern for finance" during his term. At the end of his first academic year in office, he was able to report (*News Letter*, May, 1946): "The College English Association is healthy and growing. More new members have joined in 1946 than in any year since the Association was founded." Treasurer's reports, intended primarily for the directors and secondarily for the general business meeting at annual conventions, were not routinely published in the journals, but those that did appear show continuing fiscal health during Fitzhugh's Executive Secretaryship. That of 1945, which overlapped Burges Johnson's last months, was printed in the January, 1946, *News Letter* because it had been received too late for the December meeting at Chicago. In view of dues of two dollars, receipt of $779 shown for membership in 1945 sounds odd (in both senses); however, library subscriptions at $1.50 were not separately entered. (Nowadays, we have learned to soak libraries more, not less, than monocephalous members.)

A Treasurer's report for January 1 through December 16, 1947 (printed in the maiden issue of the *CEA Critic*, January, 1948), enters memberships at $1.00 and $2.00—the smaller figure presumptively explained by a "tentative and experimental" offer in the April *News Letter* (1947) of Junior Memberships "open to undergraduate majors in English and to graduate students in English and General Literature" (with exclusion of any graduate students teaching more than half time). The report for 1947 also records expenditure of four hundred dollars for "Secretary's Salary." In one of his helpful letters to me (dated September 26, 1979), Bob Fitzhugh explained this entry—about which I had not inquired:

> It is most extraordinary the way C E A has kept going. In the beginning I was all the staff—clerk, advertising soclicitor, editor and proof reader, corresponding secretary, and mail clerk. [17] . . . Burges thought I might safely take out $50 a month, which I did, never more. It certainly did not cover my expenses.

The number of months to a "year" evidently was reckoned as eight, rather than nine (the actual frequency of the journal after 1945) or a calendar twelve. [18] Advertising revenues, which had been $728 in 1945, had risen in two years to $1,078. A later Treasurer's report, for 1948, shows advertising income actually exceeding the costs of publishing the *Critic* by more than two hundred and twenty dollars.

Regional development, given the highest priority by first President (*pro tem.*) Robert Gay as "the only hope of sustaining a national association," was strongly fostered by the younger Robert. A "Letter from Bob Fitzhugh" to the *CEA Critic* printed in November, 1959, rather luridly stated that as Executive Secretary he had promoted regional groups "by the simple process of letting them develop without answering the question how it could be done under the constitution." Of course, no constitutional issues really were involved, for as was brought out in LUSTRUM ONE the Constitution of 1939 positively, if somewhat generally, mandated encouragement of affilliates (an authorization that would be amplified and strengthened in redraftings subsequent to the Fitzhugh era).

According to an editorial in the *Critic* of February, 1949, summarizing the progress of the preceding year, in 1948 the Association

> . . . added three new regional groups, Indiana, Eastern Pennsylvania, and Southern California. There are nine regional groups, with others in prospect. . . . All regional groups were vigorous.

Eleven months later, Max Goldberg stated in the first *CEA Critic* he edited that his predecessor tripled or quadrupled the organization's affiliates in esse, posse, or potentis (I paraphrase), and (I quote) "almost tripled the national C.E.A. membership to boot." Those of us who have labored in the regional vineyards and slaved on membership committees know what an impressive record is implied in those rough estimates. [19]

The nine regional groups counted by Robert Fitzhugh at the beginning of his final year in office presumably would include, besides those named in the quotation—two of which, Eastern Pennsylvania and Southern California, were virgin; [20] the other, Indiana, evidently a reclaimed strayed sister—the following: New England, New York State, Middle Atlantic, Ohio, and Virginia - West Virginia - North Carolina, together with a Rocky Mountain CEA founded late in November of 1946 at Albuquerque (University of New Mexico) in conjunction with simultaneous organization of a Rocky Mountain Modern Language Association. I cannot document meetings in the immediate post-war period or, with certainty, the earliest post-war meetings of all those listed. Some pre-war College English Association affiliates or "sections" had become dormant; their arousal, occurring (if at all) at different times and with different degrees of formality, would not necessarily have been nationally recorded.

Middle Atlantic and New England were sleeping beauties awakened only after redoubled effort—with beastly difficulty, I am almost tempted to say. The Middle Atlantic CEA tried to meet on April 6 of 1946 at Johns Hopkins University, but for some reason (I should guess a problem in local arrangements) the date was postponed to May 4. New England, after aborting a gathering first scheduled for early 1947 at Simmons College (where CEA's co-Founding Father Robert Gay was now Professor Emeritus), actually met on October 17-18 at Northeastern University. Both Gay, who reported the meeting for the November *News Letter,* and Maxwell Goldberg moderated panel discussions. The regionals of the New England and Mid-Atlantic states, once revived, flourished mightily.

The *CEA Critic* of January, 1949—though it explicitly "establishes no precedent"—is devoted almost in toto to a detailed reporting of the New England CEA meeting of November 27, 1948, at Harvard, lauded as "a model and example of what the Association was founded to do." The chairman of the program committee for that meeting was belatedly revealed in the March issue to have been Maxwell H. Goldberg of the University of Massachusetts, who within the year would succeed Robert Fitzhugh as Executive Secretary and Editor for national CEA.

A Chicago College English Association, reported in the October, 1948, *Critic* as gestating for Spring birth, sprang forth a husky infant at the Illinois Institute of Technology on April 30, 1949, with a hundred celebrants representing eighteen institutions. I find partly equivocal post-war mentions of a metropolitan New York CEA that without any markedly evident formal structure was something of a center for CEActivities in the troubled mid-Forties. Seemingly it melded into a New York State CEA (variously named through the years) that was the apparent scion of a rather inchoate semi-organizaiton of uncertain affiliation described in the opening chapter of this Argus-eyed History. At a "C.E.A. meeting in New York," held at Columbia University on April 13, 1946, Strang Lawson of Colgate University (hardly metropolitan in situation by anyone's geography) was elected President, and Burges Johnson, late of Schenectady and "just back from Texas," presided at the luncheon. On the other hand, another session—seemingly genuinely metropolitan—of "The New York Section of CEA" was announced to be held on Saturday, December 14, of the same year, also at Columbia University. In the Fall of 1947, a "highly successful meeting" of New York State CEA was conducted at Colgate University. The group met again on May 1, 1948, at Aurora-on-Cayuga (Wells College); at the University of Rochester on October 16 of that year; and on May 7, 1949, at Elmira College. [21]

As has previously been explained, exigencies of war led to double terms for national President Henry Seidel Canby (1943, 1944) and—bracketing the Executive Secretaryships of Johnson and Fitzhugh—for Mark Van Doren (1945, 1946); [22] and also to replacement of the original town-meeting style of electing officers with a system of voting by mail. Besides Van Doren, Presidents during the immediate post-war *lustrum* of the Association were Odell Shepard (1947), Theodore Spencer (1948), and Gordon Keith Chalmers (1949). The perplexing question of Robert Tyson Fitzhugh's own Presidency, following his service as Executive Secretary and Editor, will be our anxious concern at the beginning of the next chapter. (Adv.)

As has also been related, the custom of an annual meeting, honored in the breach rather than observance after the irregularly scheduled convention of early 1943 ("for 1942," so to say), was resumed in a rather half-hearted way—except that Bob Fitzhugh's newly instituted Appointment Bureau operated actively throughout the MLA sessions—at Chicago in 1945, with the approximately fifty attendants including only a handful of national officials. At a cut-rate lunch where the Association's post-war plans were chewed over, three directors and Assistant Editor Gordon Eaker ("rhymes with Baker," the *News Letter* cautioned) spoke "briefly and informally."

In contrast, the dinner meeting at Washington, D.C., on December 29 of 1946 would appear to have been a stunning success. The topic of Training Desirable for Teachers of College English (with focus upon the soon-to-become ubiquitous theme of the doctoral program) was not only heartily canvassed at the podium by Fred B. Millett, Theodore Spencer, and Austin Warren but quickly spilled over into the pages of the *News Letter*. Besides a paid attendance of 103 diners at the unco-exorbitant price of $3.00, a hungry horde of about forty kibitzers, with or without brown bags, sneaked into the banqueting hall to listen. Even Vice-President Helen C. White, who had chosen to grace another meeting while the failthful fifty were at Chicago the year before, not only attended but this time met her commitment to preside.[23] (Whether she was a paid or non-paying attendant, the lack of break-down in the published report does not reveal.)

Although the three speakers had different things to say, they were in substantial agreement on needed changes in the preparation for college English teaching, signaled by the banner headline for their addresses in the *News Letter* of February, 1947: THE Ph.D. SHOULD BE REFORMED. Possibly Theodore Spencer came closest to verbalizing their collective view when he urged that the aim of advanced work in English should be to help the graduate student "study literature on its own terms," in order afterward as a teacher to "be able to communicate the results of his study so that the values inherent in them may be creative." A lively discussion in the journal, centering especially upon Fred Millett's urging of the primacy of an "aesthetic-critical" method for studying literature, included an attack upon it by Kemp Malone as "the most dangerous of all," and a "Comment" by Lewis Leary urging graduate faculty, in their seriousness, not to lose sight of literature as, in T. S. Eliot's equivocal phrase, "superior amusement."

If the Washington meeting of the College English Association in 1946 was an unmistakable benchmark, the next convention, at Detroit exactly a year later (once more a dinner, at an even more inflated price of $4.00 including "the use of the room"), was termed in the *News Letter* "one of the most successful the Association has ever held." A paper on "Poetry and General Education" read by Gordon K. Chalmers, President of Kenyon College, was later published as a CEA Chap Book supplementing the September, 1948, *Critic*. The Presidential address by Odell Shepard entitled "Minding Our Own Business" (the announced general theme of the meeting), printed in the *Critic* of May, 1948, was a felicitous sorting out of essential functions from the many extraneous duties laid upon teachers of college English. It had not actually been heard, for, as if to perpetuate a tradition of national meetings not presided over by the President, a blizzard in December of 1947 had prevented Shepard's journeying from Connecticut to perform his pastoral duties for delegates flocking from more clement climes.

Return of the Modern Language Association to New York City for the convention of 1948 occasioned CEA's first postwar "full program," lasting from 10:45 a.m. through the afternoon of December 27, punctuated by a luncheon in the Men's Faculty Club of Columbia University at the by then modest price of $2.50, which drew "a great many more than had made reservation." A discussion of "Shakespeare for Undergraduates" was conducted in the morning; Glenway Wescott addressed the luncheon session on "A Writer's View of Teaching Literature"; an afternoon panel considered "The Ph.D.—Past, Present, and Future." Theodore Spencer was the first CEA President to conduct an annual convention since early in 1943—when, as a matter of record, the presiding officer was called away and did not quite last out the meeting. Publication of Spencer's Presidential address about effects of literature upon teacher, student, and society titled "Agents of Relation" (in the February *CEA Critic*) was, however, posthumous, for he had died of a heart attack on January 18, 1949. *Caveant CEAE praesidentes!*

An incidental event of the 1948 New York convention at Columbia University may be taken as a fortuitous (and fortunate) closing of a wound that had been gashed ten years before. Oscar James Campbell, who had been chairman of the College Section of the National Council of Teachers of English during the disembocation of a College English Teachers Association (likewise at New York) in December of 1938, was designated to bring greetings from his own host institution. "I feel it is ironical that I am here this morning," he wryly conCEAded, "because I was one of those who vigorously opposed the founding of the College English Association. But I am happy to acknowledge to you that I was wrong and to welcome the Association here at Columbia." To which the

Critic, almost certainly in the voice of Bob Fitzhugh who had promoted the CEAsession with at least equal vigor, replied: "Graciously done, Sir, and most cordially appreciated." The lion and, if not the lamb, a Campbell had sat down together over very possibly distilled waters. Never thereafter has a discouraging word been spoken on the common range of Council and Association.

As has been hinted in a footnote not so far back, the annual meeting of 1949 at Leland Stanford Junior University was given rather short shrift by the CEA journal. For one thing, it was scheduled, not during the hallowed Yuletide but near the close of the long vacation, for Tuesday night, September 6, on the eve of a Modern Language Association convention set that year at an unaccustomed place and time. While preening itself on a widely dispersed membership, the College English Association has never had a regional affiliate centered in the Bay area, and for that matter the Southern California CEA has experienced difficulty through the years in maintaining continuity. Evidently, the national hierarchy found the convention of 1949 literally disorienting. An anticipatory notice printed in the January *Critic* had come close to apologizing for the fact that the Constitution required the annual meeting to follow MLA's traces even unto the ends of the nation. The May issue announced an easy plan whereby a major part of the program would be taken over by a group from doubly-President Chalmers' School of English and devoted to "the value of what is being done at the Kenyon School to the journeyman English teacher in his presentation of literature to undergraduates"; by September, however, when the topic was modified to the New Criticism, only one representative of the Kenyon School, who was also a student at Stanford University, had been recruited. The other speakers were Mark Schorer of Berkeley and Arnold Stein from Seattle. I fancy that relatively few brave Lochinvars rode out to the West *ex partibus Orientis*.

Whether Fitzhugh was one of those who did, I never ascertained, [24] though the silence of his journal in and after the Fall seems to testify rather loudly. By then he was winding up his CEAffairs to relinquish the Executive Secretariat and

Editorship to a slightly younger colleague, Maxwell Henry Goldberg, whom he had recruited from the University of Massachusetts and Robert Gay's first pioneering affiliate, the New England College English Association. At Max's urging, Bob agreed to continue his national service by accepting nomination to the Presidency of CEA, thus making assurance double sure for an orderly bridging of *lustra*.

On his final editorial page in the *CEA Critic* of December, 1949, under the light-hearted heading "So Long," Fitzhugh modestly evoked the "healthy condition" of the College English Association as witness that he was retiring "with good conscience." Mainly, his farewell was a cordial salute of Max Goldberg, [25] with an expression of hopeful confidence in the organization's continuing success: "The retiring Editor and Secretary has found his four years in office a rich satisfaction . . . May the CRITIC continue a free forum, and may the Association ever strengthen its resolve to make literature a vital humanizing force in the education of American young people. . . ." His concluding suggestion that the dues ought to be raised by fifty cents was humorously tagged "P.S." to mute the note of anticlimax. (Nevertheless, it was taken in earnest, and the dues did become $2.50.)

The next *Critic* [26] not only displayed prominently in a front-page box an enthusiastic tribute "In Appreciation" of Fitzhugh by outgoing CEA President Gordon Keith Chalmers, but carried Maxwell Goldberg's editorial response, headed "Your Rage I Defy," to "So Long." Wittily alluding to repetition there, and redoubling, of Burges Johnson's threat to haunt anyone who might allow the journal to become (in Fitzhugh's rephrasing) "a mausoleum for publication," it concluded: "Your double dare, Robert Fitzhugh, I take up. Your rage I defy. Your god-speed I cherish." In more serious vein, it spoke of "much help" received during the transfer of responsibilities, and with "admiration and gratitude" reviewed the multiform activities of the retiring Editor - Executive Secretary: national, regional, editorial, administrative, analytical, inspirational, and monitory or minatory. Of the transition from the age of Johnson to that of Fitzhugh, I have whispered in a quiet footnote: "Never was a changing of guard smoother or more unmistakably harmonious." Now I will proclaim, viva voce, the same about the interface of the ages of Fitzhugh and Goldberg. No transition could have been more humanly literate or more literally humane.

To wear the shoes of Burges Johnson had not been easy for Robert Tyson Fitzhugh. Always wisely walking at his own gait, without attempting to mimic another's stride, he stood tall and marched to a firm inward beat. Through difficult times of reconstruction, he bore a precious, precarious burden and handed it on safe, sound, solid, and solvent. By every evidence and testimony, his own *lustrum* in office as CEAdministrator was again worthy to be called illustrious, [27] and his memory blessed.

(Here endeth the reading of LUSTRUM TWO.)

Notae pedales for

LUSTRUM TWO

[1] The formal transfer of authority from Fitzhugh to his own successor, Maxwell Henry Goldberg, was announced to "take place during the Christmas holidays" at the end of 1949; but the first Goldberg-edited *CEA Critic* was that of January, 1950, and so I constructively treat the change as if it occurred on January 1. A *lustrum* ought to look like five years—or, as in the instance of Burges Johnson's service (1938 - 1945), five years and a bittock. (I doubt that the always generous Max Goldberg will begrudge my assigning to his predecessor what amounts to less than an added week of tenure.) Incidentally, as LUSTRUM THREE will discuss in considerable detail, Robert Fitzhugh was elected President of the Association in 1950, thus in a manner of speech succeeding himself and acquiring his own bittock (and rather more) of added CEAmanship.

[2] Johnson, who did not waste much space on complaints, did mention in the May, 1945, *News Letter* that compositors (like all crafts) had been considerably dislocated by war. Young readers of today can have no conception of how scarce things became, often suddenly, as when the civilian supply of an indispensable soft product pooped out early in 1945. We who had no access to post exchanges learned to queue up at the end of any

curling line we saw and buy whatever proved to be offered for sale at the front of it, whether we thought we needed the commodity or not. As Whistler had said to Wilde, "You will, Oscar."

[3] In an interesting editorial of October, 1943, Burges Johnson turned a jaundiced eye at "the many committees now planning Education in a Post-War World." The crystal-ball was not, however, entirely beclouded. With some prescience, in a "Presidential Message" printed in September, 1944, Henry Seidel Canby alerted the Association to a coming increased need of adult education for veterans. In the same *News Letter*, the Editor perceptively anticipated a question that was destined to arise under the G.I. Bill of Rights (offering, as it did, almost unlimited options of education or training to discharged personnel), and that for changing reasons has never ceased to be with us, when he pondered the effect of war on former conceptions of who ought to go to college.

[4] Actually, the adverse effects on civilians of unrestrained governmental expenditure for waging war were dampened, as much as possible, by legislation and regulation. Those controls worked fairly well as suppressants *pro tem.* (for example, most candy bars still cost only a nickel, though after a while some had to be unwrapped under a microscope), and in consequence the delayed effect dwarfed anything felt by 1943. I wonder what Burges Johnson may have endured when, with presumably a basic pre-war level of retirement income, he had to undergo the after-effects of repressed inflation in the Great Price Rise of 1946. I remember one blue Monday on which a pound bag of coffee nearly doubled its price of the week before. Though I had read about Germany in the 'Twenties, nothing of the kind had ever happened in my personal experience. In coming years my clever young wife, who (as neither of us could have dreamed) was to become President Doctor Helen S. Thomas of the national College English Association, had to invent a delicious bologna roast—baked, laced with cloves *au jus de pêche* (from a can)—and to generate sundry gourmet transforms of common frankfurter. In yon daze of recontruction, no mere assistant professor of English could aspire to feed his growing family on red meat.

[5] I should add "or by advertisements," which from the first issue were included in the *News Letter*, as also subsequently in the *CEA Critic* (old and new) and in the *CEA Forum*. Editor Burges Johnson attempted to control, and for all I can say really did police, the appropriateness and even size of the advertising notices he accepted. There have been later times when financial exigency compelled our management to tolerate almost anything, including one unfortunate announcement which was so unprofessional—and so offensive to a more ethical advertiser—that it had to be disowned *ex post facto*. (I may tell that story in due sequence, or perhaps I shall avoid painful memory by deep-sixing it in one of the murkier pools of my subconsciousness.)

A Treasurer's report for 1945 (to be referred to again later) shows that outlays of $812.30 for publication were, in that transition year between administrations, very nearly balanced by income from advertising ($728). Johnson was generally rather close-mouthed—if print has a mouth—about the financing of his *News Letter.* I doubt that Union College subsidized it, despite the tradition of campus encouragement of academic publications; allusion has been made in LUSTRUM ONE to his rather mysterious late mention (1952) of "how the early *Newsletter* [so spelled in the printed report of his remarks] was financed by an unexpected Santa Claus . . ." In all references to the state of the treasury during Johnson's tenure, it was reported solvent.

[6] Curiously, Johnson's announcement of retirement and cordial welcome to his successor in the *News Letter* of October, 1945, misspelled the new officer's name with a capital "H," despite the fact that Fitzhugh had been his Assistant Editor from December of 1942 through April of 1943.

[7] Fitzhugh's first *News Letter* (November, 1945) carried on the editorial page a warm tribute to Burges Johnson by CEA President Mark Van Doren, followed by the pledge of the new Editor - Executive Secretary to faithful continuation of high endeavor. Never was a changing of guard smoother or more unmistakably harmonious.

[8] Hitherto, I have refrained from calling him by the nickname that was common with his associates and that he characteristically signed when corresponding with me in the last two or three years before his death (September 22, 1981). We never met, but he seemed to know Texas well; in fact, he was famed as an inveterate traveler.

[9] The October, 1946, *News Letter* reported Eaker's move from Kansas to New Jersey as head of the Department of English at Jersey City Junior College.

[10] Fitzhugh retired to a 108-acre New York estate (Columbia County) that he called No Ruz Farm. The unique-sounding name, as I once wrote to inform him, is by no means unprecedented. Near Houston, an impressive arched gateway bears (unless the years since I discovered it have powdered the iron to rust) the following inscription in curving letters: *NO OAKS RANCH.* Anyone familiar with the bare terrain of coastal salt plains and with hopefully designated "Twelve Oaks" farms, "Whispering Pines" estates, "Deep Canyon" ranchitos, and "Valley View" or "Tumbling Cascade" suburban developments will appreciate the singular candor of the first Laird of No Oaks. May his honest tribe increase, world without end, and continue to flourish behind their iron curtain.

Candor compels me to add that No Ruz actually is Persian for "New Life"; and also that Bob's abundantly manifest sense of humor did not extend to any titters in response to my levity at the expense of his retirement home, which I now repent.

[11] While the Editor removed to Brooklyn College in September of 1947, that month's issue was still published as from Lehigh University. The first *News Letter* dated from Brooklyn was the one for October. After two more numbers, the name of the periodical was changed, for reasons to be explained in text and instanter.

[12] A grandfather-clause graciously exempted any already licensed that used the offensive word. To conform with regulations, the till then unfranked College English Association not only had to change the name of its journal but was obliged at the business meeting during the 1948 convention to resolve formally "that each member shall pay of his annual membership dues of $2.00, $1.50 for a year's subscription to 'The C E A CRITIC.'" Such bureaucratic comedy was Paar for the course.

[13] If I, for the sake of elegant variation, sometimes drop them, the gentle reader will please not to rebuke my lapse. Apropos of boots, as the French so elegantly say to introduce an irrelevancy, whether the preceding *News Letter* ought to be referred to as the *CEA News Letter* (with *CEA* italicized), as I have decided against, is a nice question. The first two lines on p. 1 read: THE NEWS LETTER / OF THE COLLEGE ENGLISH ASSOCIATION. Editor Fitzhugh, who had begun to write "C.E.A." (instead of "CEA" as Editor Johnson had written and he himself did at first), entered the new name of the journal at the head of the front page as: The C E A CRITIC, with "The" in lower case except for majuscule "T," and with extra spacing (though no periods) between the three initials. When Maxwell Goldberg took over the paper with the January, 1950, number, he immediately fully capitalized the first word and spelled the initials without special spacing: THE CEA CRITIC. The style of the title-line has undergone several subsequent CEA-changes, but never with exact reversion to the Fitzhugh formulary, which as regards treatment of "The" might have been partly imitated from the five earliest *News Letters* of Burges Johnson, where the word was set from a semi-script font of type, with only the "T" capitalized. (And I do hope somebody cares.)

[14] It was "new" only in a very nominal sense, for the numbering was continuous from the *News Letter*, the first *CEA Critic* (January, 1948) being counted as Vol. X, No. 1. Editorially, also, no sudden basic alterations of policy were evident.

[15] Near the end of his tenure, the following theme was announced for the annual meeting at Stanford University on September 6, 1949: The "New Criticism" and the English Teacher. As will be mentioned again in due course, no report of that Far Western convention was carried in any of the last three

CEA Critics edited by Fitzhugh at the close of 1949—probably (I venture to infer) because Eastern contributors who might otherwise have furnished one shirked the long transcontinental trek. I doubt that Bob himself would have found the theme sympathetic, though antipathy alone would never have impelled him to suppress commentary.

[16] With no sense of straining imagination to the breaking point, I suggest that the salary scale was derived (with some adjustment for inflation) from the fabulous pre-war $7000 of the University of Chicago; and that the ideal professor was reflected from CEA's also fabulous Editor Emeritus, Burges Johnson, even if his doctorate (unlike that of Fitzhugh) was honorary rather than "earned."

[17] "Jess Jackson kept the books." (Footnote in the letter of R.T.F.) Treasurer Jess H. Jackson's service continued from 1944 to the Spring of 1948. He was succeeded by William A. Owens, described as a Texan with a Brooklyn address.

[18] Max Goldberg, in one of his own helpful letters to me (dated November 1, 1979), mentioned that the Editor's stipend during his tenure was $48 paid ten times a year—the additional $80 annually being calculated, I should presume, to offset an estimated 20% general inflation.

[19] The one about increase in number of affiliates must have either relied heavily on prospects for future development or else reckoned revived regionals, inactive during the war, as part of the net gain.

[20] These new CEAffiliates both first met on Saturday, October 20, 1948: Eastern Pennsylvania at Pennsylvania Military College (Chester), Southern California at Occidental College (Los Angeles). As was mentioned in the preceding chapter, Indiana CEA (which actually antedated the national College English Association by several years) was a special case. It affiliated twice, first very early (May 11, 1940); again, more firmly, on May Day of 1948. Whether the original action—specified to be for "a trial year"—did not take (I draw my metaphor from vaccinia), I wish this hint to Hoosier historians might help me hit upon. I suspect that it was simply forgotten in the tumult of war; if so, score a point for George Santayana anent the fury of Clio scorned.

[21] A still later metropolitan Greater New York College English Association dissolved, a few years back, into a New Jersey CEA, leaving members in and around the Five Boroughs free to join a broader New York CEA of the state at large. I have no expectation of clarity rising from what I have said about the matter here and in LUSTRUM ONE.

The fact is manifest that an inherent vice in the place name "New York" is a formidable barrier to interpretation of historical evidence, which ought to be removed by joint action of Governor and Mayor. It is a problem that takes other forms, also. Having grown up in Kansas City (Missouri), built on limestone cliffs almost as steep as the hills of downtown San Francisco, I am still amazed and grieved to be associated with "the plains of Kansas."

[22] No simple scheme for showing the years of Presidential terms in the College English Association is feasible. I suggest the following comprehensive if admittedly clumsy schema: founding President *pro tem*. Robert Gay (who was "chief surgeon"during what Burges Johnson afterward referred to as a "Caesarian" operation at the New York birthing, though he did not attend the so-called First Annual Meeting at New Orleans the following year), *1938-39*; Howard Lowry (President for 1942, who remained in office until the delayed meeting of January, 1943), *1942(-43)*; other Presidents through 1969, by the year (or, for two-termers, years) in which they presided—or, in normal circumstances, would or should or could have presided—at annual conventions, as *1965* or (two successive terms) *1945, 1946*; after 1969, by the years of inauguration and presiding, as *1979-80* or (two terms) *1971-72, 1972-73*. By this system, the designation for Edward Huberman, who served an extended term (even though not two calendar years), presiding at both Notre Dame (1970) and Jacksonville (1971), would be *1969-70, 1970-71*.

[23] By evidently again not attending, Mark Van Doren appears to have entered a dual roll of double-term CEA Presidents never to have presided at an annual meeting, with the significant difference that there had been no meetings at the end of 1943 and 1944 where Henry Canby could have raised a Seidel.

[24] A CEAppointment operation was scheduled throughout the MLA convention at Stanford, From September 7 through 9, 1949. The general lack of reporting about that meeting in the *Critic* leaves me uncertain by whom, or how fully, the Bureau was peopled in that brave new Western world.

[25] ". . . one of the most active members in reestablishing [after World War II] the New England CEA Group. He is in full sympathy with the aims of our Association, and under his vigorous leadership we should continue to grow even more rapidly, both in numbers and influence. Success to Max Goldberg and every good wish!"

[26] January, 1950: "Re-entered as second-class matter . . . at the post office, at Amherst, Mass. . . ." This issue of the journal, marking the beginning of the Goldberg Editorship, was also the first to carry a copyright notice, a continuing practice thereafter.

[27] To my early appeal for assistance, Bob made prompt, warm response. I regret now that I did not send him preliminary drafts of this reluctant History in its formative states, while he was still alive to have read them. I hope he sensed from my letters how highly I had come to esteem his administration in the *lustrum* just before my own connection with the College English Association would begin.

MAXIMIZING THE ASSOCIATION

being

LUSTRUM THREE (1950 - 1955)

of

S A N S C U L O T T E

A NONKNICKERBOCKER HISTORY

of the

COLLEGE ENGLISH ASSOCIATION

Maxwell Henry Goldberg (1962)

CEA's Incomparable Max

LUSTRUM THREE (1950 - 1955)

Maximizing the Association

As cicerone of this leisurely historical jaunt, I now announce with Dantean reverence if less than Ciceronian eloquence: "We are entering the Age of Max." Almost as if by pattern, not only for an even ten years but for an exact calendar decade, Maxwell Henry Goldberg guided the College English Association as Executive Secretary [1] and Editor, issuing his first *CEA Critic* in January of 1950 and his last in December of 1959. From the outset, his CEAmanship was masterly; to this day, many older members still regard him as Mister College English Association. If Sir Max Beerbohm helped England dispel the Victorianism of a former era, our own Incomparable Max taught his society of American professors of English to recombine earnestness with a delightful zany spirit he could have learned from his namesake.

I must, however, as I threatened in the preceding chapter, start by attempting to unwind some obfuscating coils that enveil the CEA Presidency during the early Age of Max. The problem is somewhat like that of geology: relative sequence is easier to establish than absolute dates. The former is verifiable from successive layers of entry in the mast of the Association's journal, but those changes have not occurred with clocklike regularity. At first, as has been explained, elections were held at an annual business meeting in December; afterward, exigencies of war dictated use (which became customary usage) of a mail ballot, normally sent out in the waning year and returned and tallied early in the next. For one reason or another, the month varied when results were given by the journal, or at all events reflected in its mast.

A few instances will illustrate. A postal card ballot was mailed with the December, 1946, *News Letter*; in February, 1947, the winners were confirmed ("there was but one dissenting voice") and the names of Odell Shepard as President and others of the slate were run up on the journal's mast. They flew there (and in the retitled *CEA Critic*) through April of 1948; then, in May, President Theodore Spencer and confreres were revealed as elected successors for the current year. Because of Spencer's death on January 18, 1949, his name was removed from the mast in the issues for that month through April (without replacement, the two Vice-Presidents continuing to be so listed), until Gordon Keith Chalmers, newly and duly elected for 1949, was in the month of May awarded a restored Presidential ensign.

We are beginning to approach the heart of our mystery, which long seemed to me a riddle impenetrably swathed in enigma. In the *Critic's* mast Chalmers as President, along with Mark Schorer and Austin Warren as Vice-Presidents, bridged the transition of Editors from Bob Fitzhugh to Max Goldberg (as Odell Shepard and his fellow officers two years earlier had bridged that from *News Letter* to *Critic*), persisting through the issue of April, 1950.[2] In the May number, a report on "Election of Officers" gave the "result of the mail balloting" as Robert T. Fitzhugh, President; Joseph Warren Beach and Russell Noyes, Vice-Presidents; and the usual number of new directors.[3] Those names were still posted through January of **1952** (except that one director was dropped, without explanation, in that final month)—a continuous apparent voyage atop the mainmast only four months short of two calendar years.

Finally, in the February, 1952, *CEA Critic* a small box on the last page reported the election of President Ernest E. Leisy and Vice-Presidents John Holmes and T. M. Pearce, and also named seven new directors (including Robert Fitzhugh). All were given instant entry to the mast and remained there through November (*sic*) of 1953.[4] Nevertheless, readers who persisted to the last page of the November number could find a record there of "CEA Elections" showing William L. Werner as President and Levette J. Davidson and Lionel Stevenson as Vice-Presidents. Meantime, on October 15, 1953, Werner had formally extended greetings from the College English Association to delegates attending the CEA Institute at the Corning Glass Center in New York (a conference and program about which considerably more will be said later in another context). In the December *Critic* of 1953, President Werner appeared on the mast, with Vice-Presidents Davidson and Stevenson, for the first time. They remained there for a year and a month, through December, 1954; then in January, 1955, they were replaced by Kathrine Koller, President, [5] and Bruce Dearing and Norman Holmes Pearson, Vice-Presidents. Once again, as in 1952, seven new directors were named in the *Critic's* report of "the mail ballot on the slate of officers presented by the 1954 Nominations Committee": three for two years and four (including William L. Werner) for three years. In January of 1956, Bruce Dearing was raised on the mast from (First) Vice-President to President, [6] Harry R. Warfel and Henry W. Sams being shown as the new Vice-Presidents. [7]

I do not assume that my bedazzled readers have entered all the facts just recited into the tables of their memory or into their personal computer, or even that they have meditated them closely. The upshot can, however, be indicated very simply. Gordon Keith Chalmers was unquestionably President of the College English Association in 1949; six years later, in 1955, Kathrine Koller was President and in that capacity conducted the annual business meeting at the Palmer House, Chicago, on December 27. Only three other CEA Presidents intervened: Robert Fitzhugh, Ernest Leisy, and William Werner. But five years intervened between 1949 and 1955. It all does not, as editors say when adjusting headlines to news stories, "count out."

An easy answer seemed to offer itself when I noticed that in both *Who's Who in America* and the *Directory of American Scholars*, Ernest Leisy listed himself as President of the College English Association, 1951-53. In the latter directory, Robert Fitzhugh listed himself as President, 1950—with the date left round and unexpanded. [8] I very nearly settled for Fitzhugh, 1950; Leisy, 1951, 1952, and 1953; Werner, 1954; Koller, 1955. Still, doubts kept nibbling and gnawing. For one thing, three successive Presidential terms for the same person—even a distinguished Texan—would have been unconstitutional. Furthermore, I could not discover that the *Critic* connected Ernest E. Leisy in any way with the convention at Detroit in December, 1951, whereas a teasingly recorded feature of the

festivities was "unscheduled hog calling by Bob Fitzhugh."
Remember, also, that Fitzhugh continued to be shown on the
mast as President during all that year and even one month into
the next.

In 1952 Ernest Leisy certainly did serve as President, and
presided at the postprandial program during the annual meeting
on December 28 at Boston. Could he have been President
for two years, 1952 and 1953, if not for three (including 1951)?
The trouble with that hypothesis is that William Werner
not only had been named as President as early as November
of 1953 but was explicitly referred to as "CEA national president" in the report of the convention that year at Chicago,
where he gave what appears to have been a Presidential
address on "The English Teacher and the Sciences."
Again the next year, when CEA met at New York City on
December 28, 1954, the following entry seems definitive:
"Presiding, William L. Werner."

A type of evidence easily overlooked (I did overlook it for
a long time) has already been hinted: the number of directors elected in a given year. The normal number is three,
together with an ex-officio directorship for the retiring
President. [9] Near the beginning of two different calendar years,
nonetheless, six new elective directors were named, together
with a past President: Robert Fitzhugh in February of 1952,
who, if he had gone out of office after 1950, should already
have been a member of the Bored by 1951; and in January
of 1955 William Werner, similarly confirming the continuance
of his Presidency through 1954. Both would appear to have
been Immediate Past Presidents.

Have we whittled down the seeming claim of Ernest Erwin
Leisy for a three-year Presidency to a single term (1952)? On
a purely technical construction, evidently so. Still, the
notation of "1951-53" by that gentleman and scholar of
unimpeachable honesty (I knew him, hurray) is entirely
understandable. He must have remembered being solicited
toward the end of 1951 (or it could have been months earlier)
and, following acceptance and nomination, being elected by
ballot and so notified. He served through 1952, and then
because of an unexplained delay in the election of William

Louser Werner, or at least in the announcement, probably held a kind of informal chairmanship during the long early months of the next year, when a President of CEA did not customarily have numerous, urgent, or well-defined duties. (I speculate that the Executive Secretary may have called on him to write a few letters or sign a few papers during the second semester of the academic year 1952-53. [10]) I have to regard Werner as officially President for both 1953 and 1954, even though the temporal extent of his service appears to have been only a little more than one year. When Kathrine Koller replaced him in January, 1955, a new-old pattern was re-established: the wheeling zodiac had gone round a whole cycle and once more, after something not unlike (on a tiny time scale) the precession of the equinoxes, the Presidency of CEA was again starting near the point of transit from one calendar year to the next.

Necessary adjustment in composition and terms of directors was simultaneously made, six instead of a normal three replacements being elected. A previous adjustment similarly made in 1952 indicates that Bob Fitzhugh, like William Werner, occupied the Presidency in two successive years: 1950 and also 1951. How did it come about? The fact already brought out in an aside (fn. 8), that the two-year incumbency apparently did not strongly impress itself on his memory or Max Goldberg's, could very well indicate that it was at least half-accidental: that in the year or so following transition from the second *lustrum* of CEA to the third, some routine procedures like the nomination - election process, which under ordinary circumstances should have commenced late in 1950 and been completed early in 1951, were turned awry and lost the name of action. I conclude that the election of officers and directors for 1951 was forgotten, waived, or held in abeyance— and I wish I knew which. A similar but not so radical delay evidently occurred for some reason in 1953, when William Werner's election came abnormally late in the year. Curtailment of his total term to only a couple of months was avoided by extending it through the next year. ... Perpend!

I would quote Archimedes upon his discovery of specific gravity, except that I am never trite. Postulants of Clio, having floundered after me through so tangled a web, may now wish to apply for demission.

As was shown in LUSTRUM TWO, innovations under the Editorship and Executive Secretaryship of Bob Fitzhugh were significant but seldom startling. Those inaugurated by Max Goldberg were, if not startling, at least more instantly apparent. [11] One of the most immediate was a great increase in attention by his journal to regional activity that was of course appropriate and natural as the stringencies of wartime receded even further into the past. [12] Whole or nearly whole pages, sometimes a front page in substantial part, were given to reports of past and projected regional meetings. Editor Goldberg soon had a skein of stringers on the string, encouraged to send up to Massachusetts full accounts of action by frequent (not routine) reward of by-lines. His very first *CEA Critic* carried two probably pre-invited "Hints on the Regional Meeting" from officers of the Indiana and New England affiliates, with a linking editorial note beginning: "Let's hear how other groups handle their regional meetings. C.E.A. prides itself on its decentralization, flexibility, and adaptability." Three months later a full page was devoted to "Spring Regional Meetings," and in the following issue (May, 1950) regional reports occupied most of three of the eight pages and part of a fourth. The Incomparable Max had a sure instinct for the quintessential importance of affiliates to a thriving national organization. If his tendance of the Association could, like Tennyson's brook, have gone on indefinitely, some of the uncertainties about national - regional relations that were to become agonizing in the early 1960's might sooner have been settled by amicable understanding and compromise. But I anticipate a story yet to be told.

Maxwell Henry Goldberg was preeminently an *organizer*, in a sense hardly applicable to either of his predecessors. As administrators, Robert Fitzhugh and (especially) Burges Johnson before him tended to be loners, doing things their own way in their college office or on the family dining room table. At least in part, their comparative solitariness must have been a function of the times: in the nature of things, a small new break-away organization of college English professors could not expect to develop an elaborate table-of-organization on the heels of a great economic depression, or during and just after an all-absorbing total war. Max Goldberg began at once to *organize* Association activities and publications. His vigorous promotion of regionalism has already been implied. To judge by the mast of his earliest *Critics*, he had begun his term without an official Treasurer; [13] this gap was filled in May, 1950, with insertion of the name of Leone A. Barron. In the next issue, that of September, appointment of Albert Madeira as director of the CEA Bureau of Appointments was announced and his name placed on the mast in that capacity. The October issue reported his intention to have the Bureau in operation, as now-President Fitzhugh had been doing since 1945, during the MLA and Associated CEA conventions. At the beginning of 1953, Madeira succeeded Mrs. Barron in the office of Treasurer, [14] but throughout the Age of Max he continued also to direct placement activities with energy, persistence, and evident success.

Next to Albert Pierpont Madeira—and I cannot say for sure on which side of him—the Executive Secretary's most valuable coadjutor was Lee Elbert Holt, appointed Managing Editor in September of 1952. [15] By the time I became a contributor to the *CEA Critic* in 1954, although the mast directed all "official mail" to be sent to Goldberg's office at the University of Massachusetts, it seemed evident to me that Lee Holt was functioning pretty much as editor *de facto*. [16]

That under Goldberg virtually all correspondence was routed (I know my Businessese will be admired) to his office in Amherst, regardless of the institutional addresses of other officials, appears symptomatic of remarkable support by his university. He must have maintained a hareem of secretaries to organize his daily mail and to handle the expanding and ramifying operations he was constantly setting in motion. For a golden decade, the University of Massachusetts was a point-device point d'appui for CEA. Not lightly was a resolution passed at the Association's business meeting on December 28, 1954, extending formal thanks for "moral and tangible support of the College English Association" by that generous sponsor.

Max would, I am sure, agree—or if necessary argue—that of all the many-splendored activities during his tenure, the most imaginative, spectacular, and widely influential was his institution of CEA Institutes. The germinating idea can be quickly stated: in a post-war world that had been either saved or damned by technology (and already then, as now, the issue was in doubt), to bring into communion men and women of intelligent good will, with both scientific and humanistic bents, in an effort to survey paths to a more harmonious, less fragmented future. Maxwell Goldberg was a committed holist before most of us would have guessed that "holism" is spelled without a "w." By temperament as well as learning a follower of Plato and Coleridge (and, yes, Carlyle), he believes that mankind torn asunder, whether by bomb or bombast, is man doomed—humanity rendered helpless, hopeless, and inhumane. For him, a crew of doctrinaire technocrats at the wheel of our life's voyage could mean only that we had taken passage on a ship of fools. He is certain that the Truth to set us free must transcend alike the positiveness of mathematics and the positivism of laboratories: that it must rest upon humanistic truths hard-won by ages of searching, responsive minds interrogating an intelligible universe. So far as he is concerned, the living core of education is liberal education. In a sense which the word may almost have lost through politicization, his spirit is authentically liberal. We ought to cherish such a one, only this side idolatry. *Also sprach der Mann Thomas*.

I have remarked upon the remarkable support Max Goldberg drew for the Association from his University of Massachusetts. He convoked the Ur-Institute of CEA there on June 12-13, 1952, with himself as director and Bob Fitzhugh as general chairman. The Amherst Institute was declared by the *Critic* to have been "successful beyond expectation," with an attendance (under weather conditions reportedly "ideal") of "nearly two hundred participants." Not being then a member of the national organization, or for that matter of any local society yet affiliated with it, I was not present. By a strange chance, however, I did stumble into the third CEA Institute, [17] which was held on June 24-26, 1953, at the University of Florida. As I write, I have before me my copies of both the (probably rare) Tentative Program and the (final) Program. And yet my trip to Gainesville had nothing intentionally to do with any activity of the College English Association.

The explanation is that several years previously I had been inexplicably designated by my chairman as departmental specialist in Engineering (or Technical) English—despite the fact that I am by nature left-handed and in consequence so gauche that I have never mastered the use of common scissors, and that in sixth-grade shop my Mother's Day project of an octagonal spool-holder ended as an oblate heptagon. In my daze of developing courses of English for students of "science - engineering" (as eventually my faculty rather too neatly blended the several categories), I was driven by hyperconscience into attempting somehow to bring myself up to at least a decent level of incompetency; and so I set about wangling industrial reports and examining as many examination copies of textbooks on technical style as publishers could be persuaded to send a teacher with well up to forty or fifty, sometimes more, captive registrants.

Furthermore, I joined the American Society for Engineering Education, and even, with difficulty and pride, succeeded in getting an article published in its journal, calculated to set the English Section on fire but unfortunately seeming to fall into a layer of asbestos insulation. I did still more: for, learning of an impending Sixty-first Annual Meeting of ASEE in Florida, I submitted a ten-page paper that, *mirabile dictu*, was accepted for delivery at one of the sessions on English. Along with the printed program I received notices of an associated CEA Institute. Overlapping attendance is almost routine at such linked meetings. Although I have no clear present recollection of going to the Institute, still, as an English professor of English would say, I must have done, since in my program I marked two of its General Sessions and inked in a corrected title for one of the papers. I am sure that I learned much, but it sank in so deep that today I can not bring anything up from my subconscious. And please don't embarrass me by asking what I dropped into the collective unconscious by my ASEE performance; I haven't the foggiest notion what I sought in my "Search for the Uncommon

Denominator." O tempora! O memoria! . . . Où sont les fleurs d'antan?

By general consensus, the archetypal CEA Institute was one conducted later that same year—on Thursday, Friday, and Saturday, October 15-17, 1953—at the Corning Glass Center, not far from Mark Twain's permanent abiding place. (I did not attend, either.) The general theme was Business and the Liberal Arts: an Exchange. Several accounts in the *Critic* included a lengthy report by Robert T. Fitzhugh digesting a closing evaluation of the conference presented by President Harry D. Gideonse of Bob's own Brooklyn College. Salutary observations such as the following may be read in context on the first and third pages of the January, 1954, issue: [18]

> It is obvious to anyone who has participated in this discussion here that business and liberal arts people have a joint concern in shared problems, and it is also obvious that we are very far from any answers to questions we are not ready to formulate. But the acre ploughed up at Corning holds promise of rewarding crops if cultivated empirically. . . .
>
> Before we start preaching too loudly about industry, . . . we should see just how much of this modern economism, this spirit of "can you measure it?" has actually become dominant in the humanist citadel itself. . . . Let us be certain we do not express values that we do not ourselves live by. . . .
>
> We are not concerned with turning out smoothly polished spare parts for the industrial machine. We are concerned with raising the basic question of the kind of men it takes to carry on and to preserve a free society. . . . This is not conservatism in the sense that it is concerned with preserving the status quo. God forbid. It is conservatism that is concerned with preserving the conditions in which a free society can continue to endure. . . .
>
> [A]nother problem . . . is deeply rooted in the vested interests of the graduate schools. . . . [C]ombine financial disadvantages with a training process that sifts out

and eliminates students with natural aptitude in our direction, and we are close to a situation that will make for barren ground twenty years hence. I think that it is the present situation in humanistic scholarship in many of our leading centers of graduate study.

After Corning, though rather needless pleas for "more Institutes" were once or twice voiced in the *CEA Critic* by readers, these gown-and-town meetings greatly proliferated. One at Schenectady, for instance, sponsored in cooperation with the Association by Union College (the original academic home of CEA) and the General Electric Company in April of 1955, less than three years after Max Goldberg had inaugurated the Institutes at Amherst, was billed as "Seventh National CEAI Conference on Industry - Liberal Arts Exchange." The movement was also affecting regional activity, as I learned in Houston the year after my expedition to Florida.

Ernest Leisy, a prominent Americanist at Southern Methodist University, not only served as national President of CEA, as previously recounted, but also blasted about on his own heath setting in motion both a South Central (originally spelled South-Central) College English Association in the Autumn of 1952 and then a Texas CEA. The latter was conceived if not exactly born at a Sunday breakfast on April 26, 1953, at Austin, following the Saturday convention of the Conference of College Teachers of English (CCTE). [19] For good measure, the South-Central Renaissance Conference also met there that week-end. Texas CEA officers elected at Austin called a "first annual session" at Houston for the evening of Friday, March 12, 1954. Prime mover was John Q. Hays, designated as Chairman in lieu of the later-used term President, then of Texas Agricultural and Mechanical College (today's Texas A&M University) and now retired from Stephen F. Austin State University—not in Austin, but in the much older city of Nacogdoches [20] (pronounced "nack-uh-DOTE-chiz" and not be be confused with Natchitoches to the east, which not even natives of Louisiana can pronounce without their tongue tripping).

Hays, having assisted at both Amherst (1952) and Gainesville (1953, where his name was misspelled in the Tentative Program), deliberately put the stamp of CEA Institutes upon the 1954 program for Texas CEA, announcing as theme: The Relation of the Needs of Business and the Study of English and the Humanities. "We heard," he wrote to me in response to my query a few years back, "three or four Texas business and industry spokesmen talk about what they preferred in Texas college graduates whom they recruit for work in Petroleum, Insurance, or Merchandising." I ought to have remembered, for I was appointed to the role of moderator. I do recall that Secretary - Treasurer Mima Ann Williams exacted no attendance fee, the dinner (at a downtown Houston cafeteria) being financed as a Dutch treat.

Despite my suggestion that Lee Holt appears to have taken over effective editorship of the *CEA Critic*, never doubt that Max Goldberg still retained the function of editor-in-chief, that is to say, ultimate ideational and decisional control. [21] In other years, prior Editors Burges Johnson and Robert Fitzhugh had both lamented that more articles on literary topics were not forthcoming from the membership. Max was a thaumaturge; he, too, desired to print literary criticism and scholarship—and lo! forth it came. I believe he could have called spirits from the vasty deep as easily as lesser men fetch them up from bottles. And they would have come, too.

An early example, one that for partly personal reasons greatly interests me (it was written by a close friend and former colleague of mine at the then Rice Institute), is a leading article on "The Scholar and the Ballad Singer" that filled nearly a third of the February, 1951, *CEA Critic*. The author, Joseph W. Hendren, at that time an officer in the pioneer Middle Atlantic regional affiliate (founded years before by Robert Fitzhugh), learnedly and literately surveyed a path among the confused territorial claims of musicologists, gens de lettres, folk singers, and academicians—rectifying if not confuting the two-and-seventy jarring sects of balladry.

In the same issue, for good critical measure, "The Proof of the Pudding" by Paul E. Reynolds urged abandonment of "hysterical diatribes" against the New Criticism, [22] with substitution of "a calm appraisal of the actual worth of the new critical methods in the classroom." Reynolds' balanced conclusion, based on experience at Rhode Island State College, was that the methodology of the New Criticism "can, when used with some imagination and insight, leaven the mass of historical fact with which literary scholarship is almost of necessity incrusted [but] if employed without these two qualities it can produce as much arid pedantry as traditional scholarship ever did."

An article of February, 1952, that attracted considerable comment—surely a source of gratification for any editor—was "The Difficulties of Joyce's *Ulysses*" by Elizabeth Drew, who found "a book which is basically incoherent." [23] Among other notable contributions in the earlier 'Fifties about literature, its creation, or the teaching of it were "Milton As a Readable Great" (April, 1951) by Don M. Wolfe, a combined pedagogical - critical article; "An Invitation to the Wake" (September, 1951) by William Peery, Associate Professor of English at the University of Texas who re-joyced to identify himself as follows: *Pilliam Weery is Andsosheate Prefossil of Winglish at the Unitexity averse us*; Louis Hasley's "Meteors in December" (November, 1951), a short story of fantasy genre on a literary theme; Ellsworth Barnard's "On Teaching E. A. Robinson" (March, 1952); "The Very Thought of Shakespeare" (verse) by A. E. Johnson (October, 1953); and "Tragedy, and Also Romance" (April, 1954) by Richard P. Adams.

I do not mean to say that the *Critic* in the first half of the 1950's radically swung to literary scholarship and criticism as its dominant editorial mode, but only that those elements substantially increased under Max Goldberg and Lee Holt, moving the journal at least in the direction of a balance that would be acknowledged fifteen or twenty years later by its split into the *CEA Forum* and a new *CEA Critic* designed to be a literary quarterly. Meantime the kinds of commentary, news notes, and pedagogical and miscellaneous articles afterwards associated mainly with the *Forum* did remain dominant, but less so than formerly.

As would be expected, fall-out from the CEA Institutes was heavy—not just notices of those under plan and reports of ones already held, but frequent transcripts of the addresses. Probably never before or since has any educational society devoted such intense, sustained effort to building of bridges between Academia and the practical world of management and production, with no intention of quantifying the humanities (as, alas, has partly happened in consequence of the cancerous spread of computers) but, instead, of humanizing the executives. The current effort to find "alternative careers" for English majors is no new thing under the sun: at least two of the reprints that poured out well-nigh monthly as supplements to the *CEA Critic* in those years were on that very question, and a primary focus of the Institutes was upon liberal arts students as potential business or industrial executives.

A field in which the Goldberg - Holt *CEA Critic* came close to breaking virgin editorial ground[24] was the New Linguistics. Max Goldberg did not wait long to give the movement an airing. In November, 1950, he printed an article by John Hurt Fisher (whose name would become household in a sister Association), "On Attitudes toward Language Study," attacking by no means harshly—indeed, in tone rather mildly—"the chicanery of prescriptive grammar." The following March, Gordon Eaker's "I've Been Reading" department contained a cleverly sarcastic review by George S. McCue of a conventional grammar published in 1950 by Ralph B. Allen: "It is too bad that we had to wait so long for this *English Grammar*; it should have been written two hundred or more years ago." In a spirit of fairness, space was also given to "Prof. Allen's Rejoinder," which proved rather petulant and ineffective.

For some time, the Allen - McCue tiff continued as subject of sporadic comments in the *Critic's* pages. Three that must have been pretty promptly sent in were printed in the May, 1951, issue: one pro-Allen by another Professor Allen (Eliot D., "no relation"); one a deliberately balanced view of what is appropriate to books of grammar, by Harry R.

Warfel; and one by Donald Lloyd, whose attitude was patent in the title: "Lay on, McCue." Lloyd called (Ralph) Allen's rejoinder "negligible," and passed the following judgments upon him and his critic: "It is not presumptive [*sic*] of McCue to condemn the book . . . It is presumptive of Allen to prepare such a book . . ."

Donald Jacob Lloyd was effectively beginning his career as CEA's advocate general of the New Linguistics and, in time, an Association President to be. That Autumn a supplement in handsome pamphlet format to the September, 1951, *Critic* reprinted (from *The American Scholar*) an extraordinary interchange between him and Jacques Barzun. Lloyd's "Snobs, Slobs and the English Language" was dedicated to the propositions that "language is basically speech" and that "the essence of language . . . is its drive to adapt." Those doctrines are of course now long familiar, as is the characteristic verve with which Barzun, in "The Retort Circumstantial," undertook to "carry the war into the enemy's camp": "The enemy is not illiteracy but incomplete literacy—and since this implies pretension it justifies reproof." Those early blasts of hot and cold air upon the New Linguistics, and numerous others of increasing intensity, swept across the College English Association, helping to turn a ponderable fraction of its collective thought for a time to lucubrations upon the fundamental nature of language and the responsibilities of its teachers to their students. I need hardly say that today the basic questions remain unresolved (even though each successive "school" proclaimed itself winner in the first round by a technical knockout). Nowadays, I fancy I detect a shade less missionary zeal among aging converts to bizarre heresies, but that may be only because I suffer from combat fatigue.

I cannot attempt to digest into a paragraph or two the raging linguistic controversies in the *Critic* of the early and middle years of the 1950's. Essentially, I suppose, they differed little from those that stormed through other media and college cloisters, then and thereafter. I certainly cannot pretend that I personally came out of the fray trailing anything but tatters of indignity. The only contribution of which I am in any degree proud was my very first sortie, an effort at a sort of

Addisonian - Goldsmithian allegory about a sometime brotherhood of mandarins of manners "in the kingdom of Kweichow, which is south of Szechwan," who deserted their calling and got canned. A respondent from California found my argument "not very highminded but by no means idle, il-logical, or fanciful." Well, he was right, except that I could have wished he had called it fanciful even though not magnanimous.

Presently I found myself tangling with no less formidable an opponent than Donald Lloyd. Early in 1955, the *Critic* was publishing some papers on linguistics that had been delivered at the 1951 annual meeting of CEA at Detroit. The February issue carried Lloyd's "Needed: A New Grammar," in which he harped again on the McCue review of Allen's *Grammar* and then went on to excoriate teachers of standarized English as purveyors of "a triviality of the same kind that Emily Post decides in her books on manners." He recommended the ignoring of "all issues of 'correctness' or propriety." Because of the dates, there could have been no reference in his paper to my "Fable for English Teachers" (September, 1954) or in my allegory to a speech that I had neither heard nor as yet heard of, but the fortuitous similiarity teed me off my divot. I affected to fine-tooth comb Lloyd's article for evidences of the grand new Substandard English of which he came into an expectant world as evangel, and I shed glycerine crocodile-tears over his failure to commit comma splices, faulty accidence, and gross misspellings such as his witness seemed to foretell. To my abiding shame, the last word of my article was "bologna." To his eternal credit, Donald Lloyd used the space automatically granted him for reply, not to annihilate me with sarcasm but to express regret at the failure of "professionalism" in academic dispute. With the censured Francis Bacon, I have to bow my head and confess that "it was the justist censure that was these two hundred years."

I have mentioned that speeches at the CEA Institutes furnished important copy for the *Critic*. The Association journal, as well as an occasional Chap Book, had always freely drawn upon addresses delivered at the annual meetings, and continued to do so as in printing Donald Lloyd's paper (originally titled "Linguistics and the Teaching of English") and others from the Detroit convention of 1951. The yearly meeting preceding that of Detroit, held in 1950 at the Holland House Taverne in Rockefeller Center, New York, had yielded both a CEA Chap Book (April, 1951) titled *An Invasion of Privacy*, consisting of Robert Fitzhugh's Presidential address; and a report recommending broadening and standardizing of the Ph.D. curriculum in English, presented by a committee under the chairpersonality of William L. Werner, accepted by the membership at the meeting, "released by CEA Executive Secretary Maxwell H. Goldberg," and published on the first page of the January, 1951, *Critic*. Also, "in cooperation with Brandeis University," a brochure was issued in February, 1951, containing Albert Guérard's address preceding a discussion he led on the relation of comparative literature to under-graduate and graduate curricula in English and American literature. Attendance at the 1950 convention was reported to have "met the expectation of those who planned it" and to have included a "large number of national CEA officers—past and present." Among the former group were both Robert Gay and Burges Johnson, guests of honor at the meeting in Manhattan as officially recognized Founding Fathers.

The second Boston convention of the College English Association, on December 28, 1952, was the source of con-siderable publication in the *Critic*. During a breakfast, as has been mentioned in another context and chapter, Burges Johnson[25] was elected, aged seventy-five years and two months, on nomination of President Ernest Leisy and by acclamation, CEA's Younger Statesman of 1952. After Johnson's "witty response," Bob Fitzhugh "presented his own deuteronomic CEA declarations," strangely published without a by-line as PROPOSED CEA FIVE POINTS PROGRAM on the front page of the February *Critic* of 1953, all under a still larger banner heading: T H I S W E A R E F O R. At the dinner meeting of convention night,[26] a discussion was conducted on the question: "Teach Teaching to Teachers?"—originating in a questionnaire on Courses in Teaching for Future College English Teachers. An "occasional poem" of some length read by Vice-President John Holmes at the banquet, titled "Faculty Committee on Teaching," found its way into the March, 1953, *Critic*, together with panelist John Ciardi's address on the problem of teaching teachers how to teach literature, which had been praised in the preceding number by Brother Cormac Philip, in a critique of the Boston discussion, for its "inspirational and idealistic note." (For Max Goldberg's high view of the Boston CEA of '52, see LUSTRUM FOUR.)

The Chicago convention of December 27, 1953, attended by "a hundred and twenty CEA stalwarts," included papers by Benjamin Lease (written in collaboration with the meantime-deceased Ernest Van Keuren) on "The Student and the English Teacher," by Kathrine Koller on "The English Teacher and Foreign Languages," and by President William L. Werner on "The English Teacher and the Sciences." Their remarks and also the closing statement of Executive Secretary Goldberg about "The CEA Institute at Corning: What Does It Mean?" were digested (anonymously) with exemplary precision and clarity in the January *Critic* of 1954.

The Modern Language Association was just then beginning what we can recognize in retrospect as a tentative and uncertain move toward fairly regular shuttle between the two major convention cities of East and Midwest. In MLA's wake, the College English Association found itself in Gotham for 1954 (December 28) and back in the Loop for 1955 (December 27). CEA's theme in the former year was stated as Seeing It Whole, with division into sessions on the Undergraduate, the Adult, and the Profession. For 1955, an unusually specific (but in those times timely) theme of Teaching Translations was announced; understandably, John Ciardi was again included among the speakers, but he became ill and his place was taken by Mitford Mathews. Deviation from the usual, though not invariable, custom of dinner meetings occurred at both New York and Chicago. In 1954, instead of a dinner, "a buffet supper ... served for the convenience of those who wish to attend the business meeting" was scheduled between six-fifteen and seven. The vaguely announced cost of "about $2.00 per plate, tax and gratuity included," may suggest a sort of

English tea (in one announcement, as a matter of fact, the word "refreshments" rather than "supper" was used). In December of 1955, the official meal was a luncheon as had first happened as far back as the Boston convention of 1940, though the tariff at Chicago made it appear a rather more substantial meal (if not exactly kosher) than the two-buck collation a year before: "Luncheon price, $3.50 (all charges included). Reserved luncheon tickets may be picked up from Miss Ham . . ."

Although by then the new Institutes were tending to outbid the annual conventions as sources of printed articles,[27] frequent publication of papers from meetings of regional affiliates continued. Their use in the journal can be connected with a strong momentum in the Age of Max, already alluded to, toward laying even heavier emphasis upon regionals than the strong encouragement that had always been a fixed policy under Gay, Johnson, and Fitzhugh. Symptomatic was an invitation breakfast for "CEA officers, regional directors, and CEA staff members" at Chicago in 1955.[28] The principal topic of discussion was the afterwards perennial one of national - regional relations. The event had been authorized at a meeting of officers and directors just after the close of the academic year in mid-1955—that custom itself having been another innovation of the enterprising Max Goldberg. To anticipate events of coming *lustra*, I will mention here that in 1956 Patrick G. Hogan, Jr., having been given a "modest" CEA travel subsidy to attend the inaugural Regional Breakfast the previous December, where a yearly repetition had been voted, was one of the three committeepersons for the second of the series. Very quickly he began to be prominent in other aspects of the national Association's concern with regionalism, finding himself invested as chairman of the Committee on Regional Activity and Development (token of Max Goldberg's gift for inventing titles to spur his corps of coadjutors to high endeavor). Early in the next administration Pat was retitled Regional Coordinator, but sometime thereafter he dropped out of the national regional (no oxymoron) picture—not, however, by any means out of CEActivities generally. Then in 1965, by an extraordinary feat of legerdemain (no calembour), a sorcerer named Sears[29] caused me to appear out of very, very thin air, fully panoplied as Regional Coordinator. It was done with mirrors in the Crystal Room of the Sherman House of Chicago, mother city of the CEA's Regional Breakfasts a decade earlier. Attentive readers, possess your souls in patience and you shall hear all about it hereafter, along with the rehabilitation of Hogan.

The Incomparable Max, not only manager of CEAffairs and supervisor of the Association's servers and helpers but by temperament, in the best sense, an organization man, must have been troubled that the College English Association had always been rather loosely held together, mainly by the personality of successive Executive Secretaries. Neither Max Goldberg's scholarly knowledge of Carlyle nor the consciousness he surely felt in his own powers of leadership would have persuaded him that CEA could go on indefinitely as a chameleon image of its transitory mentors, however devoted. It must also have a fixed structure and constitutional texture. A Constitution had indeed been drawn up by a representative nationwide committee following the organizational meeting of 1938 at New York, twice published in the burgeoning *News Letter*, and then formally adopted at New Orleans in December of 1939. With a few amendments, it had served the Association for three *lustra*, but so far as I can discover was never reprinted; in later years it certainly was seldom referred to, with any great particularity, as a source of authority. Max and his constitutional committee could hardly have closely consulted the original document in the full context of early *News Letters* and then gone on to write as the opening clause of a new Preamble: "The College English Association was founded in 1939 at New York City ..."

The rest of that first sentence was truer and more recent of reference: "... and incorporated September 28, 1954, in the Commonwealth of Massachusetts." Articles of agreement toward incorporation had been adopted on June 17, 1954, and a written set of By-Laws was deemed necessary (or perhaps under the Massachusetts code may have been obligatory) to constitute, along with them, "the statutes of the College English Associaiton, Inc." Not much was said in the *Critic* about the process of drafting those By-Laws except as rather tersely unveiled in the "Secretary's Report" for 1954 and 1955 printed respectively, in whole or part, in the issues of May, 1955, and February, 1956. A Committee on Organization and By-Laws was led by Bruce Dearing and included Robert Fitzhugh among its eight members. In general, the By-Laws completed in 1955 were loosely founded on the Constitution of 1939—with, however, many provisions adapted from procedures grown traditional in the Association or else from widely customary practices (all such societies being pretty much alike in basic constitutional structure). As would be expected, there were differences peculiar to these By-Laws, and also a good number of new provisions. Of the latter, one that was to become exceedingly important was the explicit statement: "A regional affiliate shall retain its autonomy as a member of a federation, and shall not be considered as a province of the national organization."

The new document, headed BY-LAWS of COLLEGE ENGLISH ASSOCIATION, INC., consisted of a Preamble and fourteen articles; I, Agreement of Association; II, Membership of the Corporation; III, Dues; IV, Meetings; V, Officers; VI, Elections; VII, Powers and Duties of Officers; VIII, Powers and Duties of the Executive Committee; IX, Board of Directors; X, Salaries;[30] XI, Publications; XII, Regional Affiliates; XIII, Dissolution; XIV, Amendments. It was accepted at the business meeting that bracketed the lunch at Chicago on December 27, 1955, effectively became operative in 1956, and governed CEAffairs for approximately three more *lustra*. Is ten or fifteen years the normal life expectancy for any codified fundamental law of CEA? I was personally heavily involved in a thoroughgoing overhaul, consisting of separate but interlocked Constitution and Bylaws, drafted under the leadership of William James (Wild Bill) Griffin, published in the December, 1970, *CEA Forum*, and formally adopted by the membership in the Spring of 1971. Various amendments over the next decade were embodied in a Xeroxed or multilithed recension distributed by then Executive Secretary Robert E. Lee (Fighting Bob) Hacke in March, 1980. That version is notable for its codification of a basic revision of electoral timing sequences, and for a minim leap toward equality of the sexes on land and in the CEA by scattergun substitution of "he/she" or "his/her" for the more graceful but alas now disgraced unisex "he," "him," and "his" of auld lang syne.

Two previous round-numbered years, 1945 and 1950, had each brought a *lustrum* of Association history to a close with transition from one Executive Secretary - Editor to another. In 1955, no change of that kind occurred, or could have been wished by anyone. Very soon, as a matter of fact, there no longer would be an Executive **Secretary** to change, for under the new By-Laws the title became Executive **Director**, the better to impress officers of sister societies. There also were two Editors, Max Goldberg and Managing Editor Lee Holt; or even three if Consulting Editor Bob Fitzhugh is reckoned, and I am persuaded that he genuinely was consulted with some frequency.

The efficiency of the College English Association had been steadily MAXimized over the preceding five years—and with that developing efficiency had grown the value to its own members and to the profession at large. Also, beyond the horn-and-ivory towers of teachers of English, CEA was actively carrying into workplaces and countinghouses in cities of the plain luring hopes for and through humane letters. In yon halcyon daze before the shock of sputnik, leaders of commerce and industry were listening to a new - old gospel, believing (not always with full understanding), participating, even calling for more help from our guild than most of us had anticipated or were prepared to afford. I was only just beginning my own association with the Association, and my interests were still (as, indeed, they remained) primarily regional. But for those in the thick of things, which means mainly in the East and North before CEA's center of gravity began slipping and sliding southwest along the sunbelt, those must have been exciting times. UnCEAsingly, at the hub of all action—planning and designing and shaping and projecting and directing and cajoling—was the Incomparable Max: Mister College English Association.

Surely Maxwell Henry Goldberg must be pure of heart, for his strength, then and thereafter, has been as the strength not of ten ordinary mortal men but of ten giants of the earth— or CEA. Midway of the placid, hopeful 1950's, under his reassuring guidance, the College English Association was about to enter its fourth *lustrum* in full confidence of continued growth, success, and influence.

(Here endeth the reading of LUSTRUM THREE.)

Notae pedales for

LUSTRUM THREE

[1] Or Executive Director, under a new By-Law, beginning January, 1956. (See textual account near end of chapter.) The Constitution of 1970-71 reverted to the term Executive Secretary; actual usage has continued to fluctuate, partly or mainly at the whim of incumbents.

[2] Gordon Keith Chalmers signed as "President, College English Association" a front-page box of the January, 1950, *CEA Critic* "In Appreciation" of Robert Fitzhugh's service as Executive Secretary and Editor. Analogously, when Fitzhugh's Presidential address to the annual convention of December, 1950, at New York was published in a CEA Chap Book supplementary to the *Critic* of the following April, an identifying note at the front stated: "The author is [*sic*] president of the College English Association and its past executive secretary." A major difference, as will instantly become evident, is that the extent of Bob Fitzhugh's Presidential term is less easily ascertainable than that of his predecessor.

[3] Three were elective; a fourth, G. K. Chalmers, constitutionally became a director as Immediate Past President. Readers are advised to bear these "usual" data in mind until their significance comes clear.

[4] With unwitting discrepancy, an article in that month's issue about a South Central College English Association meeting on November 14 properly identified "Presiding officer: E. E. Leisy" as "past president CEA (national)."

[5] Kathrine Koller was the first woman to become President of the College English Association, though there had been an early tradition of women Vice-Presidents that began when Mary H. Perkins was elected First Vice-President at New Orleans in 1939. (While I was a director in the first half of the 1960's, and I must add not a participant in nominations, women served as President in two successive years—a record streak until tied in 1984—1985.

[6] This almost silently accomplished sequence was the first instance I have observed of our by now familiar custom of electing the First Vice-President to an immediately succeeding term as President. Although the By-Laws that went into effect after 1955 did not actually prescribe that practice (nor does any subsequent constitutional revision or amendment), the system of single nomination each for the Presidency and for the Vice-Presidency, which became a two-year term (the Second Veep automatically rising to First), must have encouraged and halfway implied it. These customs still continue, with the important exception that two nominees instead of one are offered for the two-year Vice-Presidential office.

[7] Once for all, I mention at this point that CEA's editorial use or nonuse of hyphens in "Vice(-)President" has not been completely harmonized, sometimes not even within a single issue of the journal in the early daze. I try always to include a hyphen not only because it is constitutionally seemly so to do, but to avoid any suggestion of a presiding officer who might have been committed to (or for) vicious practices.

[8] When I wrote to ask the late Robert Fitzhugh how long he had been President of the Association, he was not able to inform me with assurance. I next asked Maxwell Goldberg for help, and from Max received much the same answer about Bob's term. Manifestly, as Historian I was driven back upon surviving documentary evidence leavened by logical inference. Listen, colleagues, and you shall hear.

[9] Sometimes the Immediate Past President was named for a single year, sometimes for three, sometimes for an unspecified term. I have given myself the luxury of ignoring this problem except where it may appear critical for some other, since its resolution could require more consitutional investigation, hauling down of old masts, and interrogation of former officials than I am inclined to undertake. My impression is that in the early and middle years of CEA the succession from presiding officer to sage director was somewhat catch-as-catch-can.

[10] The interplay between calendar and academic years beclouds chronology, *ex post facto*, for all of us whose lives are thus split.

[11] A minor but useful early innovation was insertion in the September, 1950, *CEA Critic* of a "Table of Contents" (after two months the heading was shortened to "Contents") at the foot of the mast on the second page. (Some experiments toward listing contents of the journal had been made previously, but none had caught on.) The position chosen by Editor Goldberg is not the best that can be imagined, since that space obviously is valuable for major items even when not used for pure editorials. The practice of including a table-of-contents was dropped soon after Lee Holt became Managing Editor, but has since been revived and is now regular in at least the *Critic*. (The *Forum* has been in a phase of reconstruction.)

[12] A new affiliate born early in 1951 was the ancestor of two present-day Deep South CEAs: Florida; and Georgia — South Carolina. Designed as "tentatively including Alabama, Florida, Georgia and South Carolina" and called the Southeastern College English Association (SECEA), it was projected during the national meeting at New York in December, 1950; met at Georgia Institute of of Technology on Saturday, February 17; and (to judge by notices in the *CEA Critic*) continued very active. On November 3 of 1951, Michigan CEA first met at Ypsilanti and also became a vigorous affiliate, convening biannually. At the end of that year, Tennessee CEA—destined to develop into a permanent regional that would meet biennially—became at least a glint in the eye of persons "interested in Ky. - Tenn. regional CEA activities," who were invited by a box in the December *Critic* to gather at the MLA hostelry in Detroit late on the afternoon of the day following CEA's annual dinner meeting at Wayne University.

This perforce primarily national narrative simply cannot continue the attempt to record all births, deaths (or suspended animation), and other vital statistics of CEAffiliates through the shifting years. Your beleaguered Historian begs leave to beg again, as like a whining beggar he has begged many times before, that each affiliate undertake to compile, record, and if possible print its own chronicles. He pledges his assistance where appropriate and possible.

[13] The name of Treasurer William A. Owens had been removed from the mast after the April, 1949, number.

[14] Two other seemingly short-term appointments were of Rhoda Honigberg, entered on the mast as Administrative Secretary in October, 1951; and of John Waldman, added in April of 1952 as Director, Public Relations. The Executive Secretary was obviously experimenting with organization, and of course quick disappearance of names from the mast is not conclusive evidence that no further service was rendered in related or different functions. J. Gordon Eaker's name was never on the mast at all under Max Goldberg's tenure, even though he continued to serve several

years as Book Review Editor or Literary Editor and to conduct the prominent "I've Been Reading" column.

[15] By changes of title made early in the second *lustrum* of the Age of
Max (mid-1956), those two CEA-mates became, respectively, Administrative
Secretary - Treasurer (Madeira)—a combination of offices semi-paralleled
in the early 1980's with Elizabeth Johnston Cooper serving part of her term
as both Executive Secretary and Treasurer, or Executive Director; and
Executive Editor and Business Manager (Holt). Goldberg could not award
medals to his crew, but he knew the power of rank. (He had promoted
Bob Fitzhugh, for example, from Editor Emeritus to Consulting Editor.)
The skipper's own title, as has been touched on in the first footnote of
the chapter, rose from Executive Secretary to Executive Director on his
vessel's mast in January of 1956. (See also LUSTRUM FOUR for further
vicissitudes of Lee Holt's title.)

[16] Holt can be shown also to have acted as Managing Editor in the usual
sense, most particularly from the Fall of 1954, when printing, publication,
and the second-class mailing permit were transferred to his Springfield from
Northampton, to which they had been moved from Amherst early in 1952.
I am disinclined to attempt snooping out all intricacies of the business
management, but am easily persuaded that Max Goldberg left it and other
administrative functions as completely as he could to able CEAmen and
to CEAfaring women willing to make waves.

[17] The second Institute, on September 8, 1952, apparently was more a
long-range planning session than an open meeting: ". . . fifteen officers and
delegates met with forty-one representatives of university administration
and the executive world in a three-hour session," at the Johnny Victor
Theatre (RCA Exhibition Hall) in Manhattan, "to consider setting up CEA-
sponsored committees on liaison between college English teachers and the
executive world of business, industry, government, and the armed forces."
The meeting was deemed to have "marked [a] decisive advance in the
development of CEA liaison efforts . . ."

[18] Gideonse's full text was also printed as a supplement to the May,
1954, number.

[19] Non-Texans will never understand—and so should not try—that there
was already in existence since 1933 (and thus a whole *lustrum* pre-CEA)
a thriving Conference of College Teachers of English of Texas, now a Comity
Affiliate of the national Association. Texas CEA, which symbiotically meets
in the Spring with CCTE, is a Regional Affiliate, garden variety, of the
national Association. South Central CEA, also a Regional Affiliate, meets
in the Autumn with the South Central Modern Language Association that
is, of course, an affiliate of MLA. When I successively don my six hats

as a member (in some instances a Life Member) of CEA, CCTE, TCEA, SCCEA, MLA, and SCMLA (out of, well, modesty I refrain from describing still a seventh hat, for membership in TJCTE: Texas Joint Council of Teachers of English; not to mention those for AAUP and possibly still Texas AAUP, a national organization and its state affiliate that are both busy just now shedding their professional skins and trying to turn into labor unions), I must look like either a would-be comic juggler or else an indecisive Dapper Dan.

As a footnote to a footnote, I will add that the South-Central Renaissance Conference also is older than its putative parent, the Renaissance Society of America (1954).

[20] Known as "the oldest Texas town," Nacogdoches is notable for what Joseph Conrad would term "secular trees" of monstrous size, awesome beauty, and evident antiquity. While I am at it, I might as well point out that Austin College also is not in Austin, but in Sherman—which is to say, so nearly in Oklahoma that its students could appropriately be called Laters (by analogy with Sooners).

[21] Friends of plain English must not take alarm at such high astounding lingo. I just wanted to demonstrate, for once in a way, that if I wished to do so I could write Academese. I am thinking of bringing out as my next book a collection of *Snippets from the Pedagoguese*.

[22] Exactly a year before, in the February *Critic* of 1950, Martin Kallich had protested against the New Criticism, under the heading (in quotation marks) "I Must Reject," as neglecting "social man and related matters— all that makes art meaningful or 'great' ..." His article is by no means hysterical. Neither is a longer one in the following issue (indicated as "condensed" from one still longer) by Edward A. Post, essentially an unfavorable review of Wellek and Warren's *Theory of Literature*. Reynolds does not refer directly to either article, yet seems to glance obliquely at the latter in his mention of the opposition to Warren and Wellek. Several other comments about the New Criticism had appeared during the opening Goldbergian year, including two by Ellsworth Mason defending the movement ("If we continue at this rate, the New Critics will be swinging from the nearest cottonwood tree within another year ..."), and others on the subject continued to appear sporadically.

[23] The same issue ("this month marks the seventieth anniversary of Joyce's birth; the thirtieth, of *Ulysses*") contained some cheerier views of the teaching of *Ulysses*, or James Joyce more generally, by Ellsworth Mason, Howard Nemerov, and Joseph Prescott; and also an excerpt (headed "God's Gift to the English Department") from Denis Johnson's "A Short View of the Progress of Joyceanity" reprinted from a Dublin periodical of 1951. The

idea of the Special Number for CEA journals was being born, and of late has grown to be something near a hallmark.

[24] I had almost said "soil," or even "dirt," until I bethought myself not to be invidious. My personal bias against the New Linguistics is notorious among my friends (some of them, I fear, in consequence *former* friends), but I shall try to keep it out of this candid History except when I am obliged (an easy obligation) to mention myself. I could say with Swift that I heartily loved John, Peter, Thomas (Q.E.D.), and (next to Thomas) Ralph, namely the late Ralph Long of truly revered memory; but I had no high opinion of the frequent practice of certain self-styled but dubious linguists (I meanly dubbed them "linguisticists" because I doubted that as a class they were "speakers of many tongues") in sniffing at fogies like me as a litter of illiterates despite—or could it be because of?—our lifelong love, study, and devoted teaching of language as a medium for refined speech and beautiful letters.

[25] "Regret was voiced at Robert Gay's absence." In daze of yore, CEA valued its distinguished elder statemen. Incontinent readers of this cornucopia of contrarieties are permitted to peek at the peroration of the final LUSTRUM SEVEN before returning to the text of LUSTRUM THREE.

[26] Cost: $4.50 per plate "including gratuity and Old Age Tax." Diners at Wayne University the year before had paid only $2.75 for filet mignon, and a year later at the Quadrangle Club of the University of Chicago the charge was "$3.50 (no extras)." You may think the "no extras" bit a bit frivolous. Not at all! In 1950 the Holland House Taverne had affected to charge the same price, but tacked on a 15% service charge, forcing preregistrants (I swear I am telling solemn, documented truth) to send an almost unmailable $4.03. I simply can't resist the temptation of revealing these vagaries of prandial price, doubly interesting as they are in hindsight from our later high plateau of inflation.

[27] The papers from the 1954 convention, titled *CEA Symposium: Seeing It Whole*, were published jointly with, and (characteristic of Goldbergian enterprise) substantially subsidized by, the Center for the Study of Liberal Education for Adults. All CEA members received copies. I must add that, to this day, liberal education for adults has remained a passion with Max Goldberg.

[28] In the same spirit of promoting regionalism, lists of Presidents of Regionals, and of Representatives (i.e., liaison representatives to the national Association), were added to the mast of the *Critic* beginning in September, 1955. I shall have a good deal more to report about regionalism

as this whimsical History continues its oblique, not say crab-like, progress—
the latter part of fn. 12, *supra*, notwithstanding.

[29] Donald Albert Sears, to be much heard of hereafter, especially in
LUSTRUM FIVE and LUSTRUM SIX. Along with Edgar Walter Hirshberg
and Patrick Galvin Hogan, Jr., he was a member of the troika appointed
to conduct the Regional Breakfast of 1956. Ed Hirshberg, incidentally, was
always an extremely strong advocate of national action for the affiliates.
Although he served a term as director of the Association in the late '60's,
he never received nearly as much recognition as his service merited. I
hereby, herewith, and hereat give thanks for his hearty support and
heartening encouragement during my Coordinatorship. (Pat Hogan, I shall
speak of constantly.)

[30] Elective officers and directors were to serve without compensation.
"The Board of Directors may pay the Executive Director, the Editor or
Managing Editor, the Treasurer, and any other functionaries who may per-
form continuing or special services, such compensation to come out of the
funds of the corporation." As Regional Coordinator (later, National Coordinator of Affiliates), I must not have been even a "functionary," inasmuch
as I never received—or requested or desired—one cent of salary under
those By-Laws or the succeeding Constitution and Bylaws that went into
effect a little beyond midway of my term of office. I did have an adequate
expense account for stamps, stationery, and occasional visitations of affiliates
outside my own region.

RENTS WITHOUT TEARS

being

LUSTRUM FOUR (1955 - 1960)

of

SANSCULOTTE

A NONKNICKERBOCKER HISTORY

of the

COLLEGE ENGLISH ASSOCIATION

Lee Elbert Holt (about 1975)

LUSTRUM FOUR (1955 - 1960)

Rents without Tears

For the College English Association, as was rather more than intimated at the end of the preceding chapter, 1955 was notable almost as much for a thing that did not happen as for what did occur. The years 1945 and 1950, in addition to the normal rotation of elective officers, had brought a changing of the chief executive. In 1960 that phenomenon was again to recur, when after ten years of able CEAmanship the Incomparable Max Goldberg relinquished his administrative and editorial offices at the close of 1959. In 1955, however, CEAffairs flowed smoothly and imperceptibly into a new *lustrum*. [1]

Having survived a stormy beginning, terminal effects of the Great Depression, and dislocations of World War II, not to mention the ordinary birth pangs and growing pains of any burgeoning academic society, the Association was at the mid-Fifties in sound and indeed flourishing condition. It had recently become a limited-liability and tax-free corporation, and was in the process of adopting a new and improved set of By-Laws. It enjoyed the support of a great university where its Executive Secretary (or Executive Director, as he was in process of becoming) and its Treasurer and director of placement activities both taught. Its committee structure was fuller and firmer than ever before. It published a monthly journal, normally of eight pages but often thicker, nine times a year. Fifteen regional affiliates were listed on the mast, as well as seven regional representatives serving areas not necessarily coextensive with those covered by the existent affiliates. In a manner of expression that would soon be heard on the coast of Florida and in Texas, all systems were go.

As this faithful History has previously recorded, Maxwell Henry Goldberg was preeminently an organizer—an "organization man" [2] in the higher sense of that equivocal term. While the structure that shapes CEA today has been, of course, considerably modified through the years by constitutional revision and legislative and administrative change, it is still basically his legacy to the Association that he directed for a decade.

Although it might seem paradoxical, for all the firmness of his hand the intention of Executive Secretary/Director Goldberg was to spread rather than concentrate authority and responsibility. A development of the Age of Max was the occasional inclusion in the journal of a formal "Secretary's Report," in which his devotion to national and regional structures is manifest. The reports for 1954 and 1955 (*CEA Critic*, May, 1955; February, 1956), being extensive (even though the former is tagged "condensed"), helpfully exhibit the College English Association approximately midway of the Age of Max. A few quotations[3] will be of interest and information.

1 9 5 4

As in the past, our basic publication tries to maintain the tone and flavor of the forum and newsletter—the abruptness, the tentativeness, the colloquial ease, the forensic temper, and lack of definiteness of such publications. It draws its materials chiefly from (1) volunteered individual contributions; (2) regional and other CEA-related meetings; (3) occasional pieces submitted on invitation.

* * *

With one or two exceptions, we can report sustained or intensified activities among our regional affiliates.

* * *

[I have] tried to justify to my family ... my unbelievably heavy and, to me now, in retrospect, appalling investment of time and effort in the development of the Institute ... The CEA-I[nstitute] funds are budgeted separately and recorded separately—both as to income and outgo. The CEA is not financially dependent on The CEA-I, or vice versa.

* * *

In the postwar past, the national CEA has had no standing committees. In the 1950-55 [*sic*] period, it has had ad hoc committees on: the Revision of the Ph.D. Curriculum in English, Teaching Load of English Teachers in the High Schools, and the Encouragement of Undergraduate Excellence in English.

* * *

In 1954 ... a list of standing committees was adopted ... : Nominations ... CEA Institute ... Organization and By-Laws ... Research and Grants ... Ph.D. Curriculum Revision and Preparation for Teaching ... National - Regional Relations ... Publications ...

* * *

As we turn toward 1955, I voice the hope that ... we will take heart in our unofficial CEA motto: [4] *Whatever is worth doing, is worth doing inadequately.*

* * * * * * * * *

1955

Continuing under the direction of Albert P. Madeira, the Bureau of Appointments renders twofold service: (1). year-round; (2). at the annual MLA sessions. ...

Basically, we are beginning to sense the shift in center of gravity from employer's to employee's market.

* * *

... we have expanded our practice of running reprints of some *CEA Critic* articles and distributing them as separates where we think they will do good.

* * *

... this year, we have had a strong schedule of meetings of our regional affiliates ... Attendance has varied from fifty to two hundred at each meeting. Thus, through our nineteen regional meetings, we have reached about 1275 college English teachers in 1955; and through *The CEA Critic* and *Critic* reprints, the impact of the papers and the discussions at these nineteen regional meetings has gone far beyond the original regional participants.

* * * * * * * * *

From the last partial quotation, immediately above, and from much else said in the reports for 1954 and 1955 about regional affairs, it is clear that at midterm of his ten-year direction Max Goldberg was convinced of the maximum importance of that phase of CEActivity. In the later report, among all else, he mentions assisting the "recognition" of Ohio CEA; and alludes to being interrogated at meetings outside his Association about "the weight of the constituency we represent," explaining that "each time, after we have given the figures on national membership, we hastily add: but we reach and are reached by a much larger proportion of our profession."

What a pity, I have always thought, that Max did not remain in office long enough to carry out an intention he broached in that same report. For a long while—perhaps since the original President *pro tem.* Robert Gay brought into being the first CEAffiliate—the question had been rumbling, like a dormant volcano, of precisely what relation the affiliates bore or ought to bear to the parent organization. The problem was slightly complicated by the fact that in one early instance (Indiana CEA), and now in two (including the Conference of College Teachers of English of Texas, as a Comity Affiliate), the "child" is older than the "parent," if not legitimately father of the man. From the start of regional development, there appears to have been no question that the affiliates are at least quasi-independent and can, at their discretion, enroll nonmembers of the College English Association. The national

By-Laws of the middle 1950's and the later revised Constitution categorically guarantee the "autonomy" of the affiliated Associations and spell out the principle that they are members of a "federation" and not "provinces" of the national body. Still, the fact that local meetings sometimes turned out more participants than the avowedly general convocations was a galling fact to those sensitive to membership as numbers or to dues as strength. As Max Goldberg frankly observed in his report for 1955, aggregates of the regional and national membership "register" on officers of sister societies, "but not so effectively as if we could add most of the regional figures to our national membership figures."

The Executive Director made perfectly clear (if I may anticipate a phrase less current then than fifteen or so years thereafter) what he would like to do in regularizing the regional - national connection:

> . . . I tend to favor some sort of joint membership basis whereby a regional CEA participant becomes a member of the national by, say, paying a total annual fee of $3.50, up to one dollar of which, however, would revert to the regional treasury. We ought to give those who *want* [emphasis added] to join the national as well as the regional some sort of inducement and some sort of reward. The alternative—an assessment from each regional, does not strike me as so attractive. Of course, both methods could be combined, if the regional assessment were kept small.

There, in the first alternative posed (and preferred), is the germ of the plan for which I was to argue—only mildly and sporadically, I confess—during my years as Coordinator of Affiliates but which had to wait till the mid-70's to be adopted. Of course, "a total annual fee of $3.50" now sounds derisive, the present discount in joint national - regional memberships being only fifty cents less than that whole amount; but in principle the plan offered by Max Goldberg, and revived from time to time by others over the next four *lustra*, is the solution

CEA eventually found, like a blue bird in her own back yard. The affiliates remain members of a federation, not chapters of a monolithic structure. Many national members have no regional affiliation, and even more regional CEAers no national membership. Nevertheless, "those who want to join the national as well as the regional," or in whom that desire can be induced by persuasion, may now tread a *via media* that the Incomparable Max—and I and others, too, after our entirely incomparable fashion—tried to lay down. Well, not even Ruskin was a really successful road-builder. Before Max Goldberg's good intentions could be paved, a path had to be hacked through a hedge of thorns early in the first *lustrum* p.M. (*post Maxfontem*). If you thirst to be informed, you shall drink from this lesser well in the next chapter.

Meantime, CEA continued to run smoothly under Goldbergian direction. Irregularities in the timing of elections, such as have been observed during his earlier years, ceased to occur in the latter *lustrum*. With the evolving progression from Second Vice-President to First, and thence in normal practice to President, (George) Bruce Dearing—succeeding Kathrine Koller—became Association President in 1956, Harry Redcay Warfel in 1957, Henry Whittington Sams in 1958, John Ciardi in 1959, and Donald Jacob Lloyd for 1960. The College English Association continued, as it would through 1969, to follow MLA for its annual convention: to Chicago in 1955, as reported in the preceding chapter; to Washington, D.C., in December of 1956; to Madison, Wisconsin, in September of 1957; to New York City in December, 1958; and again to Chicago in December, 1959. A year later, CEA would hold its first-ever convention in Philadelphia; but by the end of 1960 Max Goldberg had been out of office for twelve months, and so the doings in that city are properly subject for a following, more troubled chapter, where brotherly love will sometimes be found in rather short supply.

At the Chicago Modern Language Association convention of December 27-29, 1955, a significant development occurred for MLA - CEA relations. Exactly a decade earlier, beginning on December 26, 1945, Robert Fitzhugh with the assistance of Joyce Kellogg had inaugurated a placement service for the College English Association during MLA in that same city. Now after ten years' observation, the host Association decided to set up its separate placement bureau as part of its own convention activities. Fortunately, as generally has happened at critical moments in our organizational history, good will prevailed over any potential animosity. As if to forestall the thought that duplication meant duplicity, *PMLA's* "For Members Only" column denied any intention of squeezing out other placement services; and, through amicable negotiation, Executive Goldberg persuaded his counterpart of MLA to agree "to help publicize our year-round availablity." For fifteen successive joint conventions, before CEA went its own way in the Spring of 1970, the two placement agencies operated in amity and, as it were, side-by-side though often (I am not sure whether I should not say usually) in different hostelries. [5]

Well did Bruce Dearing observe, albeit with no overt reference to the averted awkwardness arising from duplicated placement activities, in the peroration of his message at Chicago as President-Elect:

> All of you must know that in our Executive Director, Max Goldberg, we have the nearest thing to an Arabian Nights genie that any group wistfully rubbing the tarnished old lamp of liberal learning could hope to command. Most of you will have witnessed some of his prodigies of energy and imagination. . . . I shall then, in my role as ritual Aladdin for the year, essay to rub the lamp to the best of my ability, and we shall all see what Max can bring forth.

President Dearing and, in their turn, Presidents Warfel, Sams, and Ciardi—and also Vice-President Donald J. Lloyd as he approached the Presidency at the end of the Age of Max— were to continue to rub that **un**tarnished lamp, to the unqualified benefit of the Association winding up its fourth *lustrum* and Max Goldberg's second. A wonderful lamp it was, with a wondrous genius serving it upon—yet in—command.

The convention of 1956 was the first national CEA gathering in the District of Columbia since 1946.[6] After sustained front-page publicity in every issue of the *Critic* from September through December, attendance of the continuous program session, social hour, dinner, and business meeting at the Mayflower Hotel on Friday, December 28, was reported as "over a hundred CEA members." In addition, a second annual Regional Breakfast was held the next morning at the Washington Statler, where the CEA Bureau of Appointments also operated during the daze of the MLA convention.

The Friday afternoon program, directed by Donald J. Lloyd, had as theme English as an International Language: Implications for College English Teachers. Whereas the first Great War had been destructive of school language programs (particularly of the once-favored but then hated "enemy tongue," German), World War II had given a great impetus to foreign-language study. At the same time, however, far more than the earlier war, it had thrust English (American English, especially) into a position of primacy. Symptomatically—and also conveniently, in view of the location of the meeting—six speakers and panelists were equally divided between university professors and representatives of three government agencies: the Office of Education, the U.S. Information Agency, and the International Educational Exchange Service of the Department of State. The conclusions reached were digested to five words as opening sentence of a report of the deliberations printed in the *CEA Critic* for January, 1957: "World peace depends upon language." Presumably, nobody in Washington outside the Russian Embassy knew that a dangerous baby satellite was gestating for birth just over nine months later. Give us peace in our time!

I pause here to mention that at the beginning of 1957, with that same January issue, the *Critic* underwent one of its periodical (no pun intended) metamorphoses of typographic style, a change approved by the directors during their Summer meeting at Amherst in July of the preceding year. The number of columns was reduced from four to three, and together with

slightly larger type (changed to a sans-serif font that was pro-
gressively dropped during the next couple of years) and wider
"leading" between lines gave a more open appearance to the
layout. Whether those alterations had anything to do with the
reversion of Lee Holt's title to Managing Editor (for four
months, in the second half of 1956, he had been shown on
the mast as Executive Editor, in accordance with a
"promotion" also granted by the directors in July, 1956), I shall
allow to remain a teasing mystery. [7]

As I have said in another connection, it appears certain that
Managing Editor Holt became—as Max Goldberg himself more
than hinted [8]—to an intensifying degree the effective editor of
the *CEA Critic*, if not necessarily of the stream of brochures
and reports that the Secretariat poured out in profusion not
only for the membership but for Academia, and also Negotia
Vulgaria, more generally. I am able to attest, from personal
experiences as a contributor, to Lee Holt's continuous
dedicated service during most of the decade of the '50's, but
am not really in a position to assess it fully. His burden must
have been great, indeed, and I am not at all sure it has been
adequately appreciated.

I now pick up the thread of annals where I dropped it when
I so rudely interrupted myself across the way. On the model
of the university-hosted convention of 1949 at Palo Alto,
California, the Modern Language Association went to Madison,
Wisconsin, in September (rather than the normal post-
Christmas period) of 1957, naturally drawing the CEA in its
wake. Our Association also revived a whilom option by
substituting for the more usual dinner an official luncheon
preceding events on the afternoon of Tuesday, September 10.
"Suppers for Officers" were, however, scheduled on both
September 9 and 10, as well as the by now established Regional
Breakfast ("for Regional Officers and Directors") on
September 11. Donald Sears, who had been charioteer of a
troika that conducted a Regional Breakfast in the District of
Columbia the year before (with Edgar Hirshberg and Patrick
Hogan), was in charge of that event at Madison.

President Harry R. Warfel was program chairman at Madison for a consideration of The State of Our Profession. Appropriately, William Riley Parker, recently retired Secretary of MLA, bespoke his "Afterthoughts on a Profession." During the business meeting immediately following the luncheon, First Vice-President Henry W. Sams gave an extensive report on "what the officers and committees of CEA have been thinking about and doing during the past year," from which ample extracts were printed in the December *Critic* under a slightly opaque or at least unimaginative headline: "Report of the Committee of the Whole."

In 1958, CEA returned (with MLA) to New York for a December convention and (on its own) for an evening banquet "attended by nearly one hundred" and business session, following a general meeting announced for 4:30 p.m. as "[o]pen to all interested persons." A Comprehensive Review of English Studies was the theme for the afternoon program, arranged by President Henry Sams. Edward Gordon, Albert Marckwardt, and Willard Thorp gave a panel presentation of the deliberations during four three-day meetings, in the year just ending, of the Cooperative Committee on English Studies (Basic Issues). [9] Lee Holt's account of the panel and the ensuing general discussion (published in the *CEA Critic*, January, 1959) shows that more questions were asked than answered. "Do we have a profession?" Thorp inquired. "Edward Gordon asked whether English should include things like life adjustment and public speaking."

> During a lively discussion period ... Professor Marckwardt said that the conferees all recognized the importance of a strong subject-matter training for the teacher, but no one would deny that some teaching methods must also be learned. No agreement was reached, however, as to what agencies should carry on the teacher training.

A fourth annual Regional Breakfast was conducted on the following morning (Monday, December 29) under the chairmanship of Patrick G. Hogan, Jr., who was becoming increasingly prominent in regional CEAffairs, with Donald A. Sears serving as secretary. President Sams spoke on "The Role of National CEA" and Pat Hogan on "The Role of CEA Regionals." As has been considerably bruited already, in the late 1950's the whole question of the national - regional relationship was beginning to boil up—even though, so far, rather invisibly and below the surface—and not long after the opening of the next *lustrum* would burst upon the "federation" of College English Associations with pent-up force.

A codification important in that connection was reached by the directors of CEA during the December convention of 1958 at New York. According to a report signed by Maxwell H. Goldberg in the *Critic* of the following April, "the three men (after the executive director) who have been most active in regional work [are] Patrick G. Hogan, Jr.; Albert P. Madeira; and Donald A. Sears."

> The work of the first two is to remain essentially the same: Pat Hogan is to continue his excellent grass-roots work with the regionals through his committee [on Regional Activity and Development] and the annual breakfast which it runs; Al Madeira continues to be the clearing house at the national office for regional information. Don Sears, however, assumes a new office as middle-man, that of Co-ordinator of Regional Activities.
>
> ... The three officers (Hogan, Sears, Madeira) should operate as a team in close co-operation with one another and with the key people in the regional arena where the year's action is to take place.
>
> ... In sum, the Co-ordinator of Regional Activities is to function as an Executive Secretary of the present committee.

Once more, I ruminate ruefully: If only the great organizer, Max Goldberg, could have gone on indefinitely as planner and supervisor of CEActivities, regional (through his able agents) as well as national!

The pattern of alternating the annual MLA - CEA joint convention between New York and Chicago, though not yet (or indeed ever) fully instituted, was followed when both Associations went back to the latter city in December of 1959. President Ciardi was announced for a CEA address on the intriguing subject of "How Does a Poem Mean *Man*?" to be delivered at the Palmer House in the late afternoon of Monday, December 28, after which delegates would be "taxied to the Quadrangle Club of the University of Chicago for a social hour and dinner meeting," [10] the latter then dissolving into an unusually portentous business meeting. The by now fully customary Regional Breakfast was scheduled for the following morning. I cannot recall how my invitation came about, for though I was Immediate Past President of the Conference of College Teachers of English of Texas, there was then no direct connection between CCTE and CEA. Very likely Pat Hogan simply invited me to walk across Wabash Avenue with him to Stouffer's Restaurant, for my first-ever College English Association refection.

I would have sworn that I also heard John Ciardi's speech the day before and that it drew an unusually heavy attendance. [11] were it not that the *CEA Critic* in January, 1960, recorded that he was not present either at the Regional Breakfast (where incoming President Donald J. Lloyd substituted as panelist) or at the main meeting:

> ... the poet-president was still in New Jersey, grounded by the heavy fog that had cancelled all flights from the East Coast.
>
> With a few hours' notice, Vice-President Harry T. Moore of the University of Southern Illinois stepped into the role of main speaker. Addressing himself to the subject of contemporary literature, Professor Moore charted the realms of the Beatniks in America and the Angry Young Men in Great Britain.

And I thought I was hearing how a poem means *man*! Incidentally, but interestingly, history was repeating itself in two ways. In 1947, Odell Shepard was snowed in by an Eastern blizzard and prevented from journeying to the Midwest and delivering his scheduled Presidential address to the College English Association at Detroit; and in Chicago eight years later, Mitford Mathews had to fill in as speaker when John Ciardi became ill and was not able to attend the Association's convention of 1955.

At Chicago in 1959, the absent President missed a thorough changing of the guard: Executive Director, Treasurer, and control of editorial and placement functions. Already a year earlier, in December of 1958, Editor and Executive Director Goldberg had given notice of an "unalterable decision" to withdraw at the end of 1959, perhaps influenced by intimation or positive foreknowledge of a sabbatical leave that would be granted by the University of Massachusetts in the academic year 1959-60. As a result of a sustained "quiet search," conducted principally by Donald Lloyd as chairman of a Committee on National Staff Changes (ancestor of the Committee on Ongoing Concerns now regularly headed by the incumbent Second Vice-President, and of an occasional *ad-hoc* Personnel Review Committee), functions of the Goldbergian administration were distributed between John Hicks[12] of Stetson University and Donald A. Sears of Upsala College (both of whom were soon to find other academic homes). The somewhat irregular division of labors between these two new officers, and also the role or roles of another official, will occupy our attention at the opening of LUSTRUM FIVE.

Attentive readers may have noticed that comparatively little has been said about CEA Institutes during the second *lustrum* of the Age of Max. The fact is that for reasons never fully aired in public records, and I confess cloudy to me, they ceased to be *CEA* Institutes. A quotation several pages back from the Executive Secretary's report for the year 1954 shows an evident eagerness to confirm that "The CEA is not financially dependent on The CEA-I[nstitute], or vice versa." I sometimes seem to sense between the lines of the Association journal a feeling among elective hierarchy that the Institute tail was beginning to wag the CEA dog. With the utmost circumspection, on June 27, 1957, the Board of Directors "voted permission [*sic*] to the Humanities Center for Liberal Education in an Industrial Society[13] to organize as an independent entity." An account on the front page of the September *Critic*, signed by CEA President Harry R. Warfel, adds:

> The Board felt that this agency, which began in 1952 as the CEA Institute, had more than fulfilled its function as an arm of CEA. ...
> It is with regret ... that the Board says farewell to this offspring of CEA. But like any grown-up child it is ready to go forth alone with parental blessing.

According to a report delivered by First Vice-President Henry W. Sams during the Association's convention at Madison, Wisconsin, on September 10, 1957—and (in the quotation below) indicated as paraphrasing, at least in part, Donald Lloyd—

> The Humanities Center, as now organized, an independent organization designed to make industry and the liberal arts better acquainted with one another, is no longer a creature of CEA. A number of CEA members retain active membership in the Center committees. Max continues his energetic direction of both.
> But the CEA, as such, is free to concentrate once more on its middle initial.

How much influence the severing of his beloved CEA Institute from his beloved CEA may have had on Max Goldberg's decision to retire from managing the latter, I can only speculate. After meditating the barbed last paragraph of the quotation just above, I would not dream of asking.

Be that speculation as it may, after the Chicago meeting of 1959 the true Age of Max was at an end in CEA—though of course his interest, participation, and even office-holding did not cease. The entire Massachusetts troika (behold how I courageously resist any unworthy temptation of an alliterative "Mafia") composed of Goldberg, Madeira, and Holt (of whom only the first attended the convention at Chicago) went out of office together—except that Lee Holt was simultaneously elected to the Board of Directors. The center of administrative gravity was beginning to shift markedly westward and southward. The new Editor and *de-facto* director of placement, although a New Englander, was teaching in the Newark area and presently would remove to upstate New York, thence to Washington, D.C., and eventually (with a disastrous detour via Nigeria) to California; the Executive Secretary (within a year he reverted to this older form of the title), and also Treasurer ostensibly *pro tem.*, was in Florida and afterwards—as Treasurer—would be GTT (gone to Texas). The President and both Vice-Presidents in 1960, whether by happenstance or design, all held Midwestern academic affiliations. [14] Along with two members from New England, the directors ranged from New Jersey, Pennsylvania, Washington (D.C.), and Virginia through Florida, Ohio, and Texas to California.

Max Goldberg's concluding service to the College English Associaton as he rounded out his administrative years was preparation of a comprehensive "Report for 1950-1959: Survey and Interpretation" in three parts, published in successive issues of the *CEA Critic* beginning with the March number of 1960. [15] It is a document of the utmost importance for viewing the Association in what may be considered its golden, or at least halcyon, decade. Part I treats "A. the general content of American education (most briefly); B. the **Intra**-Organizational (Intra-CEA) context." Part II concerns CEA in relation to other professional organizations. Part III paints visions of "The Future," far as Maxwell's eye could C E A.

Although that discerning eye was not blind to dangers and problems, it was able to perceive a generally "favorable picture" of the educational mileu in the 1950's, by viewing "increased support of liberal studies by . . . corporations and . . . foundations," a "strengthened tendency toward rapprochement between the professional educators' concerns and those of the subject matter people," and "fresh emphasis on quality, rigor; the encouragement of the talented." Penetratingly, while once again noting a "shift in the labor market of our profession, from an employer's to an employee's market," the retiring

Executive Director pointed out that the new college teachers must be guided to expect, along with more opportunity for appointment and improved remuneration, that "increases in these opportunities will be largely in the underclass service courses of the four-year colleges, the junior colleges, and the community colleges."

> So far as the main academic load of a given institution of higher education is concerned, our job will be to provide service and liberalizing courses for non-English (and, to a great extent) non-liberal arts majors.

Part II of the report, surveying external relations of the College English Association to sister organizations of similar or related interests, regards the convention of 1952 (at Boston) that raised and effectively answered the question "Teach Teaching to Teachers?" as a watershed, "a critical turning of the tide," because of the participation and concurrence of "[o]fficers of the major organizations concerned with the study of teaching of English and allied studies, and of the humanities, generally ...":

> For CEA and the profession, the annual CEA meeting of 1952 marked ... the fulfillment, on the level of accepted principle, of one of CEA's chief historical missions—to get professional humanistic scholars of English and allied studies to assume once again, as they had in the past, central responsibility for the preparation as teachers of the young men and women whom they were helping to initiate into the profession.

According to Max (whose phrasing, like an electromagnet, can take on weight under excitement), "this event drastically reduced the potential of one of CEA's most readily available dynamos of programmatic energy ..." He explained this paradox of failure-and-success as meaning that by winning its battle to put urgencies of the teacher-scholar in front of established claims of the scholar-teacher, our Association had freed itself "to search for fresh sources of programmatic energy, to discover fresh dynamos to which to hook up our subsequent national and regional CEA programmatic drives."

A principal evidence of "the effort to tap fresh yet relevant energy for CEA programmatic momentum" was the development of CEA Institutes on Industry and Liberal Education.

These Institutes helped to realize a long-standing objective of the CEA—to bring the college English teacher closer to the social and cultural realities of our day and to enable the layman better to understand what the English teacher, especially as humanist, was trying to do. They also gave the CEA an alternative dynamo to which to hook up for programmatic energy during a transitional period when it was realigning its forces, its thinking, in the light of the historical moment of December of 1952. Here was a field that the other organizations were not yet preoccupied with. Here was a field where so much was in the air that needed crystalizing. Into this effort, then, in the years 1952 through 1957,[16] major CEA national executive and programmatic effort was directed.

Not only the comparatively brief section of the "Report for 1950-1959" headed **The Intra-Organizational Context** but the entire document does much, indeed, to clarify Max Goldberg's understanding of what he was about and what he considered that CEA ought to continue to be about.

We have advanced ... in number of *regional representatives where regional affiliates have not yet emerged* [emphasis added]; and in number of regional affiliates.

Together, the issues of *The CEA Critic* from 1950 through 1959 constitute a diary, a day book, a log, a journal of our professional frustrations and strivings, misgivings and affirmations, despairs and aspirations, dreams and down-to-earth doings. Above all, they have been a medium of exchange, a source book and manual for our colleagues.

In 1950 the organizational machinery of the CEA was minimal. . . . A serious lack was a rationale of the relationships between national and regional affiliates, and a definition of the limits and scope of authority and responsibility as between the national and the regional. Moreover, without incorporation [it occurred in 1954], the officers and directors were personally responsible for the Association obligations, and the foundations were loath even to consider the possibility of grants. . . . The Association sometimes honored by inviting to serve as officer or director. In accepting, the nominee sometimes honored the Association far more than it honored him. If a given officer wanted to work, there was plenty of work. But there was no systematic demand or provision for such work.

. . . one of the ruling concepts of the CEA in the past decade [has been] a strong and flexible federation of virtually autonomous affiliates. . . . What I propose . . . is an expansion of the present pattern of national secretariat organization to include several administrative assistants at different places—men [*sic*—Fi donc, Max!] who have a feel for what we have been trying to do regionally and nationally, and who already have records of commendable—in some instances strikingly devoted and otherwise superior—work for CEA—work involving at least some degree of leadership and responsibility.

A master-concept . . . has visualized a network of vitally interrelated regional affiliates, nourished but not dominated by *The CEA Critic* and other national publications, and by the annual national program, together with a flexible, energetic, resourceful, dynamic central headquarters; a federation encouraged, but not pampered or coerced, by the national office. It was to be an image of a nation-wide federation of regional affiliates concerned with grass-roots needs, problems, and opportunities seen within a national context.

... Among the organizations sharing our professional responsibilities, the CEA should continue to be what it has become more and more explicitly and pervasively during the latter years of the 1950-59 period—a "third force"—alert, flexible, imaginative, and, above all, with a deep and realistic sense of basic responsibility to the student, the profession, American higher education, and American society and culture.

... At one time or another in the past decade, almost every *-ism* connected with our profession has sought to gain for itself the official and exclusive sanction of the CEA and to make of the CEA its official instrument. ... CEA has tried to keep clear of final and absolute commitment to doctrines or dogmas.

Remembering the way in which both the New Linguistics and the loyal conservative opposition were given fair, impartial hearings throughout the Age of Max, when one of the most prominently vocal members of CEA and ultimately of its hierarchy was (in my term) a New Linguisticist, I honor Maxwell Henry Goldberg for the words quoted just above, and for the truly *liberal* spirit of mediation they reflect, as much as for anything he ever said or did.

We now have provision for a number of committees, together accounting for almost all the central concerns of our profession and our association. ... We now have a body of national officers and directors, most of whom have had a number of years of experience—regional and national—in CEA work, and who, therefore, are available for effective CEA service beyond the conventionally expected deliberative services of an office holder in such a professional association as ours.

I cannot go into the extensive and at times interlocked work of the committee network of CEA in the Age of Max—far more complex than the modest phrase "a number of committees" might suggest. [17] I must, however, name two in particular: Bruce Dearing's Committee on Constitution and By-Laws that carried through a "revision" (analyzed in LUSTRUM THREE) that was very nearly an original enterprise; and the Committee on Ph.D. Curriculum Revision, headed by Alvan S. Ryan. The latter committee's report, on "Doctoral Studies in English and Preparation for Teaching," was distributed in various forms for preliminary consideration during its interim stages; it was completed in June of 1957 and published in full in the March, 1958, *CEA Critic* (and also as a separate). It was the subject of long and wide consideration, not only in the pages of the *Critic* but as far abroad as sessions of the Committee on Basic Issues in the Teaching of English, where it reportedly "figured substantially in discussions of the committee." It stands as one of the seminal acts of the Association during the Age of Max, and has generally been so recognized.

Reading today the text of "Doctoral Studies in English and Preparation for Teaching" is not a startling experience, but that fact may only be a measure of the fourth (plus) of a century since issuance of a highly regarded proposal that fit the advanced spirit of its time. The main recommendations are conveniently and clearly summarized near the beginning of the report: 1. Broader and more flexible programs, "including opportunities for inter-departmental study, with emphasis on evaluation and criticism as the final aim of literary study." 2. Critical review and reappraisal of "the meaning of concentration or specialization." 3. "The encouragement of foreign language study," tempered by refocusing of the *requirement* upon "knowledge of one foreign language and **literature**." 4. "Less stress on the doctoral thesis as an 'original contribution to knowledge,' and more encouragement of theses aimed at interpretation and criticism." 5. "Continued efforts throughout the graduate program to prepare candidates for a teaching career . . ." 6. "Such study of modern linguistic scholarship as will give the candidate a command of linguistic methods and of the explicit structure of modern English, so that he [*sic*] can deal in a scholarly way with language problems from simple literacy to the critical analysis of literature." [18]

As I have pointed out previously (cf. fn. 8), among all else the revealing "Report for 1950-1959" of the retiring Executive Director lends some support to my judgment that during most of the Age of Max it was Lee Holt, even more than the master himself, who effectively edited the *CEA Critic*. It hardly is to be doubted that the "promotion" which Holt was offered in 1956 and which for a time was written into his title flown from the mast of the journal as "Executive Editor," was recognition of services he had already been rendering as Managing Editor for several years, and marked a reassessment rather that reassignment of duties. Assuredly, the editorial transition between the first and second *lustra* of the decade of the 'Fifties was as smooth and nearly invisible as the conversion of Max Executive Secretary to Max Executive Director.

Still, our working assumption has to be that to a degree Lee Elbert Holt "grew into" his editorial functions as Max Goldberg found his own multiplex and mounting activities more and more and more time-demanding. [19] One indicator was the increasing formal attention to editorials (which had been comparatively unimportant or casual, at any rate, for Max [20])— both unsigned and, especially in the last year or two of Holt's service, flagged with the increasingly familiar initials "L. E. H." One of the editorials thus signed (January, 1959), containing, in the writer's words, "gloomy comments" on the "inhumane and anti-literary atmosphere" in which "gifted students are now forced to read everything but the primary texts with which they fell in love under our tutelage and which are the reason for their going on to do graduate work," aroused the kind of sustained lively response that had traditionally characterized interchange of opinion in CEA's journals. Among other replies, this editorial brought forth the maiden contribution from a future Association President, Howard O. Brogan, titled simply "On Graduate Study" (September, 1959):

... I read that editorial with surprise ...

This sort of thing is of a piece with the wholesale condemnation of scholarly publication of which some CEA
members appear to be fond. ...

Let us improve graduate study if we can. We are not
going to improve it by removing the scholarship. Let us
value good teaching highly, but let us not suppose that
good teaching could possibly be divorced from good
scholarship. Nobody can teach well what he does not
know, and this is at least one of the reasons why good
teaching is a rare and difficult art.

Lee Holt's even-tempered tolerance of opposition was also
fully in the tradition of the Association. To an earlier attack
than that just quoted, he had replied mildly (April, 1959): "If
we are going to have discussion, we must have generalizations without being understood to say that there are no
exceptions to the generalizations." And he had gone on, quiz-
zically, to quote Thoreau's advice to the Society for the
Diffusion of Useful Knowledge: "Go to grass. You have eaten
hay long enough. The spring has come with its green crop."

If the journal had a weakness in the Age of Max (and Lee)—
but I protest I do not count it as weakness—it would be that
the *Critic* did not strongly advance on the side of the literary
essay. Until recent years, when a tilting of interest carried
that bob far into the yon side of its arc, it had always been
so with the CEA journals. The College English Association
originated partly in dissatisfaction with underemphasis by other
organizations, in particular the Modern Language Association
(which has since mended its ways), of the pedagogic side of
our profession, and so with imputed overemphasis of purely
literary scholarship.

I must not be misconceived as intimating that Editor
Goldberg or Managing (and quondam Executive) Editor Holt
was hostile to literary history and criticism. I refer only to
a traditional, continuing weight of emphasis—with overcompen-
sation, if one chooses to view it so, for what was seen as a
comparative neglect of the teacher in the teacher = scholar
equation. Nevertheless, literature was far from neglected,

much less ignored, during the second lustrum of the 1950's.

I will mention (without implying lack of merit in other such contributions) the following titles because of their varied interest: George S. Wykoff, "Walden Pond 1955" (December, 1955)—not "literary," exactly, but an account of an inspection of the mid-twentieth-century reality; "The Speaker of the Evening" (January, 1956)—a brilliant little piece of light verse by Robert T. Fitzhugh on the surprising model of Alexander Pope; E. L. Jacobs, *"The Emperor Jones* and Aristotle" (October, 1956): ". . . in spite of whatever of the bizarre is in it, [the play] is true tragedy"; Frederick J. Hoffman, "Katherine Anne Porter's *Noon Wine"* (November, 1956): "The experience of *Noon Wine* lies in reading it in the rhythms of understanding that its style and form dictate"; "Der Jammerwoch" (December, 1956; attributed to Hermann von Schwindel—not an original contribution but a reprint of the enormously amusing Kauderwelsch version of "Jabberwocky": "Bewahre doch vor Jammerwoch! / Die Zähne knirschen, Krallen kratzen! / Bewahr' vor Jubjub-Vogel, vor / Frumiösen Banderschnätzchen!"; Robert G. Tucker, "A Remedy for Criticism" (April, 1957)—a venture into theory: how to temper judgmental criticism with mercy; Morris Freedman, "Sound and Sense in Faulkner's Prose" (September, 1957)— a defense against animadversions of Edmund Wilson; J. Mitchell Morse, "Browning's Grammarian, Warts and All" (January, 1958)—a witty example of reading with one's wits about one ("Browning was always rich in irony. Like the Mesabi range. . . . And yet. And yet. . . . To contradict the disciples flatly would be as unperceptive as to take their estimate at face value. . . ."); James A. Fuller, "The Humanism of Thomas Mann" (October, 1958: "Throughout the works of Thomas Mann there is found a continuous struggle of mankind in this world. In depicting this struggle Mann is being essentially humanistic. . . ."); Willis D. Jacobs, "Carlyle and Mill" (February, 1959): "This note . . . suggests that the [phrase in the eighth paragraph of "The Everlasting No"] 'Mill of Death' . . . is a deliberate reference to John Stuart Mill and his doctrines, by a man brought to anguish by them"; Harry R. Warfel, "The Mathematics of Poe's Poetry" (May, 1959)—despite the title, an essay in literary criticism (though with particular reference to Poe's use of language).

Famine? Rather, an appreciative reader might feel thonself impelled to exclaim "A feast!" (If he or she is not acquainted with the useful locution "thon[self]," may Women's Lib cry shame on his or her head.)

Several observations and comments may be in order. The literary essays (along with other articles) published in the *Critic* (1) continued to come frequently out of regional meetings, from which contributions were welcomed and indeed solicited; and (2) as often as not were of the kind named by a later Editor of CEA, Earle Labor, "usable criticism"—that is, studies of writings especially suited to undergraduate teaching and considered, at least partly, in that aspect. (3) After J. Gordon Eaker ceased to be Literary Editor during the first half of the Age of Max, book reviews became exceedingly uncommon in the *Critic*; in fact, I half suspect that Seymour Rudin's laudatory review of Doris V. Falk's *Eugene O'Neill and the Tragic Tension*, titled "Sane Criticism" (March, 1959), was offered and accepted as a more or less independent article, instead of being commissioned in the conventional way as a book review.

Besides literary matters, the subject of linguistics (new and old) continued presenting itself to be tossed and gored in the pages of the journal, including a spirited exchange between the comparatively "traditional" Ralph B. Long, "Is Trager-Smith Linguistics What We Need?" (March, 1957):

> ... we must never forget that a phonemics is not a grammar, and it is only one part of a "structure." We cannot really substitute analysis of pitches, stresses, and junctures for syntax.

—and Robert P. Stockwell, "Trager-Smith Linguistics Is What We Need" (May, 1957):

> ... I must first acknowledge that I still remain in doubt as to the exact nature of the contribution which any kind of linguistics can make to the composition class. ...

About all it can do is to pour a good concrete foundation
to support the cross of grammar.

. . . not one book is mentioned in which an attempt
has been made to apply Trager-Smith-Fries-etc.
linguistics to teaching English composition: Whitehall,
Roberts, Lloyd and Warfel go unscathed. . . . I am sure
their measure has not yet been taken, and it is obvious
that they, at least, along with many others, find that the
tools of structural linguistics produce fruitful statements
for the student who is interested in composing better
prose.

The September, 1957, *Critic* printed a letter by Keith
Hollingsworth of Wayne State University commending Long's
article but not referring to Stockwell's. Hollingsworth's principal intention was, however, to reassert "the values of
historical study," particularly of Old English.

Speaking of Wayne State University, I must quote from a
somewhat grudging bicentenary lecture titled "A Wreath for
Noah Webster" that Wayne's Donald Lloyd delivered to another
scholarly society on December 6, 1958, and published in the
CEA Critic of March, 1959:

According to Professor Harry Warfel, Webster's affec-
tionate and careful biographer, we have reason to see
Noah Webster as in effect the morning star of modern
American linguistics. Let us remember that the morning
star does not itself give light; it only forewarns of the
rising sun, which may be long in coming. It is the sun
that brings the light.

I must also mention a (to me, at least) delightful satire
by Milton Kalb—printed in the same issue with Robert
Stockwell's reply to Ralph Long—of the everything-goes school
of linguistics, headed "Leave Your Cooking Alone": [21]

. . . the dietitianist has eliminated the words *stale, fresh,
insipid taste, smell, look, aroma, savor, appeal, tempt,
stimulate, piquant, good (cooking), bad, better, worse,*

> *mouth-watering, disgusting, manners, standards, vulgar,*
> etc. ... Dietetics is entirely concerned with the chemical
> and physical composition of the food, and hence is not
> an art or a pseudo-science, but a true science, a branch
> of chemistry, botany, zoology, and physiology, with a little
> physics and anthropology thrown in.

(You will either love or hate that last touch of anthropology,
which I confess struck me as a stroke of genius.)

The *CEA Critic* for January, 1960, the first offered by Editor
Donald A. Sears, was a very hopeful number. Graced by the
innovation of halftone illustrations,[22] it showed on the front
page a smiling Max Goldberg handing over some presumably
official paper to his sober-miened executive successor,
John Hicks, and on the op-ed page a modishly flat-topped
President Donald J. Lloyd proclaiming sweetness and light for
all. A theme of the whole issue, including Pat Hogan's new
"Regional Exchange" column (soon to bear his portrait, also),
was successful search eventuating in orderly transition. All
functions of the Association were represented to be in able
(if generally new) and willing, nay eager, hands. Suitable
sentiments about the delicate, only slightly tested, national -
regional balance in CEA were attributed to both the incoming President ("a loose federation which non-joiners feel
somehow moved to join") and the newly appointed Executive
Director ("He stressed that there will be no tampering with
regional autonomy ...").

That a bright new day was breaking for the proclaimed
federation of *pares inter pares* constituting the College English
Association, metropolitan and dispersed, appeared very nearly
self-evident. Who could dream that such a dawn might be
brightest before the gathering of darkling clouds? Was it the
sun that shone, or the flash that foretells rumbling thunder?

(Here endeth the reading of LUSTRUM FOUR.)

Notae pedales for

LUSTRUM FOUR

[1] It may be of interest for what I have called a phenomenon of round-numbered years in our Association that the transfer of the Secretary-ship of the Modern Language Association from William Riley Parker to George Winchester Stone, Jr., occurred in 1956, and from John Hurt Fisher to Executive Director William D. Schaefer in 1971. I do not attempt to account for the lapse of one year in each instance, except to suggest that CEA has perhaps always been more timely than MLA.

[2] I am reluctant to say "organization person," for Max Goldberg was and is every inch a man.

[3] This whole chapter is more full than others of extended quotations, particularly musings and communications of Max. Since faithful preservation of thoughts is the main point, I have allowed myself a modicum of liberty in slightly consolidating matter where I felt that clarity and economy are served without distortion of intent or style. (I am conscious of having sometimes blurred the original paragraph structure.) May the blessed shades of Ronald B. McKerrow and W.W. Greg, who telepathically guided me in a quarter century of effort to teach the complex composite discipline called Bibliography, pray for the repose of my textually sinful soul.

[4] The witty but too-modest Executive Secretary ought, rather, to have called the slogan a *MAX-im*—or (related to a phrase he was to fix on CEA elsewhere) a *zanyism*.

[5] The candor for which this truthful History achieved an underground reputation in manuscript, during several years of compilation, obliges me to record that Max Goldberg was quoted by CEA's placement director, Albert P. Madeira, as feeling "that MLA's new placement service, set up for the duration of the MLA conference, cut into our 'act' at Chicago." Madeira predicted that adjustments in the joint operations would be worked out, as indeed they were over the course of time. In 1957, for instance, the notice in the *CEA Critic* of the September convention at the University of Wisconsin stated: "The CEA Placement Bureau will be run in connection with the MLA Placement Bureau . . ." For the 1958 convention at New York, a similar announcement read: "To ensure close co-operation between the MLA and the CEA, the CEA Bureau of Appointments will staff a desk in the interview room of the MLA Faculty Exchange . . ." I hazard the guess that Madeira, who kept what is called a low profile, poured as much oil on roiled waters as Goldberg.

With regard to the imputed fifteen years of amicable "side-by-side" operation, the reader should defer judgment until (s)he reads LUSTRUM FIVE. There were to be, certain evidence suggests, some lean and hungry years for CEA placement.

[6] In a sense, that previous Washington meeting of 1946 had been a long-delayed convention. In 1942, MLA had first planned to go to the District of Columbia, then because of wartime conditions in the capital changed the place to New York City, and finally aborted the December meeting altogether because of holiday congestion of transport. Readers of LUSTRUM ONE will recall that our more resourceful CEA actually did meet, taking its separate show to New York in January of 1943.

[7] A proposed amendment of the By-Laws to change the title officially was announced for vote at the annual meeting that December. Did it fail? Or did Lee Holt decline the intended honor? At any rate, his old title of Managing Editor was restored to the mast of the January, 1957, *Critic*.

Readers probably are already so annoyed by my habit of not soliciting gossipy information of this kind from still-living worthies of our corporate past, that I can hardly suppose they will wax appreciably more wrathful if I retain one more little mystery. An old professor of mine in the field of Education (with a capital "E") had a slogan about the responsibility of a teacher in each grade: **Save something.** I feel that I must *save something* for gleaners of my stubble field after this vegetable love has been harvested—or, should I say, for skimmers of froth off my a-bounding CEA?

[8] In a comprehensive report of his decade of service (to be mentioned more particularly hereafter), Goldberg generously stated: "While retaining ultimate responsibility for *The CEA Critic*, especially for over-all policy, the executive officer has come to rely almost completely on his managing editor—in effect an executive editor—for seeing that this aspect of CEA enterprise functions adequately and tries to develop." (I opine that the last two words may be especially significant.)

[9] Cooperative undertakings marked CEActivity during the whole Age of Max. For lack partly of information and partly of space, I am sensible of having done scant justice to Goldbergian enterprise of that character. From time to time, it shines from the record like shook foil.

[10] I should be a little happier to confirm from a report in the January *Critic* of 1960 that "the sumptuous buffet was still as good as it had been in 1951 when last the CEA had met at the Club," except that the annual meeting of 1951 was held in Detroit, not Chicago. (I infer a misprint for 1953.)

[11] In view of my evident lapse of memory, it is possible that I am confusing 1959 (even though I most certainly did attend MLA/CEA that year) with some

other convention at Chicago, both for a Ciardi lecture and for a breakfast at Stouffer's. Or am I confounding Harry Moore with John Ciardi? Such is the gauzy fabric of biographical-historical evidence delivered by eyewitnesses.

[12] Not to be confused with John Harland Hicks of the University of Massachusetts, then as for years to come a prominent regional and national CEAer—and a walking antithesis of the "dour New Englander" of legend.

[13] The year before, that name had been taken "primarily to indicate as clearly as possible in the title the nature and scope of the Institute activities. The name *Institute* is now the title in use for the large conferences only."

[14] Himself a native of Massachusetts, Goldberg observed enthusiastically, in a final account of his stewardship (to be discussed in text immediately hereafter): "As it rounds out its twentieth [actually twenty-first] year, CEA is truly a **national** organization."

[15] Part II (April) was misheaded "Report for 1959-60 . . ."

[16] The year when the Institute (renamed Humanities Center), though remaining under Goldberg's direction, was detached from the College English Association. Somewhere (so let it be here), I must mention that Part III of this report points up a certain tension between "Those who prefer to regard the CEA as, chiefly, an organization" and "Those who prefer to regard CEA as, chiefly, a movement." I have several times referred to Max himself as a great *organization* man, but it is clear that he also was a tremendous prime *mover.* He saw himself as a mediator between those two concepts.

[17] I am reminded of a "Happy Thought" I plucked years ago from Stevenson's *Garden:*

> The world is so full of a number of things,
> I'm sure we should all be as happy as kings.

[18] Along with its restrained approval ("Such study . . .") of the New Linguistics, the committee allowed one of its members, Donald J. Lloyd, to "form a separate committee" and furnish an addendum to the report, strongly endorsing structural linguistics.

[19] Lee Holt certainly was in charge of the journal in the Fall semester of 1959, when Max Goldberg was on University leave-of-absence "for study and writing."

[20] It could be said that pretty nearly everything the prolific Goldberg has ever written has been a sort of continuous, long-running editorial. Yet he never seemed especially taken with the opportunity to display his thoughts on the

cramped platform at the foot of the second page, where the editorial mast was stepped, but tended to use that space much like any other in the journal.

[21] It occurs to me that I have underplayed the role of satire in the *CEA Critic* during the Age of Max. Just for instance, in the same May, 1957, number with Kalb's "Leave Your Cooking Alone," Edgar W. Hirshberg contributed a piece of futuristic fiction, "A Visit to Alma Mater," predicting the disappearance of the Ph.D. in favor of a new degree of Et.D. (Doctor of Television Education), with replacement of teaching faculty by "teleclerks." This issue was unfortunately marred by several misprints, including a misspelling of Hirshberg's name. (In the general Index for 1939-1958, the name was again misspelled—in yet another variant.)

[22] They were already in use, at least in some boiler-plate technology, for the likenesses of "The [wo]man who reads dictionaries" in World Publishing Company advertisements.

THE WALRUS SAID

being

LUSTRUM FIVE (1960 - 1965)

of

S A N S C U L O T T E

A NONKNICKERBOCKER HISTORY

of the

COLLEGE ENGLISH ASSOCIATION

Donald Albert Sears (about 1980)

LUSTRUM FIVE (1960 - 1965)

THE WALRUS SAID

Readers who have bated their breath since the end of the preceding chapter of this rarely dramatic History, expecting the College English Association to produce a big bang early in 1960 followed by a prolonged whimper, will be either relieved or (depending upon their temperament) annoyed to hear that the new *lustrum* embarked into destiny on a fairly even keel.

No catastrophe, certainly, yet a difficulty of the kind vulgarly called snafu did arise in the transfer of authority to a new crew of CEAmen. When Robert Fitzhugh had taken over from Burges Johnson in 1945, I fancy that there was comparatively little "paper work." Maxwell Goldberg speaks almost humorously of his own succession to Fitzhugh a *lustrum* later:

> . . . Somewhere in the battered filing cabinet that contained the CEA records when the headquarters were moved to the University of Massachusetts, was a copy of a pre-Second World War constitution . . .

It sounds delightfully informal and personal. Moving out of Massachusetts after another whole decade was, however, serious business, with part of the by then extensive College English Association records being destined for John Hicks in Florida, part for Donald Sears in New Jersey, and part for Patrick Hogan in Mississippi. In the general shuffling of executive duties, Pat Hogan was replacing Don Sears as Regional Coordinator, [1] besides retaining his chairmanship of the Committee on Regional Activity and Development and assuming Albert Madeira's former function of maintaining a "clearing house . . . for regional information."

Matters were complicated by the fact that documents of CEA and those of the Humanities Center (formerly the CEA Institute, but for several years detached though also directed by Maxwell H. Goldberg in the manner, *mutatis mutandis,*

(137)

of dual monarchies) had been imperfectly separated. The assumption was that all persons concerned could wait upon leisure and fair weather to straighten everything out, but the resignation of an administrative secretary who had been in charge of both files precipitated a crisis. Prompt action became imperative.

In the last days of February, 1960, therefore, Max Goldberg returned home to Amherst from a "sabbatical hideout in Connecticut," while Don Sears set out from New Jersey and John Hicks from De Land of Florida. It was a stormy season, with even the turnpikes and throughways precarious. Hicks decided to relieve Winter of discontent by flying instead of attempting to drive nearly a thousand miles north. President Donald Lloyd and Second Vice-President John Ball, "next to snowed in" at a seminar on communication (then a fad of college English teachers) in Virginia, on hearing of Hicks' change of plans drove to Washington, D.C., with the intention of conferring with him between flights; instead, they took him into their car and despite "a dull and threatening day" and ominous weather forecasts fetched him to Amherst. There the whole party including Don Sears and Max Goldberg "sat around in a room at the Mt. Pleasant Inn . . . , talking CEA futures into the small hours." I spare my readers the subsequent odyssey of Lloyd and Ball in "a fifteen hour drive through snow, sleet, freezing rain and fog to Michigan."

At Amherst, where John Hicks had first intended to "load his car with the most immediate essentials" to be selected from the CEArtifacts that he and others would sort for three days, he had no car to load. As *pis aller*, ". . . Don Sears carried the most vital equipment and records to Upsala for the time being, with others to be moved at convenience." Pat Hogan reported that "the major portion of the records and correspondence directly related to regional matters was separated and shipped to the present Regional Coordinator."

Difficulties were compounded by the fact that John Hicks was planning to migrate in July from an old-hat John B. Stetson University to a bouncing four-year-old University of South Florida; so, according to Donald Lloyd, the bulk of materials pertaining to a central office were "disentangled . . . gently from those of the Humanities Center, and marked ... for transfer ultimately to Tampa." Evidently, the "most vital" papers carried off by Don Sears must have included vital statistics on membership, for the *CEA Critic* directed that dues "be mailed to the Editoral Office, Upsala College, East Orange, N.J.," to which he took the journal as part of the general shift. Somehow, he also fell into superintendence of CEA's placement services. While the rather odd combination of duties on the part of an official designated only as Editor could, to be sure, have been made according to some predetermined complex plan, I fancy that fans of *A Midsummer Night's Dream* will concede that weather can vex this vale of tears at least as strongly in Midwinter as in Midsummer. Be that as it may, when Donald Albert Sears later received an amplified title and entered upon more extensive administrative duties for the Association, the change was not so extreme as might have been assumed by someone unaware of his multiple chores from the early part of 1960 through the Spring semester of the academic year 1961-62.

Meantime, CEAffairs went on pretty much in accustomed grooves. For the Philadelphia convention of 1960, a variation was made in the pattern that had been developing of a more or less continuous program starting with a late-afternoon session followed by a social hour, dinner, and business meeting, together with a Regional Breakfast early on the following morning. At Philadelphia a reception, dinner, and business meeting were deferred to the day of the breakfast, thus more effectively separating what was explicitly billed as a public meeting in the afternoon of December 27 from a partly social affair limited to "CEA members and guests" on the night of December 28.

The topic for the public meeting was ostensibly based on a complaint about graduate schools in the *NEA Journal* of April, 1960; however, it also pointed back at least obliquely— whether consciously and intentionally or not—to an editorial by Lee Holt in the January *Critic* of 1959, which as was shown near the end of LUSTRUM FOUR attracted considerable attention and controversy. A panel composed of Warner Rice, Joseph Doyle, John Ball, and Bruce Dearing threshed out the question: "Are the Graduate Schools Ruining Undergraduate English?" (reflected in a CEA Chap Book issued September, 1961, titled less tendentiously *The Ph.D. Today*).

Following breakfast the next morning another panel, consisting of James Barrs, Charles Clark, Joseph Doggett, and Edgar Hirshberg, mulled the topic: "The Regional Responsibility in 1961." A specifically practical contribution, offered by Ed Hirshberg, was a renewal of Max Goldberg's idea for "a package deal on the payment of national and regional dues at the same time." Sensible as it was, the scheme did not come into effect in 1961, or for a good number of years thereafter. Neither did Henry Adams' proposal from the floor that a "fall newsletter containing national developments should be sent to all regional officers." However, though I was not present to hear his suggestion,[2] as Regional Coordinator beginning five years later I did issue multilithed bulletins in an irregular and wild way. Since my time, they have been regularized (though frequency of issue has continued irregular), in an attractive printed form, as *The Regionalist*.

At the banquet that evening, a will-o'-the-wispish John Ciardi, having taken an excused absence from his own Presidential address the year before, this time did present himself as speaker. Donald J. Lloyd also delivered the current Presidential address. At the following business meeting Harry T. Moore, who as master of ceremonies had introduced Lloyd and Ciardi, was himself introduced as incoming President of the Association for 1961.

With the issue of January, 1960, the *CEA Critic* had moved its editorial office to Upsala College in Essex County, New Jersey, with the new place of publication being at nearby Livingston. Change of printshops tends to bring changes of typography and sometimes of format, but in this instance the journal continued to look—except for considerable use of halftones furnished out with capsule captions—surprisingly like its former self. The basic type face for text was closely imitated, though in a slightly larger point size. A predilection of Max Goldberg—or, more probably, Lee Holt—for use of italic capitals in headlines was no longer evident. Editorially a revitalized practice, not of course really innovation, was the frequent, becoming virtually regular, inclusion of miscellanea (ordinarily not in-house news) as NOTICE(S) OF NOTE. Letters to the Editor were encouraged, and one or several under that heading came to be expected in a normal issue of the journal. More unconventional was yielding of editorial columns to the President; Donald Lloyd several times availed himself of the opportunity. Other guest editorialists signed in from time to time, whereas an occasional signature "DAS" identified an item by the Editor. The *Critic* was becoming distinctly fuller, more often twelve than eight pages and commonly ten. A scene in a medieval scriptorium, from the first edition of Holinshed's *Scotland*, that had been printed as line cut for the Association's pioneering *News Letter* in December, 1939, was reproduced on the front page of the April, 1960, *Critic;* that Autumn it was adopted as a logograph and placed (in reduced size) at the head of the mast on the editorial page, and also in the address panel on the back page. [3]

To anticipate, two years later a change was made that not only affected the journal but had wider administrative implications. In March, 1960, a "DAS" editorial column headed "Ground Rules" had usefully indicated some data about the Association of a kind that members of academic organizations often find hard to obtain, including this statement: "The CEA year is the calendar year (i. e. from January through December). There are nine issues of *The CEA Critic* published during each year." The nine issues were then January (No. 1) through May (No. 5) and September (No. 6) through December (No. 9). In 1962, however, by special ballot a radically different "activity year" was instituted that made excellent sense: "a fiscal year that coordinates with the academic work of the membership." [4] Now payable to the Treasurer at the University of South Florida, Tampa, dues fell due in the Fall—you will pardon the jingle. The *Critic* was to be numbered beginning with the October issue, becoming the first of each "activity year," through a new June number in the following calendar year. The journal would no longer be published in September.

The College English Association went back, with MLA, to Chicago for the post-Christmas jollities of 1961. CEA's pre-

Philadelphia pattern of a basically one-day gathering was reinstated (though early announcements seemed to imply repetition of the Pennsylvania plan of 1960): a session open to the public beginning at 4:45 p.m. followed by a reception and dinner meeting that same evening, together with a Regional Breakfast early the next morning—presided over, as usual, by Patrick Hogan—at which he and President Elect John Ball spoke. The topic for the afternoon panel of Albert Marckwardt, Robert Gorham Davis, and Marvin Mudrick, with Seymour Betsky as chairman, was "Cultural Influences on the Teaching of English: Some Crucial Issues." President Harry Thornton Moore again acted as master of ceremonies for the banquet, at which William Van O'Connor spoke on "Aristotle and Modern Criticism." [5]

As panelist at the opening open meeting, Albert H. Marckwardt ("in my capacity as a historian of the language") had attempted to survey a middle passage between the extreme claims of the New Linguistics and the reluctance of traditionalists to accept the new gospel, against a background consideration of the effects on English of an upwardly mobile society both in twentieth-century America and in eighteenth-century England. In his easy persuasive way, he pointed out what I have occasionally attempted, more stridently, to demonstrate out of my profound fund of technical ignorance: the difference between the wholly proper scientific refusal of value-judgments and the absolute social necessity of making choices among competing values:

> ... Operating as a scientist, the economist is obligated to take a long-term, objective, and impartial view of our present economic situation. Behaving as a consumer he must make up his mind whether to buy domestic or foreign; as a voter, whether to support a protectionist or a free-trade candidate.
> ... I may consider inevitable the ultimate disappearance of the conjunction *as,* but for the present I may choose to align myself with the precisionists and eschew *like.* On the other hand, I may choose to hasten the equally inevitable disappearance of *an* before a host of

words beginning with pronounced *h* ... Every time I choose a semicolon as a point rather than a comma, or substitute one word for another, I am making a specific linguistic judgment. So must every linguistic scientist, every teacher of English.

John Waldron Ball's Presidency in 1962 was important for me in a special respect upon which I shall expatiate by and by. For the annual convention in December, he took CEA to Washington, D.C., where his sucessor-to-be, First Vice-President Charles Marston Clark, taught at the American University. The pattern of a late-afternoon public session followed by a social hour and dinner meeting was continued, but with designation of the breakfast gathering the next morning as a formal Council of Regional Delegates in substitution for the previous plain-jane, rather catch-as-catch-can Regional Breakfast. After Patrick G. Hogan, Jr., who had been Regional Coordinator and chairman of the Committee on Regional Activity and Development, was elected to the national Board of Directors for a three-year term beginning in 1962, his designation as Regional Coordinator disappeared from the *Critic's* mast. Why, I do not know; he himself appears to have forgotten, or chosen to forget. In the December *CEA Critic,* without reference to him in the immediate context, [6] mention was made of the Council of Regional Delegates that was "soon to be established." The chairman of that body, at least *pro tem.,* turned out to be John Ball, who also turned up as chairman of a CEA Committee on Regional Development. Presumably that was a shortened name for "[a]nother committee soon to be established" mentioned in the December, 1962, account of "New National Committees" as "one on Membership and Regional Development." Presumably, also, it stood in succession to Pat Hogan's old Committee on Regional Activity and Development.

At the Regional Council Breakfast, given on Friday morning, December 28, 1962, at the Hotel Lafayette in the nation's capital city,

... Donald A. Sears spoke on the new concept in

national - regional relations constituted by the establishment of the Council of Regional Delegates. Each regional
provides an elected member to the national council. In
such a way cooperative action can be taken on vital issues
at both the regional and national levels. Also a forum of
debate can thus be provided whereby national information can be more readily made available to regional
meetings.

Both Pat Hogan and I were present. I cannot remember (I
had caught a very bad cold from the wretched weather in
Washington) whether he or I took any prominent part in the
discussion conducted from the chair by national President Ball
that was recorded to have lasted *(déjeuner compris)* for two
long hours by the West Room clock, from 7:30 to 9:30 a.m.—
ending "with a spontaneous expression of renewed vigor and
interest in regional - national cooperation."

The principal events at Washington were, of course, not seen
as regional but as national, embodied in the meetings on the
day before the Regional Council's marathon morning conclave.
In the afternoon open meeting on Thursday, December 27,
a panel moderated by the ubiquitous President Ball and composed of Thelma Gray James, Edwin M. Moseley, and John
Hicks[7] discussed as theme "'The Individual Student." The
nature of their inquiry was spelled out as a query, printed in
the notice of the convention, that demonstrated how a question can be rhetorical without being merely a rhetorical
question: "In today's maze of courses and schedules,
textbooks and syllabi, administrative pressures and legislative
pressures, new media and programed learning, research and
recrimination, what of the student—the *individual student
himself?*" (Italics textual.) At the dinner that night, Robert
Richman, Director of the Institute of Contemporary Arts
(touted by Charles M. Clark as "the man who has civilized
Washington, far in advance of the New Frontier, and who has
succeeded in relating the Arts and Humanities, far beyond
the dream of most teachers of English"), spoke on "Literature
and the Other Arts."

A seeming problem never fully acknowledged in public print

Came to a seeming head at Washington in 1962, and a month or two later to a seeming (and ultimately seemly) solution. Some evidence suggests that CEA placement activity during MLA conventions may have been slacking off since 1960,[8] though in 1961 promise was bravely made that "The Bureau will operate during the national meeting, December 27-29, at the Palmer house, Chicago." A cat seems to peek out of the bag—actually, a box headed BUREAU OF APPOINTMENTS on the editorial page of the November, 1962, *Critic:* "For a nominal $2.00 to help defray clerical costs, a CEA member may be listed for a full twelve-month period. *At the same time he avoids the slave market aspects of the annual meeting."* (Emphasis added.) Nothing in that announcement, or in one of December concerning the convention in general, mentions a station or officer explicitly assigned to placement duty; however, the issue dated January, 1963 *(sic),*[9] in another box also headed BUREAU OF APPOINTMENTS, states: "Inquiries and registration may . . . be made during the MLA convention in Washington, Dec. 26-28, 1962, at the CEA Suite in the Statler-Hilton Hotel." (Other notices located the suite in the Mayflower Hotel.)

At all events, a new director for CEA's Bureau of Appointments was announced "with gratification" and the name of Edward Huberman of Rugers University at Newark placed on the *Critic's* mast in February, 1963. The entry lasted only through the remainder of that second academic semester, after which a happy Huberman was off to Austria for a full, bright Fulbright year at the University (and inns) of Innsbruck. The serviceable Donald Sears stepped back into the breach, and announcement was made that "The Bureau will operate as usual both during the year and during the annual meeting in Chicago at Christmas." the phase *as usual* may indicate that there had been no slacking of activity during the recent conventions, after all.

In the Fall of 1964, Huberman returned and resumed his teaching service in Novavacca, and also his interrupted placement service for the College English Association, though his name was not restored to the mast of the *Critic* for several months. For more years then his one successor or any

predecessor saving a near-tie with Albert Madeira, [10] he continued, and expanded, the traditional practice of twelve months'
registration and correspondence with both seekers and the
sought, combined with moderate, informal, always individual
and personal contacts at the annual conventions—never smack-
ing of inhumanity, much less slavery. Placement was very far
from being Ed Huberman's only service to our Association,
but it remains a shining jewel in his crown of glory.

I have been dodging, or dodging about, a nexus of events
which particularly concerned me and with which I have
frequently piqued the impatient reader in previous chapters
as well as this one. I have even been so devious as to conceal
the fact that Donald A. Sears, quoted in connection with the
convention of 1962 in Washington, D.C., was then Executive
Secretary besides continuing ("for the time being") as Editor,
and had been since shortly after he transferred his academic
person and CEA's editorial operations to Skidmore College
in the middle of that year. The October, 1962, *Critic* (Vol. XXV,
No. 1), the first published from Saratoga Springs, New York, [11]
announced to the membership that the national headquarters
were now situated there. The "considerable package of
approximately simultaneous changes" in 1962, to which I have
previously alluded in a footnote, was indeed large and fully
packed.

I must hark back to the incumbency of Executive Secretary
Max Goldberg. As we have seen, one of the things that deeply
concerned him when he took charge of the Association was
a pervasive uncertainty about relations between national CEA
and its regional affiliates. The early Constitution of 1939 that
he found in the "battered filing cabinet" of CEA records
inherited from his predecessor committed the organization
to fostering regional meetings but did little or nothing to define
the relationship to be "encouraged" (the word used in text). [12]

Among the first things the Incomparable Max did in office
was to begin going into the field to visit and talk with regional
members and officers, and also to scout the possibility of new
affiliates. Becoming "acutely aware" of the unsettled national-
regional relations as being a "serious lack," he drew up a

position paper that he put on the editorial page of the *Critic* in March, 1952, headed "CEA National and Regional," with the subtitle "The Grass Roots Concept." It begins "The College English Association is a federation of regional units, and, as such, it encourages the distinctive individuality of each of the affiliates as an autonomous entity . . ."; and explicitly states in the next paragraph: "Membership in the national CEA is not a prerequisite to membership in any one of our regional affiliates." Manifestly, what went into the final clause of Article XII (Regional Affiliates) of the new By-Laws of the College English Association, adopted midway of his tenure, was in full harmony with the Goldbergian philosophy: [13]

> A regional affiliate shall retain its autonomy as a member of a federation, and shall not be considered as a province by the national organization. However, coordination and mutual support between regional affiliates and the national organization, and among regional affiliates, shall be earnestly sought and encouraged.

That is phrasing which Max Goldberg himself could have composed, and undoubtedly did at least help to inspire. Just the same, determined as he was that the College English Association should be a countervailing power—a "third force," he liked to call it—among major organizations open to college teachers of English, he was troubled that the total enrollment of the federation, with its increasing number of increasingly far-flung affiliates, could not be engrossed as the headquarters roster of CEA's membership. More than once, he expressed "If only . . ." thoughts of that kind, without ever— so far as I am aware or believe—having any even half-serious intention of attempting to dragoon regional CEAers into compulsory national enlistment.

The official position, echoed for example by President Donald Lloyd in a *Critic* editorial of May, 1960—beginning: "Membership is a perennial problem for the CEA"—was: "It must attract its members one by one." If I may intrude at this point (and when have I hesitated?), my own view always has been that the regional affiliates are national CEA's prime recruiting grounds; to which I add, I trust needlessly, that recruitment and conscription are different and opposed procedures.

In ending LUSTRUM FOUR, I quoted from the paraphase in Pat Hogan's "Regional Exchange" of a pledge "that there will be no tampering with regional autonomy . . ." made by John Hicks at the Regional Breakfast of December 29, 1959, just as he was succeeding Max Goldberg as Executive Director. I did not see fit at that point to expand my ellipsis. The rest of the sentence, following a comma, ran: ". . . although it would be good to see regional membership imply membership in the national or a closer tie therewith." Similar sentiments, usually similarly ambiguous and iffy ("**or** a closer tie therewith"), had been voiced by many persons on many occasions through the years but had never crystallized in a serious threat, or even concrete proposal. I for one, sitting at table in Stouffer's stuffy establishment under the rumbling "L" in Chicago that grey December morn, felt no uneasiness. Nor did I when I read above John Hicks' signature on the editorial page in the February, 1960, *Critic* this observation: "Some of you may be perfectly satisfied with everything that has been done. If so, I am surprised." Why should a vigorous new executive officer not be eager to institute beneficial changes?

There is no way to keep myself out of this part of the annals of CEA, and so I shall boldly and unashamedly continue employing the big *I*. At that time in my life, I was (as I have continued to be) more concerned with geographically limited than with country-wide organizations, partly because Houston is close to being at the end of the earth for traveling to the formerly **conventional** places. The South Central (then spelled South-Central) College English Association—founded in 1952, largely by urging of national President Ernest Leisy of Southern Methodist University, to serve five states and part of an elongated sixth—inaugurated a regional journal, *The Round Table*, in February of 1960. In the first issue eight unexceptionable "tenets" that Executive Director Hicks had formulated the month before in the *Critic,* under the rubric QUESTION OF FAITH, were reprinted as "Greetings from

CEA." Here, with a funambulist's funny amble, I will quote a passage from my booklet of 1980, *À la Recherche du Temps Perdu*, that was distributed as a preamble to this ambling History:

> ... Not surprisingly, he was invited to Waco, Texas, to address the 1961 meeting of SCCEA ... on Armistice Day, which I have never learned to quit calling November 11. Meantime, seemingly innocuously but in retrospect ominously, as it now sounds to me, an article in the January, 1961, *Round Table* reporting a regional breakfast given on December 28 by the national College English Association, during MLA's 1960 convention at Philadelphia, began: "Stepped-up active cooperation between CEA regionals and the national CEA organization was forecast ..." I do not know whether any of us then connected that report with a short, unobtrusive, certainly unabrasive letter which the executive officer had contributed to the *Round Table* in October of 1960, mildly raising, only for discussion, a little question: "Should we not ask [*sic*] that all members of regional groups be at the same time members of the national organization ...?"

Looking back now, I am still uncertain whether there was any connection between the Hicks letter of October, 1960, and the breakfast in Philadelphia two months later, which was the one where Edgar Hirshberg renewed a suggestion for a voluntary choice by which dues to regional and national CEA could be combined, with a monetary saving on the dual membership. I am, however, convinced that the lettter to the South Central affiliate was a feeler toward forced conscription, or what I have called attempted dragooning, of regional members into the national roll. Floating "Wouldn't it be nice if ...?" thoughts had apparently begun to tack in a tacky new direction: "Why don't we ...?"

At the Waco meeting of SCCEA in November of 1961, I was present to hear the national executive officer speak. An excellent communicator, he expressed himself clearly and earnestly. I listened attentively, and heard him through to the end. Two months later, in the January *Round Table* of 1962, I read what purported to be the text of those remarks. The final sentence ran: "There are problems on a national level which require thinking, which require analysis, and which ought to call for inter-participation of regional and national groups and people." To that conclusion no CEAer, national or regional or both combined, could possibly take umbrage. Unfortunately, it was an inconclusive conclusion. From the platform, I was absolutely certain, I had heard considerably more. I appealed to the resourceful Editor of the *Round Table*, whom I had observed taking down the proceedings on magnetic tape, and from his transcription was able to recover the speaker's ipsissima verba.

I rushed into the next *Round Table* (March, 1962) a burning paper headed *Et Quo Tendis?* I quote it here in part:

> Mr. Hicks came to the Waco meeting bearing a threat from the organization for which he is now official spokesman. Evidently a good many of our 244 members do not belong to the CEA, which views each such non-member as a loss of potential revenue of $4.50 per annum. Why, asked Mr. Hicks with winning candor, should not paid membership in the CEA be prerequisite to membership in our organization? He invited the S-CCEA officers to "consider" this question gravely, adding that in the failure of an accommodation the CEA would have to "consider" establishing a rival organization affiliated with the national Association.
>
> The present situation is, indeed, ambiguous because of our use of a name implying without defining affiliation with the national organization. ... If the secretariat of ... the CEA ... published terms of affiliation for regional or sister associations, such as the payment of an annual fee of (say) fifty cents per capita, we should long ago have entered into a regular arrangement or else never have presumed to infringe ... The CEA, however, has waited until we have reached a flourishing condition, and now invites us to "consider" standing and delivering our

entire membership into its hands. This technique is known as a Regional Membership Drive.

The proper answer to threats is a posture of defense and defiance. Accordingly, I have proposed to [the regional] President . . . that an *ad hoc* committee be established to resist any pressure to destroy the present complete autonomy of the regional Association. As a first modest proposal, I would suggest that we undercut the only tenable ground occupied by Mr. Hicks, by "considering" a change of name. . . .

The Editor, just a shade uneasy, did two understandable and proper things. In a box beside my article he cautioned that John Hicks' closing remarks had been "off the cuff" and urged that "readers . . . accept Joe Thomas's blast in the tradition of the Southern Rebel yell . . ." More importantly, he gave Executive Secretary Hicks (who had reverted to that humbler title of office early in his administration) an opportunity to respond on the same front page of the same issue. Instead of blasting at me, as I should have done in his place, he affected to doubt that my "modest proposal" could possibly have been serious. At the same time (and here I commend him most heartily and sincerely), he did not attempt to extenuate but, instead, defended the position he had taken:

Membership at once regional and national in CEA would simply enhance personal participation in that forum. The *CEA Critic* would speak not only for individuals, but also for regional groups in disseminating and exchanging regional views. It would of course also follow that each regional group holding close association with the national organization would have a distinctive voice in the government of the national CEA.

Manifestly, the issue was joined—honorably on the part of John Hicks and, I must confess, rather less so on my part. [14] I had no status (beyond membership) in either CEA or SCCEA. I expected scant support beyond, perhaps, a little lip salve and a light pat on the head. Then, a strange thing happened on my way to oblivion.

The next meeting of the South Central affiliate, at Fort Worth, Texas, on November 2, 1962, was addressed by national President John Ball. In the intervening year, I had wangled appointment to head a study committee for SCCEA on its relations to other organizations (I am sure my strategy must be transparent), and had sent a "courtesy" copy of my questionnaire to him as chief official of national CEA. In his own presence at Fort Worth, I was able to quote from his written response: "I feel that individuals should be free to form or join any group they wish to form or join, and that groups may be free to interpret their degree of affiliation as their members may determine. ...Before we rule on the interworkings of our affiliated organizations much listening will have to be done and much grass-roots discussion carried on." The trial balloon launched at Waco—if that is what it was—had gone amazingly flat. Was it arrogant for me to assume that a voice crying in the bundocs[15] had been heard and, yes, heeded in the hierarchy? Another heartening, if unrelated, event of the meeting in 1962 was my election as Secretary of the South Central College English Association, leading to the Presidency in another year.

I have no way of ferreting out the headquarters discussions that may have taken place among officers, directors, and executives of CEA about the project of moving toward compulsory national memberships by regional participants, assuming that there had ever been such an intention outside my teeming imagination. I can only report from the printed record *(CEA Critic,* October, 1962, *s.v.* "Change of Executive")* that not long after my *Et Quo Tendis?* and John Hicks' "Modest Proposal—Modest Answer" had appeared in the March, 1962, *Round Table,*

> Because of his heavy duties as Chairman of Humanities at the University of South Florida, John Hicks—for the past three years executive secretary of The College English Association—last spring [*scil.*, 1962] asked the directors to name a replacement. Regretfully they

accepted the resignation of John, but happily were able to gain his consent to keep the office of CEA treasurer. Donald Sears was elected by the directors as the new executive secretary.

In an "Executive Report—1962" printed in the February, 1963, *Critic,* Donald A. Sears stated that "actual plans for the transition of the executive office" had been made in June of 1962, following which he had officially entered upon his added duties in September.

Here I must mention to the credit of John Hicks that as executive officer of the College English Association he had continued a policy important during the administration of his predecessor, Maxwell Goldberg: cooperation with sister organizations. Two notable instances are reflected in CEA Chap Books published, respectively, in December of 1961 and June of 1963: *If Articulation Succeeds—A Cautionary View;* and *Humanities Courses and English Staff: And or Versus.* Both derive from panel discussions provided by CEA for other meetings: the first at the Conference on College Composition and Communication in Washington, D.C., on April 7, 1961; the other at the National Council of Teachers of English convention in Miami Beach, Florida, on November 23, 1962. Hicks was prominent in arranging both and in bringing the papers to publication, though by the time of the second he identified himself as Immediate Past Executive Secretary. [16]

As mentioned, John Hicks continued as Treasurer of CEA at the University of South Florida. In September of 1963 he took that office to Southern Methodist University in Dallas, Texas, [17] where he had been called to design a new University College that was to be opened a year later as an interdisciplinary honors school for undergraduates. After the College came into operation, "Pressures of his office as dean ... made it necessary for him to ask the Directors for relief ..." Beginning in the Fall of 1965, Edward Huberman added the office of Treasurer to his direction of the Bureau of Appointments, as Albert Madeira had done in the 1950's; and John Hicks ceased to be an administrative officer of CEA.

Readers will not suppose that while they have been enticed into ogling a comparative sideshow, the big top had closed down and tied its flaps. On the contrary, the main performances went on in regular schedule. In succession to President Charles Marston Clark (1963), Elisabeth Wintersteen Schneider was elected President of CEA for 1964, and Muriel Joy Hughes for 1965. [18] The three presided over successive December conventions in the respective years of their incumbency: Charles Clark at Chicago, Elisabeth Schneider at New York, and Muriel Hughes at Chicago once again.

Just in those years a period of more than a decade was commencing when I was to be privileged to rub mind and shoulders with the national hierarchy. To my genuinely unfeigned surprise, I was nominated in 1963 to become a member of the Bored, and even more amazingly elected. I did not technically take office as a director until the beginning of the next year, but by then election results were customarily being announced during the business meeting of the annual convention—and of course the successful candidates were informed as soon as possible. At Chicago in late December, 1963, invited to sit, well, maybe a little below the salt but at least in reach (the occasion may have been a luncheon of officers in the Palmer House), I came to know Charles Clark, "withouten other companye," and to observe the way things were done behind the unironed curtain.

The 1963 program was ambitious and, in no pejorative sense, irregular. The Regional Breakfast and the social hour and following banquet were all scheduled on Saturday, December 28. The College English Association's usual public meeting gave way to participation in a General English Meeting on Sunday morning arranged in cooperation among the Modern Language Association, the National Council of Teachers of English, and the American Studies Association. Main speakers were Francis Keppel, U.S. Commissioner of Education, and Northrop Frye; Donald Sears presented a report specifically for, and about, CEA. [19] At the banquet Saturday night, Kenneth G. Wilson spoke on the "The Portable Liberator: A Right Role for College Dictionaries." Beginning with a rather unsupportable attack on Jacques Barzun's "ignorant" view of the quite unportable *Third International,* Wilson went on to present some sensible generalizations about what portable dictionaries must and may include, to compare in those regards the available rivals, and to indicate an English professor's role in teaching young undergraduates to use them:

> . . . we can show our freshmen how a dictionary is made. We can help them compare dictionaries so that they can learn to *respect* the good ones without *fearing* them. We can teach them that dictionaries are intelligent tools, not prayer wheels to be spun hopefully in times of wonder and fear. Ultimately we want to teach them their language, and all of it—even the grammar—is in the good dictionaries . . . , if only we know how to get it out. We want to give our students a sound basis for judgments— not a helpless reliance on some supposed "expert."

That (if a scribe, mayhap even a linguistic pharisee, is permitted to comment) was worth saying, and well said.

After the big show at Chicago in 1963, the convention of 1964 (the first I ever attended in New York) marked a noticeable pulling in of horns. 'Twas strange, 'twas passing strange; for a considerable effort was mounted to make it a notable event—ramrodded, I should think, at least in part by Ed Huberman, newly back to (metropolitan) New York from Innsbruck. At least I am fain to fancy that like Browning's fictive Claus of that Austrian city he caused to be cast in bronze (color) a gummed oval commemorative seal reading: "College English Association 25th Anniversary 1939 - 1964." As a matter of fact, the anniversary was the Associations's twenty-sixth (December, 1938 - December, 1964). Yet, by an astounding serendipity, the *convention* was itself really CEA's twenty-fifth if the break-away meeting from NCTE that occurred at the same city in 1938 is included in the reckoning, as in my view it ought to be. Our Association had met in 1938, 1939, 1940, 1941, and 1943 (*sic*—in January) and from 1945 annually. Count 'em through 1964: precisely twenty-five national gatherings.

The only events announced in the *CEA Critic* for the 1964

convention were a reception at 5:30 p.m. on December 27 in the Colonial Room of the Sheraton-Atlantic Hotel in Herald Square and an immediately following dinner. The speaker was Norman Holmes Pearson, but his topic was not stated nor the text afterward printed in the journal. I must have heard him, yet with valorous discretion I beg off attempting to iterate his utterances. You will wonder if I was even there (it was my first official attendance as a director, and I am absolutely certain that I never missed any meetings in that capacity) when I admit that I also have no record or recollection of any sort of Regional Breakfast, beyond a feeble feeling that one was conducted by Don Sears. My only excuse for such vagueness is that I have eaten a great many official CEA breakfasts, national or regional; and, as everyone knows, one plate of bacon and scrambled eggs is much like another. I do not, however, forget the breakfast a year later in Chicago.

The rather slender format used for the meeting at New York in 1964 was not imitated but radically altered for the Chicago convention of 1965. CEA's traditional public session was restored for Monday, December 27, but the traditional dinner was abandoned. The open meeting was scheduled at night instead of in late afternoon, and was followed by a smoker (old-fashioned term—and with a lady President, at that!) and cash bar for "CEA members and guests" that more or less corresponded to the tradional "social hour" or reception that commonly preCEAded our banquets. In addition, a Breakfast for Regional Delegates (sounding as if hybrid between the Regional Council Breakfast of 1962 and the vulgate Regional Breakfasts) was scheduled for the following morning.

Both parts of the CEA convention were (a bit confusingly) announced for Crystal Rooms, but of widely separated hostelries: the evening meeting and smoker on Monday at the Palmer House; the Breakfast for Regional Delegates considerably to the northwest at the since-razed Sherman Hotel ("the gracious Sherman House," as the *Critic* denominated it), on Randolph Street two or three blocks beyond the main theater strip. At the Crystal Room of the Palmer house, a panel of Maxwell H. Goldberg, Donald A. Sears, and C.L. Barber discussed a topic interesting to members but possibly just a shade less relevant for a proclaimed public meeting: "CEA and the Profession of English Today." [20]

The breakfast at the Crystal Room of the Sherman Hotel (or House) was attended by thirty-three persons who reached it by one of the narrowest public elevators ever designed. Having been alerted by Don Sears several months before that in my capacity as a director of CEA I was to be in charge, I addressed the throng with a prepared text on "Time to Think Little?" (with a question mark), professing to foresee "the coming demise, from after-effects of gigantism, of conventional conventions"; and then opened the meeting not only to the question of whether smallness might not be an advantage, but "to all aspects and activities of the Association, with special reference to regional problems." In an anonymous account of our transactions, furnished for publication in the March, 1966, *Critic,* I attempted to report that "The pervasive tone was familial but not crass, and eloquent but not ostentatious." Alas, some printer's devil up in Upper New York State scrubbed "familial" and triumphantly substituted "familiar," for the greater inglory of Addison, Johnson, and the College English Association, Inc.

In the report quoted and misquoted immediately above, I identified myself as "Director and Regional Coordinator." I was commencing my third and final year with the Bored in 1966; and furthermore I was indeed Regional Coordinator for CEA, though I had gone to the Sherman's mirrored Crystal Room in December, 1965, innocent of any such title or intention. In an expression that I would not dream of using in a formal writing like this stately History, I was slickered. My translation—to borrow the Bottom line of Shakespeare—had been accomplished by prestidigitation and with mirrors. Without investiture except of emperor's new clothing, and with no by-my-leave whatsoever, the sly sleight-of-hand artist Sears simply assumed a *tour accompli:* that by arranging and conducting the breakfast I had allowed myself to be passed into a continuingly responsible official for the Association's regional affairs. Being a fast learner, I promptly worked the same trick on Patrick Galvin Hogan, Jr., notifying him before he quite caught the boorish calembour that he had been galvanized into

Associate Regional Coordinator. [21] Our names did not get into the mast of the *CEA Critic* until the Autumn of 1966. By then, Don Sears was off on African safari with high astounding "plans ... afoot for an international CEA conference in Europe next summer," and with a new Managing Editor installed more or less (rather less than more) in charge of the Association.

Without more fully anticipating the exciting events of LUSTRUM SIX, I think I ought to say of Donald Sears during the *lustrum* which is under present consideration that he administered CEAffairs with a flair and seeming ease. Personally (in an archaic but always complimentary term), he is an extremely *genteel* man, the proverbial "gentleman and scholar." I never saw him otherwise than tastefully dressed and impeccably groomed. Sometimes, in a mataphorical sense only, official papers seemed to hang loose out of his pockets, or an annual report had to be collated while we directors or functionaries waited; still, things got done, always without flurry, fuss, or feathers. He is considerably my junior, and so I may have treated him at times like a little boy, but I think he liked me. I not only liked—I admired—Don Sears.

As Maxwell Goldberg had been before him, Executive Secretary Sears was something of a projector. Early in 1964, for instance, he arranged for CEA to sponsor, wrote a blurb for, and helped to sell out of Skidmore (at a discount to members) a revised standard self-help book called *Good Reading,* [22] described on a flyleaf as "The 21st Edition" but in other front matter indentified as "This edition, the 19th," and by Sears in the *CEA Critic* as "the fifth complete revision since 1947." (It had begun as a mimeographed list in 1932.) Later in 1964, he brought the Association into an arrangement with Twayne Publishers for the subsidized issuing of scholarly monographs, in "an experimental attempt to ameliorate the 'publish or perish' dictum that threatens academic survival," under a complicated formula that would cost the typical author around five to eight hundred dollars in editorial and production expenses, [23] with the College English Association assuming responsibility for refereeing manuscripts offered. How many perishing CEAmen may have been rescued from watered-down publication in inferior outlets, I have no bibliographical data to help me estimate. A few years later came a Book-of-the-Month Club Writing Fellowship undertaking deeply involving the College English Association, but belonging to the next *lustrum*.

Donald Sears as Editor, the capacity in which he served a full decade *et plus* (longer than anyone else, before or since), was energetic and resourceful. He pleased me by being always eager to reflect regional activities in the journal; among other ways, in succession to Pat Hogan's "Regional Exchange" of the early '60's he devised a "Regional Roundup" (with minor variants of the rubric) that continued beyond his own Editorship into the next decade. Like Maxwell Goldberg, he never developed the lower second page into a regular Editor's corner, but he did continue to accept frequent signed guest editorials. A notable instance occurred in 1963 when Immediate Past President John Ball contributed two (or one in two parts, the first being in narrative - dialogue form) to successive issues of the *Critic:* "English: Is It Subject Matter or Discipline?" (May), which plumped for "subject matter" but went beyond a simple either/or decision; and "English As Interdisciplinary" (June):

> At the *undergraduate* level, it can almost be said that English is inevitably interdisciplinary—that the question is not   to be or not to be   interdisciplinary, but how to cope effectively with the fact that in significant ways English overlaps or relates directly to every other subject-matter area and every discipline.

Editor Sears made some progress toward solving the perennial problem of house organs, which afflicted the *CEA Critic* particularly hard because of the dual national and regional biases: a problem not exactly of identity but of satisfying the rhetorical trinity of unity, coherence, and emphasis. In childhood and youth *(News Letter* growing into *Critic),* and it must be conceded to a considerable degree in middle age, the journal was a decidedly miscellaneous organ; indeed as we have seen, the original Editor, Burges Johnson, rather gloried in that character. Member - subscribers really did not know what they would pick up in their mail from month to month, although they must have found what they did receive to be engaging, each issue in its own way. I have said that the *CEA Critic* did not acquire a strikingly new appearance or novel format after Donald Sears took it over.[24] I must, however, describe an instant regularizing of front-page makeup that in retrospect impresses me as having been important for continuity.

Starting as a publication in four columns, the journal had gone to three at the beginning of 1957. Previously in the Goldberg - Holt era, many different arrangements of type matter had been employed for the first page, from single columns to four columns. Reduction to three as the maximum available clearly invited, though it did not absolutely force, unbalance. Among other arrangements prior to January of 1960, sometimes a two-column headline was run at the left and sometimes at the right. From his first issue, Editor Sears made the latter arrangement so nearly uniform (with variations in typographic style of the two-column headline) that it became something like a hallmark of the journal, an element of expectation. Clearly, it signaled a leading article at the right, with a less weighty or meaty one-column article, report, or department (often, not invariably, giving in-house or at least factual information) to the left. Consciously or unconsciously, readers of the Sears *Critic* became accustomed to its face, and to looking for something of major or considerable consequence at the upper right. Of course, I do not intimate that they never suffered disappointment, for such a journal as ours could hardly hope to shake the academic underpinnings of the world nine times a year.

Nor do I imply that merely by partial stylization of its makeup the *CEA Critic* could expect to become—or that it did become—perfectly unified and coherent, with every aspect of the multitudinous CEAffairs given appropriate emphasis in each issue. The journal still served a great variety of not easily miscible interests: national, regional (for various regions, from CEA to shining CEA), professional,[25] pedagogical (a factotum word blanketing an enormous range of different kinds of concerns), linguistic (a critter of many horns that all the jarring sects love to blow), literary, even philosophical. [26] The Editor was alert to trends of the times such as the use of case books and of television in teaching, and to special problems such as those arising from expansion of mass education into colleges and even into university graduate schools. [27] During two years (1964-66) in the District of Columbia, he was in strategic position to prepare or commission articles like "English and Federal Aid" (February, 1965; first delivered by Sears as a speech at a regional meeting in December, 1964) and "English Institutes" (June, 1965; anonymous), which could be used as permanent models for the furnishing of such information by CEA to its members.

I am sure that no one would have viewed the *CEA Critic* as specifically or primarily a literary publication between 1960 and 1965—or, for that matter, at any time before a mitosis of the journal in 1970, to be recounted in detail hereafter. Just the same, partly (but certainly not wholly) because of increase in average size of issues, readers of strongly literary - scholarly bent could usually find matter to engage their interest—if not in the leading article, then among the numerous others, large and small, spread through inside pages.

Book reviews, however, were generally against policy and therefore remained about as scarce as they had been in the previous several years. By coincidence, as I suppose it to have been, Doris V. Falk, whose *Eugene O'Neill and the Tragic Tension* had in 1959 been the subject of a substantial (and favorable) review mentioned in the preceding chapter as so atypical that I suspect it to have been an independently submitted article rather than a commissioned review, was herself author of a very long and very scathing book review in the May, 1962, *Critic* about which I am inclined to draw the same conclusion. Another extensive unfavorable estimate of a book was contributed by Patrick G. Hogan, Jr., to the October issue of 1963; the two-column headline, "Faulkner Scholarship and the CEA," and the position starting at the upper right of the front page would indicate that the Editor regarded it in the character of a leading article. Short notices of books were sometimes included in NOTICES OF NOTE columns or under other headings, but with no regularity and little frequency. Hardly to be assimilated to book reviews, though perhaps vaguely ancestral to a long-running feature called "Minireviews" that would later be devised by Edward Huberman, was a sporadic yet at times frequent column contributed tõ the Sears *Critic* (on request) by J. Sherwood Weber and Olga Svatik Weber under the heading "Paperbound Previews"—giving author, title, and publisher, without critiques.

Literary contributions to the *CEA Critic* in this period ran a wide gamut of topics and types. Among them I mention (not exlusively but indicatively):

APPRECIATIONS—like Weller B. Embler, "The Sanity of True Literature" (on *Sir Gawain and the Green Knight)*, May, 1964.

CRITICAL THEORY—like R. W. Stallman, "Aristo & Tottle vs. Criticus" (a sophisticated if brief Drydenian dialogue between Criticus [*scil.*, Novus] and two spokesmen for the "Chicago School"), October, 1962.

Explications de texte—like R. B. Smith, "Sexual Ambivalence in [a] Tennyson [Poem]"*(Princess*, vii.161-174), June (repr. October), 1965.

LARGER INTERPRETATIONS—like David M. Rein, "Hamlet's Self-Knowledge" ("To attempt . . . to find Shakespeare's explanation of why Hamlet delayed is to seek what does not exist"), March, 1960.

"USABLE" CRITICISM—like Leonard Jerome Moss, "Transitional Devices in Henry James" (close analysis of a long single paragraph from *The Portrait of a Lady* to demonstrate how transition can be exhibited and taught), February, 1960.

TEACHING EXPERIENCES—like Robert Henson, " 'Howl' in the Classroom" (Ginsberg "communicates excitement"), February, 1961.

"SCHOLARLY" ARTICLES—like Joseph Gold, "Two Romantics: Jim and Stein" ("The novel ends with Stein because Stein is what Jim would have become, had he run away from Patusan"), May, 1962.

GENRE STUDIES—like Harry T. Moore, "Campus in Wonderland" (on the college novel), May, 1961.

ETHICAL INTERPRETATIONS—like Mildred Brand Munday, " 'For saying so, there's gold': A Note on Price and Value in *Twelfth Night*" (". . . the characters' inadequate sense of emotional values is reflected in their attempt to place human relations on a monetary basis; to substitute purses for warm responsiveness"), March, 1961.

UNCLASSIFIABLE PAPERS—such as William Coyle's amusing account of two variant "highly simplified" texts of *Huckleberry Finn* for teaching English as a foreign language, encountered in Brazil: "Never the Twain," November, 1963.

Speaking of amusing contributions to the *CEA Critic,* I have to say that satire won a considerable, if by no means major, place in the journal of this period. Don Sears had a twinkle in his own eye, as may be illustrated by a box of **DEEPEST REGRETS** in March and April, 1963, very heavily black-bordered, in memory of "all good CEA'ers who forgot to renew their membership . . ." A subset of the category of humor and satire, burlesque (including parody), had some vogue from time to time both in prose: e.g., Laurence Perrine, "Fifteen Ways to Write Five Hundred Words" ("or, How to Stretch a Penny'sworth of Wit into a Pound'sworth of Paper"), November, 1962; and in verse: e.g., Trudy Drucker, "The Love Song of Any Graduate Student" (". . . In the rooms the teachers sit and read / Books on Beowulf or Bede. / . . . / Shall I document from Poe? Do I dare a ribald line? / I must write the proper preface: 'Any errors here are mine.' / I have soaked my ballpoint pens in table wine / To bring a bit of spirit to my prose. / . . ."), March, 1965. [28]

Controversies, sometimes conducted casually as Letters to the Editor, sometimes more formally, were frequent—as indeed they have always been in the publications of CEA. An unusually sustained instance was a running debate in 1965 about the courage, or lack of it, in Holden Caulfield. It began with an article in March by Deane M. Warner, "Huck and Holden": "The hero of *The Catcher in the Rye* never found such courage" (*viz.,* as that of Henry Fleming in *The Red Badge of Courage*). Boris Burack replied two months later in a leading article headed "Holden the Courageous":

"... Holden Caulfield is not searching for courage. He does not lack it. He already has a kind of courage—an unusual courage but nonetheless, courage." In another considerably longer leading article (October), Charles D. Peavy wrote of "Holden's Courage Again": "What Mr. Burack sees as courage ... are the symptoms of Holden's sickness. ... An adolescent in a ridiculous red hunting cap, he represents not so much a courageous rebel as a frightened, pathetic Peter Pan." Then, in the last *Critic* of the year, Boris Burack contributed an even-toned Letter to the Editor defending his position by taking "a few exceptions" to the "persuasive" comments of his opponent of two months before. One was an objection to the contention that "What Holden wants to do is to keep the 'little kids' from falling over the precipice into adulthood ..."; Burack countered: "For one thing, it's difficult to intrepet the tumbling of children from a cliff—a violent, tragic descent—as an *ascent* into adulthood. Consider the fallen angels in 'Paradise Lost,' or Dante's descent into Hades." [29]

Before I drop the curtain on the great *Catcher* controvesy just calendared, I will point out that it started in a "Junior College Supplement of the   C E A   Critic" inserted as a leaf numbered 4-a and 4-b between the regular fourth and fifth pages of the March *Critic* in 1965. (The author of the initiating article taught at Cape Cod Comminity College.) It was the third such supplement. Later to be reheaded TWO-YEAR COLLEGE SUPPLEMENT, edited by Selma (Sally) Stonberg of Newton Junior College, and integrated into the regular pagination of the *CEA Critic,* it had begun in December, 1964, as a "Supplement of Assoc. of English Teachers in 2-Year Colleges" occupying part of a single page in the journal. Originating in 1962 and "officially launched" in 1963, this organization—its exact name was, or became, Association of English Teachers at Two-year Colleges—was mainly active in New England and the vincinity of New York City, though it had members in about half the states. It voted in 1964 to become an Affiliate Organization (what now would be called a Special Affiliate) of the College English Association. Its checkered fortunes thereafter will be part of the story related in LUSTRUM SIX.

I have observed with dogged, damnable iteration that years ending in zero or five have tended to mark turning points for the College English Association. Contrariwise, I have rather underemphasized a dilemma that I have sometimes had to dehorn in deciding whether such "round-numbered" years should be treated as part of the closing *lustrum,* or instead as part of the new one looming over the horizon of time. If I were given to arrogance, I could exalt the morning of Tuesday, December 28, 1965, as a pivotal point between the first and second *lustra* of the 'Sixties because, as already reported, before thirty-two witnesses in the city called Windy my own CEActivities were turned into an unexpected channel. With infinitely more potential significance, on the other hand, the close of the preceding year might have become a major turning point for CEA in consequence of a proposed change that, as things turned out, did not actually occur.

I must digress, and partly turn back, to explain that shortly before the "25th Anniversary" convention previously described, in the Autumn of 1964 still another move of the national headquarters had been made: to the national capital— although the *CEA Critic* continued to be published from Saratoga Springs, New York, with a Managing Editor at the Skidmore College English Department, Devra Rowland, now named on the mast. The reason for taking the main office to Washington was that Donald Sears had been appointed a staff associate of the Commission on Plans and Objectives for Higher Education of the American Council on Education. Then, a twelvemonth later, at the beginning of the academic year 1965-66, he conducted an intra-urban migration of the CEA headquarters (but again not the publications office, which still remained at Saratoga Springs with Devra Rowland as Managing Editor) to Howard University, where he was to be concerned with a new Ph.D. program in American literature. In October, 1965, the *Critic* exulted: "The location in the nation's capitol [*sic*] will greatly aid the work of CEA in our new era of Federal concern for English." [30]

Meantime, about when the original move from New York State to the District of Columbia was occurring, Don Sears had requested that search commence for his successor. He might well have been influenced by the fact (already recounted) that simultaneously John Hicks was moving toward retirement from the office of Treasurer. Or could it be that CEA's chief executive was heeding the rumble of a distant equatorial drum? At any rate, he informed the Executive Committee that he wished to be relieved, and asked that the matter be a "major item of business" at the directors' meeting in December, 1964.

In bumptious assumption of an authority I could scarcely claim as only a fledgling director of the Association, I made myself a living demonstration of the adage about fools rushing in, by loudly proclaiming a candidate (one eminently qualified, I hasten to add, by experience, dedication, and ingrained habits of industry beyond any call of mere duty) whom I pushed and touted to the point of antagonizing some officers, one in particular belonging to that division which used to be known as the "gentle sex." What with one circumstance and another, my candidate—the only live body really in sight—was nudged aside, and Don was persuaded to reconsider and carry on. Thus the Sears Decade was undivided, as the Age of Max had been, at the middle of an extended tour of duty.

And yet it was divided, and wrenchingly so, in ways that could not have been predicted when the reappointment was negotiated. Would it have been better for the Association if I had not conned my candidate out of contention? I do not say so, only that troubled times lay ahead for CEA. But that, as Scheherazade used to tease the sultan, is another story.

(Here endeth the reading of LUSTRUM FIVE.)

Notae pedales for

LUSTRUM FIVE

[1] I find that I have hitherto neglected to mention the first holder of a similar title, Arthur Williams of the University of Massachusetts, whom Executive Secretary Goldberg apppointed in 1954 as coordinator of regional - national CEA relations (Max gave the title in lower case in his annual report). From insufficient yet compelling evidence, I infer that the appointment was local and functional (and seemingly short-lived), without the broader freedom of action entrusted to later Coordinators. Williams was not, for instance, formally named to the policy Committee on National - Regional Relations.

[2] I mention my non-attendance of the 1960 convention partly to allay suspicion that my imagined hearing of John Ciardi (a non-show at Chicago) in 1959, confessed in LUSTRUM FOUR, might be derived from his presence as a speaker at Philadelphia.

[3] With the February issue of 1960, the envelope in which the journal had been enclosed was discarded; thus—as a measure of economy (especially of time)—the paper became a self-mailer, as CEA publications are today with the further aid of computerized address stickers.

[4] The innovation was part of a considerable package of approximately simultaneous changes. Donald Sears had moved to Skidmore College in July, 1962, taking to Saratoga Springs, New York, the office of Editor and also that of the Bureau of Appointments. (Alteration of typographical appearance in the journal resulting from this move was again minimal.) One major item in the "package" of organizational changes remains to be revealed hereafter.

[5] The address was published in the January, 1962, *CEA Critic;* a tart Letter to the Editor about it in March by Harry C. Schnur drew a Tartar retort from O'Connor that was printed immediately below it.

[6] Elsewhere in the notice, Pat Hogan was reported to be "assembling members of a new Committee on CEA Plans and Policies," of which I discovered little or no mention thereafter. In the journal, I hasten to add, committee reports and reports of committees were only sporadic.

[7] Hicks' attitude was implied in the title of his contribution as published in the *CEA Critic* a year later (December, 1963): "The Human Relationship." Two issues still later (February, 1964), Moseley's "The Individual Student Himself" was printed.

[8] I am not sure I should not say "since 1959," for Albert Madeira did not attend the convention in Chicago that December when the old administrative guard was yielding place to new. Present mainly for MLA, and in the excitement of being on a program, I had no occasion to observe how, or whether, CEA placement activities were conducted there.

[9] For several years, the January *Critic* carried notices—obviously intended to be prospective, not retrospective—of a convention belonging by date to the preceding month and year. The journal must have been mailed (or at least intended to be mailed) very early then, as nowadays it is mailed late. I suspect that when the first issue of the academic year was ostensibly moved from September to October, the old rhythms refused to subside— much as one eats at an improper clock hour when crossing time zones or changing to or from Daylight Saving.

[10] Without resorting to computer hardware and software, I have calculated with a soft pencil and some hard research that Al Madeira served eighteen continuous semesters in charge of placement, to Ed Huberman's interrupted one in 1963 plus sixteen from 1964 to 1972. (The placement service itself lasted one more year, as will be recounted in LUSTRUM SEVEN, before being buried at CEA in 1973—an unfeeling act of oblivion to the fruitful pains of Robert Fitzhugh, who inaugurated it in 1945, and his successors.)

[11] Because of the change of "activity year" already described, the immediately preceding Volume XXIV terminated in May, 1962 (No. 5). If minute details of that kind irritate you, pray remember my quarter century as druid in the bibliographical Grove of Greg, and be tolerant if not charitable.

[12] The language ". . . whenever a large enough group of the members find it possible to assemble . . ." might well seem—and most probably was, in draft, so regarded—appropriate to chapters of a closed national organization. Nevertheless, subsequent records make clear that the regional affiliates really were autonomous, as they were constitutionally defined as being in the revised By-Laws of 1955. The second meeting, in April, 1940, of CEA's primal affiliate (New England) decided that whoever paid the registration fee could attend, though those who did were to be "strongly urged to join the national C.E.A." That has been the typical pattern in our regional Associations.

[13] The first of the three clauses proclaimed an Association policy of "establishment and support of strong regional affiliates"; the second specifically authorized use of "funds of the Corporation" for "establishing and maintaining regional affiliates."

[14] While my fenceposts carry no skulls, like Conrad's Kurtz I lack restraint, as I doubt not that readers have discovered for themselves.

[15] "Boonies," if you don't recognize the word all dressed up for the dictionary.

[16] I do not, in this eclectic History, take notice of every particular CEA Chap Book, but will remind the reader of an invaluable listing of those published through April, 1970, in the *Critic* of that date (Vol. XXXII, No. 7, p. 15). Not many have since been issued. At least two more of the period included in this present chapter ought to be mentioned: W.K. Wimsatt, Jr., and others, *What to Say about a Poem* (December, 1963); and Leland Miles, *Where Do Y o u Stand on Linguistics?* (January, 1964; a second edition, revised, was published in February, 1968).

[17] And why not? He was a birthright Texan (born in Port Arthur).

[18] During part of the preceding year the mast of the *Critic* had separated her name and President Schneider's by that of Second Vice-President Allan H. MacLaine, as if two women officers back-to-back might appear indecorous to organizational male chauvinists.

[19] Published in the February, 1964, *Critic* under the sanguine title "The CEA, or How to Cut up a Bullock," it was a useful summary of broad historical trends and of then-current tides in the College English Association.

[20] Their remarks were printed as a CEA Chap Book the next Spring (April, 1966), with the title *College English—Past, Present, Future.* As might be guessed, Goldberg was the spirit of CEA Past; Sears, of CEA Present; Barber, of CEA Future. What Max Goldberg revealed about former times has been enormously helpful to this Historian. Those who have never served in the retinue of Queen Clio cannot conceive how dependent the story that gets told often is on almost accidental disclosures.

[21] In the Autumn of '65, Hogan went to the University of Houston, and so became my cross-town associate and presently Associate Coordinator. We had already known each other for several previous years, and unless I have a tin ear were developing sustained chords of harmony. (By the way, the name Galvin is pronounced GAV'n, as I knew very well and Pat knew that I knew.)

[22] Another edition, identified as the twentieth, was brought out in 1968. I have not looked into the subsequent bibliographic fortunes of this "MENTOR BOOK PUBLISHED BY THE NEW AMERICAN LIBRARY [and] *Sponsored by* College English Association ..."

[23] "... and that is all!" (exclamation point textual), added an enthusiastic notice in the October *Critic* (page one, column one) about "A New CEA Project."

[24] The halftones that have been mentioned were less and less used after the first year or two, I suppose because of cost.

[25] I cite leading articles by George Sherburn, "Perspectives on the Profession" (December, 1961); and Philip B. Daghlian, "College English Teaching Becomes a Profession" (November, 1962)—the latter so exceptionally "leading" that it was given all three columns of the front page under a banner headline. Beginning at the upper left of the first page in October, 1960, appeared a discussion of teaching evaluations by John Hicks, headed "If We Yearn to Be a Profession ... " (ellipsis *sic)*.

[26] I cite an inside (not front-page) article by Maxwell H. Goldberg, "The Humanities As Heuristics" (June, 1963).

[27] About that time, or it might have been in the '70's, I heard of a state university offering Advanced Remedial English for verbally deprived graduate students. In the *CEA Critic* of November, 1964, Ernest Earnest (another of Sears' catchtwentytwoish contributors was named Minor Major) wrestled under a two-column headline, "Students in Limbo," with the question: ". . . what are the graduate schools to do about poorly prepared applicants?"

[28] Verse played a comparatively minor part in Don Sears' *Critic* (or in any CEA journal up to the time now under consideration), but did increase in frequency and modest magnitude. Generally, whether serious, "occasional," satiric, or casual, it was of fair to excellent quality.

[29] Another, immediately following, note (under the same **Letters to the Editor** heading) also dated (by a different writer) from Burack's Middletown, Connecticut, made the same point—with references likewise to Dante and Milton. I gather that lively discussions must have been going on at Wesleyan University during the Yule CEAson.

[30] I do not quite know how to take the word "capitol." On its face, it resembles a simple misprint or editorial blooper, yet Sears' and CEA's official address had already been at the *capital* for a year. I must tentatively assume that some allusion was intended to the close administrative ties of Howard University's corporation to the Federal government. (How physically distant the campus is from Capitol Hill I did not happen to know at the time at writing, and was too ornery to inquire.)

FOAM OF PERILOUS CEAS

being

LUSTRUM SIX (1965 - 1970)

of

SANSCULOTTE

A NONKNICKERBOCKER HISTORY

of the

COLLEGE ENGLISH ASSOCIATION

Edward Huberman (1975)

Earle Gene Labor (1983)

LUSTRUM SIX (1965 - 1970)

FOAM OF PERILOUS CEAS

The College English Association, having sailed into 1960 with a crew of new administrative and editorial officers, ended the year 1965 with a full complement of CEA-worthy officials. The incoming President for 1966, Allan Hugh MacLaine, would be "new" by definition, but by a partly constitutional and partly customary order of succession he was already experienced by two prior years of Vice-Presidential office, as was incoming First Vice-President Henry Hitch Adams by his one as Second Veep during 1965. The "new" second Vice-President was the most highly CEAsoned of all, for he was none other than Maxwell Henry Goldburg, the Incomparable Max.

As for appointive offices, those of Executive Secretary and Editor remained in the hands of Donald Albert Sears, who had been conducting the journal and variable other affairs of the Association since January of 1960. If Edward Huberman was new in the office of Treasurer, he had been around considerably longer in direction of the Bureau of Appointments, a function which kept him in close year-round touch with all aspects of CEA's operations—as was most fortunate, for reasons that will not be long in coming to the surface. I suppose it would have to be admitted that the Regional Coordinator was an utter novice; still, even that function had the counterweight of an Associate Regional Coordinator, Patrick Galvin Hogan, Jr., who for several years in the late '50's and early '60's had been close to being Mr. CEA Regional.

All in all, I think a soothsayer (though we employed no seers other than Don Sears) would have found the omens favorable for as placid a second half of the 1960's as the second half of the 1950's had been. For the first year or so, if anyone had spoken such a soothing prophecy, we should all have agreed that he was saying sooth.

The preceding chapter observed that during the prior years

of the Sears-edited *CEA Critic* no one would have regarded it as primarily a literary journal, but perhaps the perceptive reader caught an intended implication that it was moving noticeably in that direction. Throughout 1966, that movement accelerated, though I do not in the least suggest that other interests—pedagogical, linguistic, organizational, and miscellaneous—were being neglected. The front pages of the first three issues of 1966 are illustrative. In January a left column headed "Biographies of CEA Nominees for Office" was flanked at the right by a two-column leading article, "Test of Language Attitudes"; in February "New England CEA Fall Meeting," by "A Shaw Story and Brooks and Warren"; in March "Greater N.Y. CEA Meets on Ph.D.," by "Literature on Closed Circuit TV." Other leading articles during the year (under two-column headlines at the upper right of the first page) included "Critical Clichés," "Stylistics—A Bibliographical Survey," [1] and "Chaucer's Perplexing Pardoner." The left-hand column was mainly, not exclusively, devoted to in-house or regional affairs. In reviewing a file of the journal for 1966, one senses an intention to achieve an improved order and regularity, with increasing attention to literary or related themes, even in a situation where completely standardized form and unified content were ultimately impossible of achievement.

The June *Critic* of 1966 was something of a Faulkner Issue, although not specifically so designated. On the front page (next to a factual, but enthustiastic, account at the left by Ed Huberman of his Bureau of Appointments), is a leading article titled "Faulkner's 'That Evening Sun'" by Mel E. Bradford. Despite focus upon the servant Nancy's relation to the white community, to her race, and to herself, the author contends that "The theme of this story is the potential for tragedy in the human condition, not the tragedy of being Negro." Picking up a phrase from Bradford's essay about Nancy's being "'failed' [the word is in quotation marks] by the community, and especially by the Compsons," Patrick G. Hogan contributed "Faulkner: A Rejoinder," demurring that "There is considerable question as to the validity of reading the story as either a condemnation or a justification of the failure of the community or of the Compson family." A long inside article by Thomas R. Gorman on "Faulkner's Ethical Point of View" defends the short stories, in particular, against the charge of offering "only a nightmare of nihilism." By coincidence or design, this markedly literary number of the *CEA Critic* contains back-to-back with Gorman's argument another article, "A Return to Hardy's Native," in which Robert F. Fleissner defends Thomas Hardy against much the same charge. There are also pieces of light verse by James McNally and Richard L. Loughlin, an *explication de texte* headed "The Rhetoric of 'Tract,'" by Eugene McNamara, and even a quickie quotation from R. B. Sheridan purporting to glance at the publish-or-perish syndrome.

After an absence of five months, the TWO-YEAR COLLEGE SUPPLEMENT, made available by Editor Sears to the College English Association's Affiliate Organization, reappeared in April, 1966, re-headed "Junior College Supplement to the CEA Critic." It consisted of a single article, about an experiment in having Freshmen write verse as an approach to better understanding and appreciation of poetry. The supplement contained no special news (or even mention) of the Association of English Teachers at Two-Year Colleges. The fact is that the organization, which had only sixty-five members at the time of its affiliation with CEA, was not in flourishing condition, despite devoted effort by its officers and eager, though I dare say ineffectual, tendance on my part after I became Regional Coordinator. As will be seen, I gave the Two-Year Association some prominence at the Regional Delegates Breakfast in 1966, the first one I planned and carried through from A to Izzard. I may as well go on at this point and record its demise a year later.

First, though, hear some sobering words of Jacques Mitchell speaking as President of the Association of English Teachers at Two-Year Colleges in December of 1966 (words in brackets supplied from context):

> So far, our affiliation has been a disappointment, prob-ably because the special problems inherent in the col-leges I represent have not yet been fully understood by four-year college people.

> To begin with, we are not the first two years of a four-year curriculum . . . We have different problems and different goals.
>
> . . . I wonder if the real question before us is not: Does the CEA want an affiliate of two-year college English teachers? If the answer is "we do," then by involving us in [national] committee work, by including a special two-year college section at [regional] CEA meetings, and by supporting the ["teaching"] Ph.D. program that two-year college people most need, the CEA would encourage a truly enthusiastic and valuable affiliation with the thousands of two-year college teachers of English.

During ensuing months, it became evident to President Mitchell and his associates that the battle to make the Two-Year Association a viable nation-wide organization had been lost. A headline deep within the November, 1967, *CEA Critic* announced: "CEA Affiliate Disbands." Writing over his initials, D(onald) A. S(ears) put as good a face as possible upon the catastrophe:

> Having served its purpose of establishing professional identification and concern, the Association of English Teachers at Two-Year Colleges is now officially disbanded effective December 31, 1967. We would regret the passing of this organization did we not know[2] that all of its members continue as full-fledged members of the College English Association.

In dissolving, the Two-Year Association directed that any funds remaining in its treasury should be transferred to the foster-parent College English Association. Here I am moved to quote myself (as is bound to happen once in a while) writing in 1980:

> Apropos of regional development, I should like to urge that one of our priorities for the 1980's ought to be resurrection of a short-lived affiliate of the 1960's in the so-far vacant category of Special Affiliate as provided by our

since-adopted Articles of Affiliation—described there as
an organization representing "a particular interest or
branch of the college-teaching profession not
geographically defined." I refer to the Association of
English Teachers at Two-Year Colleges, which on its
untimely demise bequeathed the remnant of its treasury
to the College English Association and thus laid some
continuing obligation upon our shoulders. Although a . . .
Carnegie report speaks of a decline of private junior colleges of the old breed, I am convinced that two-year
institutions generally, including those primarily dedicated
to vocational education, are entering their most important era, and that their English teachers belong with us
rather than with associations centered at the secondary
and lower levels of instruction.

The "sobering words" of Jacques Mitchell, cited a page or
two back, were spoken during the CEA convention of 1966.
For it, the College English Association returned to the
Sheraton-Atlantic Hotel in New York City, and closely imitated
the pattern first cut for Chicago in 1965. Again, there was no
banquet. An open meeting beginning at 8:30 p.m. on Tuesday,
December 27, was followed by a "social" (*vice* smoker, reception, or what you will) on the same night, and by a Breakfast
for Regional Delegates the next morning beginning at seven-
thirty. The program for the open meeting was genuinely
interesting to guests, curiosity seekers, and drop-ins as well
as to members: four representatives of different publishing
houses, together with Dean William E. Buckler of the
Washington Square College of New York University, performed
a biblio-obstetric anatomy on the Birth of a Textbook.

In planning the breakfast for December 28, I did two things:
I made a sincere and sustained effort to attract officers or
officially appointed delegates from as many affiliates as possible
(and did attract forty-four jentaculants, including national
officers and directors); and I stole a leaf out of Max Goldberg's
chapbook. As "CEA Past" in the panel discussion at Chicago
the year before, reflected in a CEA Chap Book that had since
been published and distributed to the membership, he had

spoken of a certain "Zany Element" which he said had always set our Association apart from her more solemn corrivals.[3] A thousand-watt bulb had suddenly illuminated my spirit. I almost cried aloud: *C'est mon métier!* Instanter, the Zany Element of CEA became an article of faith for my performance as Regional Coordinator.

Almost every Regional Breakfast, Regional Council Breakfast, Regional Delegates Breakfast, or breakfast at a regional meeting I had ever eaten was followed by speeches or exhortations on the theme (variously phrased) of how to improve national - regional CEA relations. It was obvious to me that there remained a great gulf fixed between the national Association and its affiliates. What we needed was a mating of minds, a marriage, a proper wedding.

And so, at New York on that Wednesday morning of 1966, the nuptials were solemnized. Having equipped myself in advance with a black book dangling an extra-long notched crimson marker-ribbon, I summoned to stand before me Karl Kiralis (CEA) to be wedded to Cortland Auser (CEA Affiliates). I also contrived to include Jacques Mitchell, representing the two-year colleges—I forget now on what pretext but presumably best man, as the man Jacques may very well have been. "Dearly beloved," I intoned—

> we are gathered here within sight of the Empire State Building, and in the face of this company, to join together the College English Association and its regionals in holy Affiliation; which is an honourable estate, instituted of Max, signifying unto us the mystical union that is betwixt CEA and her members; which holy estate Pat adorned and beautified with his presence and first miracle, and is commended by Don, to be honourable among all men; and therefore is not by any to be entered into unadvisedly or lightly; but reverently, discreetly, advisedly, soberly, and in the fear of trembling . . .
>
> Wilt thou, Cort Auser, have this College English Association, after Don's ordinance, in the holy estate of Affiliation? Wilt thou love her, comfort her, honour her, and keep her in scholarship and pedagogy; and forsak-

ing no others, keep thee also unto her, so long as ye all shall teach?

After each of the three principals, in turn, responded "I will," he addressed the congregation—with at least moderate seriousness—on attitudes and behavior appropriate to the segment he specifically represented, and on its relations with the others. The ceremony concluded with this reverend pronouncement:

Forasmuch as Cort, Karl, and Jacques have consented together in holy Affiliation, and have witnessed the same before this company and Ed Huberman, and thereto have pledged their dues—by virtue of the authority vested in me by the Board of Directors of the College English Association, Inc., and by the Commonwealth of Massachusetts, I confer upon them and upon each of you here present, respectively, with all the rights, privileges, and duties appertaining thereunto, the certificate of *Jentaculum jentaculorum*, regions without end.

There you have an unfair working sample of my conception, which I fear you may deem misbegotten, of the office of Regional Coordinator that I held from the end of 1965 to the middle of 1974—with a slight change of title (to National Coordinator of Affiliates) in the second half of my term. I was convinced, rightly or wrongly, that if I could make colleagues around the country feel that CEA was an oasis in Academia Deserta—that we furnished fellowship, fun, fancy, and yet a feast of reason and a fount of inspiration—then I was doing my best, and all the hierarchy had any right to expect of me, to compound the several hundred dollars of annual expense money generously allotted by the Bored with few if any strings attached to the purse. An unsympathetic observer might have wished to put it more bluntly: that I used corporation funds to goof off. If so, at least I tried to goof grandly, spreading CEA's tidings as widely among regional Associations about the country as typewriter and duplicating processes and travel by automobile, air, and train would permit. For example, four months after the nuptials in Parlor F of the Sheraton-Atlantic in Manhattan, I addressed the biennial meeting of the Tennessee College English Association at Lambuth College in Jackson on "What Have We Done for You—Lately?" [4] Routinely (and at my own expense) I attended the South Central CEA meeting every Fall and that of Texas CEA each Spring, and was always granted time for "a few words about the College English Association."

At New York in that December of '66, I carried zanyism into still another dimension by handing to Allan Lefcowitz a burlesque *explication de texte* of Clement C. Moore's "A Visit from St. Nicholas." He sat down on a red-plush hotel bench, and after a quick perusal said succinctly: "I'd like to use it." You may well be asking—unless you were a member of national CEA in the late 1960's or happen to know him outside the pages, thus far, of this sometimes less-than-methodical History—"But who was Allan Lefcowitz?" Donald Sears discovered him as a bright young colleague at Howard University, and Allan had given his maiden contribution to the *Critic* (in collaboration with his wife, Barbara) in February, 1966. By the time I encountered him at the December convention, he was Managing Editor, and to (for him, regrettably) an indeterminate degree in charge of some executive affairs for the Association. "But how . . . ?" Once again, I quote you, the perplexed reader: ". . . how did that come about?"

As I more than hinted in LUSTRUM FIVE, but did not consider appropriate to elaborate at that point, sometime in the middle of 1966 Don Sears heeded the rumble of a distant drum and accepted an appointment to teach for a year at Ahmadu Bello University in (Northern) Nigeria. Although as Regional Coordinator (an office of which the By-Laws then in force were ignorant) I gradually became a sort of courtesy member of the Executive Committee, [5] I have no recollection of participating in the discussions that must have preceded confirmation of interim arrangements for the academic year 1966-67. Presumably on recommendation of Editor Sears, Allan B. Lefcowitz became Managing Editor, with William Washington (also of Howard) as Editorial Assistant. Through January of

1967, the mast of the *Critic* showed the national headquarters as a post office box address that appears from the zip code to have been that of Howard University; beginning in February, the address was given as Rutgers University at Newark. Lefcowitz was explicitly designated to be in charge of the Book-of-the-Month Club Writing Fellowship program for CEA,[6] but I do not know how much else besides routine conduct of the journal. My impression is that he expected to be in constant touch by international air mail with his superior Editor and Executive Director,[7] and to receive continual advice and directives.

I am also not well informed about the reception of Don Sears in Africa, for I always felt it would be indelicate to quiz him about the unpleasantries he suffered upon arrival. Apparently his plane landed at the Kano airport just as a contigent of Southern bad-guy Ibo rebels from the Niger delta were shooting up a troop of good-guy Northern Nigerians (or it may have been vice versa). Rumor had it that Don lost a substantial part of the personal possessions he had taken with him to make life tolerable at a latitude of twelve degrees, and I vaguely got the impression that for a while he was considerably less then personally safe. At any rate, he bravely hung on and stayed out his year. Meantime, though his CEA titles were preserved intact, communication was uncertain and caretakers on the home front were obliged to muddle through. A hope expressed in the *Critic*, over the initials "DAS," for an "international CEA conference in Europe next summer" came to naught.

By the tone and appearance of *CEA Critics* through December, and by dead reckoning from general knowledge of the process of editing, I take it that before leaving on safari, Don Sears probably had chosen manuscripts and perhaps even dummied-up layout for several issues. With the January number of 1967, however, a new hand was distinctly evident. For one thing, Allan Lefcowitz gave himself the privilege of throwing his weight around with a long editorial, or long signed article beginning in the conventional spot for editorials at the foot of the mast on page two.[8] For another, he not only included a book review (with rare exceptions, excluded by

THE CEA CRITIC

THE COLLEGE ENGLISH ASSOCIATION

IN THIS ISSUE

VOL. XXX—No. 6   Published at Saratoga Springs, N.Y.   March, 1968

THE CEA CRITIC

THE COLLEGE ENGLISH ASSOCIATION

IN THIS ISSUE

B.O.M.C.
Poems and Reviews
Bradbury on Ahab
McNelly on Bradbury
Mulqueen on Sister Carrie
Asmundsson on Fiedler
Earnest on Computers
Weigel on Communications

Vol. XXXI–No. 6   March, 1969

Regional Roundup

FLORIDA CEA
Date: April 12
Place: Stetson University
Local Chairman: Elliott Allen
Program: The Negro Writer in America

GREATER NEW YORK CEA
Date: April 26
Place: Finch College
Program Chairman: Samuel K. Workman, Newark College of Engineering
Program: Literature for the Non-Major
Speakers: Dean Sterling Olmstead
Dr. Floyd Zulli

MIDDLE ATLANTIC CEA
Date: May 3
Place: Goucher College
Program: The Crisis of the Cities in Modern Literature
Speakers: Alfred Kazin, Kenneth Lynn

PENNSYLVANIA CEA
Date: April 18-19
Place: Hershey (Pa.) Motor Lodge
Area Chairman: Richard L. Jordan, Harrisburg Area Community Coll.
Program: The English Major
Dinner Speaker: Daniel Hoffman

TENNESSEE CEA
Date: April 25-26
Place: Middle Tennessee State U.
Local Chairman: William Beasley
Luncheon Speaker: Earle Labor

The Humanities Department at the State University of New York Maritime College will sponsor a conference on "Science as a Humane Discipline" on March 28-29, 1969. The premise underlying the conference theme is that many of our colleagues tend to see the portion of the curriculum devoted to science and technical training as largely if not entirely isolated from liberal education and a liberal point of view and that such a view of the matter is incorrect. Featured speakers will be Dr. Bentley Glass of Stony Brook and Professor Joseph Mazzeo of Columbia. Anyone desiring further information should contact Professor Joel Jay Belson, State University of New York Maritime College, Fort Schuyler, Bronx, N. Y. 10465.

Sonnet 155 by William Shakespeare

(Recently Discovered in England by

Professor Charles R. Larson of Indiana University)

Oaths of thy love, thy truth, thy constancy
Which have no correspondence with true sight:
For all that beauty that doth cover thee,
O'ercharged with burthen of mine own love's might.
In our two loves there is but one respect.
Where beauty's veil doth cover every blot;
The ornament of beauty is suspect,
Thou mayst be false, and yet I know it not.
So shall I live, supposing thou art true,
Now that the summer is less pleasant now:
No marvel then, though I mistake my view;
With all-triumphant splendor on my brow:
    Look, what is best, that best I wish in thee,
    Make thee another self, for love of me.

Sears' editorial policy) but rather defiantly, as it now seems to me looking back, headed it with the rubric REVIEW. [9]

At even a glance, the February issue was slightly shocking to regular subscribers: the two-column "leader" was at the *left*, not Don Sears' customary right, of the front page. Furthermore, it was shocking to hypersensitive CEAers in a more basic way. Headlined "Not Even a Mouse: An Explication," and signed with a transparent pseudonym, an outrageous burlesque of archetypal - mythic criticism purported to find "The Night before Christmas" a revival of pagan worship, "an apocalyptic Dionysiac poem" spoken by "a naïve *persona* incapable of recognizing and interpreting the ancestral memories that flow back upon him during his sleep at Christmas Eve." Two characters of the vision ("To the blind dreamer, the visitation is only 'A Visit ' ") are identified. Saint Nicholas, whose "stump of a pipe" is a "a stump (broken relic) of the pipes of Pan," is demonstrated to be Silenus. Pan himself "is the acolyte, who accompanies him silently into the room and who is so vastly overshadowed by the 'right jolly old elf' that the dreamer barely notices him, mentioning him only at the end:

. . . then turned with a jerk,

. . . obviously, it is Santa's helper, the jerk, who is being beckoned to follow him up the chimney."

Forgive the extended quotation of frivolity, but I really needed to show the incredulous reader why some officials were outraged at what appeared to be going on behind the back of an absent D. Africanus Sears.

Before I document that point further, I must mention that also in February there was an article or report (on the Writing Fellowship program) signed by Managing Editor Lefcowitz at the foot of the mast. More intriguingly, an entirely new department was introduced with the heading in Old English type (then an oddity for the *Critic*):

Gazetteer

In it, a fictive Gaz wrote discursive paragraphs on the sorts of things that had been stated briefly and barely in previous

NOTICES OF NOTE columns, and also on in-house affairs: "From this point forward, he is responsible for all general College English Association information (elections, meetings, dues, and so forth), brief letters to the editor, general professional business, news of members, and such matters of interest that individual CEAers may wish to communicate to their brethren." In a final NOTE FROM MY CUBBY, he called for "squibs, quips, and quiddities for future *Gazetteers*," adding: "And this, for the nonce, is my quietus."

No, Allan, not for the nonce but for the future. Unhappily, Managing Editor Lefcowitz spoke more than he knew in that last sentence, which happened to fall (in a continuation) on the last page of the last issue of the journal he edited for CEA. Where his name, title, and professional address (followed by an entry also for his colleague William Washington) had been appearing at the *Critic's* masthead, the next number (March, 1967) substituted "Guest Editor: Edward Huberman, Rutgers at Newark."(The journal continued to be "Published at Saratoga Springs, N.Y.")

It is clear beyond question that when Allan B. Lefcowitz was editing the February, 1967, *CEA Critic* he had no inkling of any approaching end of tenure. A feeling of verve and confidence and eager planning stands out glowingly from its pages. I do not know who gave him the bad news, or how or when or by whom the decision was made. He partly blamed or seemed to blame me—but whether he held me guilty of corrupting his youth by handing him the typescript of "Not Even a Mouse" at New York, or whether he mistook my status of lowerarchy for hierarchy and imagined that I was instrumental in his separation, I simply wot not. I personally thought very well of his services to CEA, and always said so to anyone who would listen. I sympathize with any subordinate on whom responsibilities are thrust without matching authority. I still regard the "Gazetteer" page as a splendid editorial idea, highly worthy to be revived whenever the right conductor can be found, sufficiently eighteenth-century in spirit and imbued with just the right tincture of zanyism. [10]

During the Chicago convention at the end of the year, I said something of the kind in the presence of Second Vice-

President Francis Utley. (It may well have been following the Breakfast for Regional Delegates, to which he brought "greetings from President Henry Adams," who had booked an early flight to Florida to play golf lest CEAing Illinois in frosty December completely elude his game.) Fran replied, it seemed to me unnecessarily pointedly in view of my manifest authorship of the most glaringly offensive article in the short, unhappy Editorship of Allan Lefcowitz: "The *Critic* was becoming a sort of high school humor magazine." From that remark, which I am certain I paraphrase closely and perhaps quote verbatim, I assumed that indignation had been whipped into action as much by Francis Lee Utley as by any other member of the Establishment. If that be true, I do not—to employ a very faulty expression—"fault him." He had high ideals for the organization he was due to preside over two administrations thence, and must have strongly felt that it was time for a change. At this point, lest I forget later, I want to say that Fran Utley was one of the great scholars who have not regarded being an officer of CEA as a semi-honorary position. [11] He always worked hard and conscientiously in every position he filled, and continued active interest and participation until his lamented death. He once filched my raincoat, but it fit so poorly that he brought it back to my hotel room at midnight and retrieved his own.

Although Don Sears' entry in the mast of the journal continued to show him as Executive Director and Editor, Guest Ed. Ed Huberman was from March through August, 1967, effectively in total charge of CEAffairs: executive, fiscal, placement, editorial. Even after Sears had returned to America—with such momentum that he carried the executive headquarters to California State College (now University) at Fullerton, constructively arriving on September Morn—Huberman continued temporarily as Guest Editor, bringing out both the October and November issues. Then, in December of 1967, the name of a new Managing Editor, Earle Labor of Centenary College of Louisiana, flew from the mast. Even earlier, Ed Huberman was being assisted as Treasurer by an understudy at the neighboring Newark College of Engineering (later New Jersey Institute of Technology), James

J. Napier, who succeeded him in that office at the end of the year. Beginning with the January, 1968, issue of the *Critic*, Edward Huberman—on whose "capable shoulders," according to a report by Executive Director Sears printed in that same number, "[d]uring my leave in Africa, most of the duties of the national office eventually fell"—was shown in the mast to be bearing only a residual administrative burden of the Bureau of Appointments. He was, however, just then entering upon a Vice-Presidency that would lead in two years to his rising to President at what proved to be a major turning point of CEA's history and, *pari passu*, of this heedful History.

For his brief Editorship of less than a year in 1967, Ed Huberman showed a sure hand and brought some new ideas to the journal. Instead of reverting to the often clustered "Notices of Note" entries, he distributed through the journal ruled boxes giving discursively some of the kinds of material that Allan Lefcowitz had intended his Gaz to present, and also introduced an occasional NEWS OF MEMBERS column. In his second issue (April, 1967), he invented another column which instantly became a regular and popular feature, and which he continued to furnish to the *Critic* after he ceased to be its Guest Editor. "Minireviews: Something for Everybody" he first headed it, afterward wryly (and needlessly) altering the subtitle to "Something for Almost Everybody." Before long, he began to include audio-visual materials as well as books.

The Huberman *CEA Critic* retained essentially the Sears front-page makeup, though with more frequent occurrence of two-line (as well as two-column) headings over the leading articles at the right. The Guest Editor also sometimes used a "teaser" line in smaller type above the headline of a major article, e.g., A Fresh View (underscored) above a two-line, three-column heading of an essay about *Miss Lonelyhearts* on page five of the June, 1967, number. In both front-page leaders and the inside pages (the articles in or at the head of the left column of the first page were normally informational or pedagogical), strong interest was shown in literary topics, including one leading article on style, another on "Parallel Scenes in *Tom Sawyer* and *Huck Finn*," and two on literary criticism (one of which was an account by Earle Labor of a classroom "Experiment in Criticism"). Verse, both serious and light, was used with considerable frequency, and often given a position of prominence at the head of a page. Letters to the Editor were run in some abundance. An amusing blend was a (very free) verse "Letter to the Editor: LEAVES OF CHAFF" by George P. Zirnite in the April issue, a lampoon (inspired by a *Critic* article in January) of a "learn'd linguistician" with his "puffs and disfigurements . . . ranged in charts and graphs before me" at the convention of a sister organization.

Among the boxes appearing in several Huberman *Critics* were offers of shopworn remainders of CEA Chap Books and old copies of "The Basic Issues in the Teaching of English." Thrift, thrift, Eduardo! Perhaps by such economic shifts, Treasurer Edward Huberman was able to afford Guest Ed. Huberman increased space for maneuver in the journal. The first two numbers he edited ran to a record twenty pages each, and the thinnest of the five contained fourteen. I must add that this opulence continued into the next regime: Managing Editor Earle G. Labor's second, fourth, and fifth issues (January, March, and April, 1968) each had twenty pages. I must, more pointedly, point out that those were flush times when publishers still believed in lavish advertising in professional journals, and when even double-page spreads were not just dreamed of but verily sold.

With its harassed hunter home from the hill, [12] and the heavy Edwardian burdens redistributed on several pairs of shoulders (including Ed Huberman's own), the College English Association returned for its annual convention of 1967 [13] to Chicago and the storied Sherman Hotel or Sherman House. (The *Critic* impartially referred to it as "the Sherman House Hotel.") The scenario played there two years before and followed at New York in 1966 had, by now, become fairly well established; the main deviation (besides introduction of a necessarily novel Luncheon for Book-of-the-Month Club Writing Fellowship Program Regional Judges) was that the open, public meeting on the night of Wednesday, December 27, was promoted from eight-thirty to seven o'clock. [14] Speakers were Louis

Kronenberger and Henry Adams. The latter had just been elected CEA's President for a second term, to continue through 1968.[15] For personal reasons into which I have never penetrated, or seriously tried, First Vice-President Goldberg had declined an otherwise assured nomination to the Presidency. Luckily, two successive years (not more) in that office were constitutional, and in fact such double terms had occurred several times in the 1940's and 1950's. Fortunately, also, Barkis Adams proved willin'. Regrettably, however, Maxwell Henry Goldberg, like Burges Johnson, his rival as All-time Man of the CEA, never occupied the Presidency of the organization which hardly can be thought of apart from those two grand old names.[16]

The Regional Delegates Breakfast was served on December 28, 1967, not in the Crystal Room where Sears' sorcery of 'Sixty-five had put me under spell, but in a Gold Room (much better hidden by the architects than an entirely separate and readily accessible Gold Coast Room, where I first mistakenly laid out my paraphernalia), on the same *soi-disant* first floor reached from the second stop upward of the same strait and narrow elevator mentioned in the previous chapter. With the aid of sentries posted at the elevator door, thirty-seven participants finally found the right place to break their fast. An account of the proceedings in the January *Critic* called them "An assemblage so widely representative of the widely flung College English Association that an atomic device carelessly detonated that morning could have deflowered the chivalry of CEA." (In those days, as now, we were all half-expecting small fission apparatuses to fall into the hands of terrorists and malcontents.) "The Idea of a Newsletter" had been announced as the postjentacular topic. Seven regional publications were exhibited and discussed by their Editors, together with a presentation about the *CEA Critic* by Donald Sears, Edward Huberman, and Earle Labor. It was agreed that the Regional Coordinator would thenceforth prepare and distribute "a regular Exchange List, to enable the Editor and/or Secretary of each branch of the Association to receive all publications, programs, and miscellaneous bulletins of information from all others on a regular and continuing basis."

Beginning that December, I have every reason to believe, or even to be certain, that Managing Editor Earle Gene Labor was at least as effectually in charge of the *CEA Critic* as I judge managing Editor Lee Elbert Holt to have become in the latter 1950's, even though during the tenure of each the title of Editor was formally attached to the Executive Directorship held by another officer. An instant radical change of appearance occurred with the December, 1967, issue: the paper now had a front cover. (See illustrations.) Actually, the remarkably curvaceous design came through the influence if not the hand of the Immediate Past Guest Editor, for it was created by Ed's daughter Jamie Lyle Huberman. As can be seen, it encouraged at least a suggestion of a table-of-contents (something that had been halfheartedly attempted in the past, even as recently as June of 1967 by Huberman himself, but had never permanently caught on), and when reduced to corner size permitted other editorial matter to be given top display. Later, in the April issue of 1969, the Earle of Labor instituted a genuine table-of-contents, with full entries including page numbers, on the second page of the journal.

The new Managing Editor picked up and expanded or modified the use of some technical devices from practices of his predecessor. An isolated occurrence (so far as I have noticed) can be seen in the final Huberman *Critic*, to which Earle might possibly have contributed some appropriate labor, of the modern equivalent of an old-fashioned type ornament: a small, simple drawing that by photographic process could be enlarged or reduced at need, used for combined decoration and "filler." Commencing with the December issue in 1967, a variety of these ornaments was kept available in the bureau of Labor, some of whimsical character such as a pair of Beardsleyan Wilde eyes. I do not suppose that the Managing Editor was reluctant to accept contributions in verse—as a matter of fact, quite the contrary was true[17]—but the employment of these ornaments did cut down on the casual insertion of short jingles to piece out small gaps between longer items. Edward Huberman's successor at first imitated his teaser lines used over headings, but soon in effect transferred them to the lower right corner of the new front-page design. In typographic style, he went further (in part, though not necessarily deliberately, by reverting to usages of earlier Editors of the journal) in choosing variety types for headlines, including script and church text.

About this time, the industrious Labor participated in completion of a project that had been proposed many years before,[18] and that had been undertaken by Lee Holt as early as the Summer of 1958. Exactly ten years after Managing Editor Holt had reported its beginning in a *Critic* editorial (November, 1958), his *INDEX to NEWSLETTER* [sic] *of the College English Association, June 1939 through December 1947 a n d THE CEA CRITIC, January 1948 through December 1958* was published as a Special Index Issue of the *Critic* in November, 1968. The Earle and Lady Betty Labor took up the task at that point: their *INDEX to THE CEA CRITIC, January 1959 through June 1967 Volumes XXI-XXIX* became a second Special Index Issue in June, 1970. From 1968 the *Critic* and after its founding the *Forum* have been indexed year by year in the final number of each volume of both journals. (Omission of most indexes in 1983 and 1984 resulted from circumstances of publishing difficulty and editorial transition.)

Earle Labor continued as Managing Editor to the end of Volume XXXII of the *Critic* in the middle of 1970, when it was split into two quarterlies with leapfrogging monthly dates of publication, the (new) *CEA Critic* and the (even newer) *CEA Forum*. He became Editor of both. I happen to have known him better than any of his predecessors (he is easy and pleasant to know), and have an abiding sense of his professionalism about editing. He understood by instinct, observation, ratiocination, or a combination of all three that the focus of the College English Association was, always had been, and always would (or should) be upon the scholar - teacher: the scholar in the classroom. From the first *Critic* he edited, or "managed," he openly solicited "particularly short critical essays ... which cast new light on how literary material can become effective and remain viable in the college classroom," adding that "Creative work which has some relation to the teaching of English is also welcome." Like Don Sears—and also at first *with* him as designated Editor—Earle had an excellent sense of balance among the multiple interests necessarily served by an in-house publication for a teachers' "federation" having both general and parochial entitlements. He continued the "Regional Roundup" and, at a less major level, restored "Notices of Note." He had a good ear for genuinely funny humor, such as an ironic transcription by John Schmittroth of the introduction of one "Doctor Ross, who has dedicated his life to the study of language . . ." and who, called upon to "begin these exciting finals by pronouncing the first word," offers to an expectant speller: "Hunnert."

So far as the use of literary and scholarly material was concerned, Earle Labor's temperament agreed closely with that manifested by Don Sears when he had been fully in charge, or supported by at most a functionary Managing Editor based near the printing press; once again, I do not have to trouble myself greatly about who was "really editing" what I call the Laborite *Critic* of 1967-1970. It may be significant for that question, so far as it is a question, that under Managing Editor Labor book reviews, and not just the continuing "minireviews" now acknowledged and signed by Edward Huberman, became increasingly important—as a glance at the annual indexes of June, 1969 and 1970, for example, will quickly reveal. Quality of reviewing was generally high. Having spoken of Ed Huberman a moment ago, I think that I ought to mention that Oscar Cargill, whose first contribution was made to one of the issues Ed edited in 1967, was to become an important firehorse in the Sears, Labor, or Sears-Labor stable, specializing in substantial essays of the type known as review articles.

In a casual parenthesis some pages back, we left Henry Hitch Adams, at the end of 1967, playing golf in Florida to refresh himself for a second hitch as President of CEA during 1968. In December of the latter year, he beckoned the College English Association to New York City. There, "special-rate accommodations" were offered to members "at the gracious Barbizon-Plaza Hotel . . . [j]ust a pleasant stroll from the Americana Hotel, where the crush of MLA English meetings will be held . . ." I have always felt that I was robbed at this convention, but not of my purse (*Othello*, III.iii.157).

The attentive reader will remember that for several years no official banquet or general luncheon had been included in the new formula which had been developing for the Association's conventions. During those same three years, I had conducted a Regional Delegates Breakfast that, if I say it myself who oughtn't, had become a popular event. In 1968, the whole format was radically overhauled, with disappearance of the evening public meeting—together with smoker or social hour, lock-and-stock, and cash bar barrel. Now, the central event of the convention was to be a breakfast on Saturday morning, December 28, with President Adams presiding, not at CEA's Barbizon-Plaza hostelry but at MLA's Americana—crush or no crush—and not free to invited regional delegates but offered for "a token $1.00 to CEA members (others may join)." The program would consist of "A celebration of the 20th anniversary and the 20th reprinting of CEA Director Mark Schorer's germinal essay 'Technique as Discovery.' " Perhaps as token concession to expectations of the Zany Element from remembered previous breakfasts, Mark Schorer would make a "rebuttal" to lauds by R. W. B. Lewis. Fran Utley was cast as moderator, to pick up any fur that might fly.

I do not remember that breakfast well, unless it was the one—which I am pretty sure came a year later, at Denver—where we made a fast break to only Danish and coffee (*period*). Perhaps I was sulking in my hotel room, or trying to quiet *Katzenjammer* from the night before. Yes, it most emphatically was the morning after the night before. Instead of a Regional Delegates Breakfast, a Regional Delegates Reception was scheduled for the CEA Suite in the gracious Barbizon-Plaza Hotel, to which I was permitted to bid my usual guests to take something slightly more than a stroll on Friday evening, December 27. I ought to have said "Pat Hogan and I," for he was co-host. Either that year, or it might have begun in 1970, I was to learn the fine art of snooping out cut-rate Manhattan liquor stores and stockpiling mixers, Edam cheese, junk snacks, paper napkins, and plastic cups without having to call on room service (prohibitive in price at metropolitan hostelries). It takes a lot of lugging to throw a proper party;

rustling ice, alone, is a labor of Hercules. Dr. Helen Thomas seems to recall that at this first one the supplies were provided by the management (Don Sears). Among us, anyhow, we managed to keep glasses full around the not especially crowded room that very cold enchanted evening, and to initiate a new tradition.

The trouble was that the hierarchy envisaged a "meeting" somewhere midway of the bash, a procedure I regarded as unfeasible. Still, I made an effort to gavel the revelers into attention, and maliciously called on those most vocal about having a serious meeting of minds to stand and deliver their wisdom. I flatter myself that attendants generally did enjoy the party. I know that many stayed late, some carrying off handfuls of popcorn or wedges of cheese to eat in street or elevator, and not a few helping with the disposal of partially empty bottles. We almost had to set up a lost-and-found station for hats, topcoats, and umbrellas left behind or exchanged. Be advised that I am here blending memories of several of these affairs as they developed through the remaining years of my tenure, either while we were still meeting jointly with the Modern Language Association or when (after 1969) CEA had gone its separate way but I still chased MLA in December and called apart, for a little night musing, regional and national worthies of our own Association who also happened to be attending.

As I have passingly mentioned before, Francis Lee Utley became President of CEA for the year 1969, which—I hardly need remind any readers out of their nonage—was a critical time for academic organizations. The business meetings of the Modern Language Association had turned into chaos as early as 1968 in New York, where I can remember migrating from one protest gathering to another (as appalled observer) with a sense of "After this, the deluge." Under conditions of sanity, the 1969 convention would have rotated back to Chicago; but threats, or at least vituperative manifestos and abusive speeches, caused MLA to fly in the face of prior commitment and a poll of its members, and move to the fastness of the Rocky Mountains. Of necessity, the College English Association went along with the gang, and so I bought a pair of snow tires and prayed (successfully) for unseasonable December weather in mile-high Denver. Although the business meeting of MLA was more stormy than the weather, it was conducted (if that be the word) in such a detached location that trouble-makers found themselves somewhat divided; and so, despite a comparatively low general attendance, the panicked displace-ment can be deemed on the whole a successful strategy of the divide-and-survive kind.

The College English Association's own sessions were not much affected, at least overtly or obviously, by the dissidence of dissent, since dedicated malcontents had plenty to do elsewhere hustling petitions up and down hallways, peddling sleazy "literature," grabbing microphones, electing their ilk to high office, and generally disrupting the dignity of MLA. Our own convention pattern at Denver was closely imitated from that of the preceding year in New York. A Regional Delegates Reception in the late afternoon and early evening on Saturday, December 27, included a showing by Charles E. Linck, Jr., of *The Scarlet Woman* , a vintage silent motion pic-ture ("the archetypal underground movie," I called it) made in 1924 by Evelyn Waugh and featuring him, Alec Waugh, and Elsa Lanchester (not in the title role). The "serious" section of this gathering—I do not say "session" because the February, 1970, *Critic* reported a "standing room only" attendance—centered on discussion of the impending creation (or revival[19]) of a Rocky Mountain CEA.

The announced Annual Meeting of the next morning was again a breakfast for which CEA members paid one dollar, others six including five for joining up. President Utley spoke—"From My Side of the Generation Gap"—a balanced plea in troubled times for understanding, responsibility, and (yes, he used the word) love. [20] Also scheduled for the morning program was a Recital of Songs from the Plays of William Shakespeare Set to Music by Composers of Five Periods of Music History by William R. Diehl and David A. Karp, pianist. Unhappily, the Diehl fell through (illness) and the recital was canceled. President-Elect Ed Huberman stepped up to the musical chair with an extempore intermezzo in which he "affirmed that the CEA of the 70's would move in new directions to assert its integrity and independence."

In the not entirely logical yet hardly mistakable phrasing of a song popular some years ago, the incoming President was "not so very far from wrong." Things were stirring in the councils of CEA. Largely at then Vice-President Huberman's urging, yea insistence, the directors had formally ratified at their meeting on December 26, 1969, a decision which had been in the works for some time: that the College English Association would at long last break away from Mother MLA and conduct its own independent, full-length meeting on April 24 and 25, 1970, at the University of Notre Dame du Lac, in **association** (you should pardon the ineluctable pun) with its Indiana affiliate. A formal topic (a custom more or less abrogated in the later years of the 1960's) was announced: Contemporary Relevance and the Teaching of Literature.

It seems to me appropriate to divide between *lustra* two successive "annual" gatherings that were held only four months apart and yet symbolized old yielding place to new in College English Association history. It will also give the final chapter of this climactic narrative the opportunity to open on a high note, which I shall do my best to sustain to the end. I will, however, mention here that to keep the termination of CEA Presidencies in phase with the yearly meeting, as it had been before by the simple expedient of having both coincide with the close of calendar years, Edward Huberman agreed to fill an extended—not exactly the same as a double—term. Instead of retiring on December 31, 1970, he continued as President until the second New Style Conference held at Jacksonville, Florida, in early April of 1971,[21] when he was succeeded by William James Griffin—who also, but from an entirely different cause, was destined to serve two (full) terms as President of the Association.

The greatest project of Projector Donald Albert Sears, not even excepting his abortive grand intention to promote an international over-CEA meeting during the Summer of 1967, was undoubtedly a fellowship program in creative writing that he negotiated in 1965 with Harry Scherman, founder of the

Book-of-the-Month Club. It was presented to the directors of the Association and then announced to members at the annual meeting that December in Chicago. In February, 1966, a box announcement was placed in the middle of the *Critic's* front page for information of those who had not been present to hear the glad tidings, and in June what by form seemed to be an advertisement was inserted on the op-ed page: "'The Book-of-the-Month Club and the College English Association are pleased to announce the First Annual Book-of-the-Month Club Writing Fellowship Program," identified as being in celebration of the fortieth anniversary of the Club. Fourteen fellowships of three thousand dollars each would be available for college or university undergraduates.

A year later, in February of 1967, Allan Lefcowitz, who had been left in charge of the BOMC project when Don Sears went to Africa, reported that CEA had already "received over 2,000 inquiries about the program," and that "students applying for fellowships (which includes sending in a portfolio of writing)" had submitted "over 425 completed applications." He also revealed: "The smallest portfolio contained two sonnets; the biggest contained two novels, one play, twelve short stories, and twenty-two poems." The immense bulk of these submissions was parceled out among CEAppointed judges in seven geographical districts; the best entries in each area were then funneled to three national judges, all distinguished as creative writers; in the end, fourteen fellowships[22] were awarded to graduating Seniors of the class of 1967 in nine states (the "mode" being Iowa, with five winners).

After February of 1967 until Executive Director Sears' return that Autumn, the BOMC Fellowship program was administered for the College English Association by Edward Huberman as *factotum pro hiatus rebus*. Thereafter, Sears was to testify that "a large part of my time has been devoted to directing the Book-of-the-Month Club Writing Fellowship Program." As a spin-off, he pushed a cooperative survey by the BOMC and ADE of creative writing courses in colleges and universities, leading to his editing of a *Directory of Creative Writing Programs in the United States and Canada* as a CEA Chap Book published in December, 1968.[23] Another offshoot that year, intended to become annual, was an anthology of *New Writing* (by BOMC Fellows) brought out by the Washington Square Press.

In the March *Critic* of 1968, Don Sears made a statistical analysis of the forty regional winners in the first year (1966-67) of the Writing Fellowship program—of course including the fourteen national winners—by birth, age, sex, secondary school background, number of colleges attended, and institution from which graduated. Conclusions:

> While it is obvious that talent—including creative talent—is where you find it, it is possible to suggest from this analysis certain probabilities. The current college graduate who has already demonstrated a high creative writing productivity is relatively young (21.3 years old) and may well have trained in a private preparatory school. At least half of the number will have attended more than one college, and the group is one-third female. In most instances he [*tsic*] will be the product of an urban environment.

A "Report of the Executive Director" for 1968, printed by the February *CEA Critic* in 1969, was almost pathetically optimistic. Not only did it allude generally to "the period of affluence into which college English has moved in the late 1960's," but it spoke with confidence about the Writing Fellowship program, then well into its third year, as a growingly important force in Academia Americana. There was no hint, or rather not the sighest suspicion, of any *terminus ad quem* for the project. In October of 1969, Managing Editor Labor joined in rejoicement over the program (in an editorial plurally signed "Eds."); and Editor Sears performed another analysis based on that of March, 1968, but now covering all three years and differing in some statistical procedures. The last words of his article were ". . . the program continues into its fourth year."

It did, indeed, but no farther. The fourth successive (academic) year of the program began normally in the Autumn of 1969; and in April of 1970 the *CEA Critic* announced thirty-five regional winners for that fourth year, five in each of the seven districts, adding that fourteen national winners would be selected. Actually, twelve were named in the June issue. The rest was silence.

A heavy blow had fallen on November 12, 1969. Harry Scherman, who had been Mr. Book-of-the-Month Club since the founding in 1926, died aged eighty-two. The annual report for 1969 of CEA's Executive Director printed in the February, 1970, *Critic* stated in measured words: "With deep sadness I report the recent death of Harry Scherman, founder and chairman of the Board of Book-of-the-Month Club, and, to us of CEA, guiding *and funding* spirit behind the BOMC Writing Fellowship Program, which for the past four years has sought and found outstanding writing talent." That was the total entry (except that I have added emphasis to a significant phrase); those were also the last signed Sears words I remember seeing about that soaring scheme.

During the bell-shaped trajectory of the BOMC project, I was only slightly aware of it except for what I read in the *Critic*. Its first announcement at Chicago in 1965 was nearly simultaneous with my impressment as Regional Coordinator. From then on, for close to a decade, I was heavily engaged in my own specialized CEActivity—with a finger or often both hands, and sometimes I fear a foot and mouth, in regional affairs.

For the month of December, 1965, when that activity began, the mast of the *CEA Critic* listed sixteen regional affiliates, [24] together with the Association of English Teachers at Two-Year Colleges as an Affiliate Organization, which (as has been revealed previously) was to disappear after a couple of years. For a year and a half, until the October issue in 1967, the list remained unchanged, except that Western New York had been redesignated Upper New York State. Nevertheless, by then it was slightly out of date (as I regret to say information nailed to masts always has been, is, and shall be). In the Spring of 1967, to my great exultation, I had helped (by remote control) Keith Rinehart and his colleagues Anthony Canedo and Frank Collins, all of Central Washington State College (now Central

Washington University), to beget a Pacific Northwest College English Association. About eighty persons showed up at the initial meeting to hear papers on "Three Oblique Views of College English," to organize, and to plan another meeting for the next year—with many more to follow.

I am, of course, proud of all my children (which, to my chagrin, are very few), and not least of one I helped to engender during a period of months after the Pacific Northwest (and by even remoter insemination): a Caribbean CEA—you will readily guess how I pronounced the name—fathered mainly by John Zebrowski of the Inter American University of Puerto Rico, who was first entered in the mast of the *Critic* as its Coordinator in April, 1968. Other islanders, including Virgin Islanders, were welcomed to membership. Activity has continued vigorous.

My appetite grew by what it had been feeding. I could hardly emulate Don Sears' sometime vision of an international CEA, but why not one in our Fiftieth State? I enlisted (once again by almost infinitely remote control) the interest of Gloria Glissmeyer of the University of Hawaii; her name appeared on the *Critical* list in June, 1969, as Liaison Officer. I am sorry to report that she was never able to sandwich in a meeting at the Islands before her remove to California. Meantime, in March of 1969, another new Liaison Officer had appeared in the mast: Paul T. Bryant of Colorado State University (afterwards to become national President), for a proposed Rocky Mountain CEA that was brought still closer to ultimate being (as has been hinted) following screening of Evelyn Waugh's *Scarlet Woman* at Denver on Saturday evening, December 27. I count that healthy affiliate as a child of my parentage—though Paul Thompson Bryant and I sometimes drop into a tenderloin bar during conventions and dispute whether a Thomas or a Thompson was the real father.

My greatest disappointment in my ambitious program of covering land and CEA with affiliates was a mush (by mail) into Canada, where an organization acronamed ACUTE had been in being since 1957. When I talked with a member in Houston and referred to it by saying uh-CYOOT, he looked at me with unaffected puzzlement until he finally caught my drift, smiled sourly, and asked: "Oh, do you mean the Association of Canadian University Teachers of English? We pronounce each letter separately." That experience may help you to understand why, although I wrote reams of persuasive letters over the course of several years, winningly explaining that nothing could come but good on both sides of the border if their Association became a Comity Affiliate of ours—with no loss or cost to either except the moderate expense of bandying ideas, exchanging publications, and encouraging mutual participation by traveling delegates (at, for instance, MLA conventions)—they simply did not cotton to my fustian gab. When they found they could not freeze me out by ordinary polite coolness, I received a stiff, formal letter from an officer of ACUTE stating that they had carefully considered affiliation and declined to consider it further. I backed off, unhonored and unstrung.

I will spare you from sharing my embarrassment in certain attemped negotiations south of the border, and of course must omit from this chapter any regional triumphs belonging to the next *lustrum*. I am obligated, however, to cite a statement by Executive Director Sears in his annual report dated December 26, 1969: "Regional Coordinator Joe Thomas has started development work in the following areas: . . . Hawaii CEA . . . Midwest CEA . . . Alabama CEA . . . Mexico City CEA . . ." After each citation, in my copy of the February (1970) *Critic* where the report was printed, I have written "No result." At the convention of the Midwest Modern Language Association in St. Louis on October 23, 1969, I had obtained from a cooperative MWMLA Executive Secretary (himself an English professor) a spot for a pitch from CEA by Fran Utley and Associate Regional Coordinator Pat Hogan. If they attended, they brought back no commitments for any MWCEA. I myself had previously carried on unavailing correspondence with a "contact" in my close-to-native Kansas City; also, a fellow CEA director during my own term (though I never met him) did not reply enthusiastically to my letters about the desirability of founding a Midwestern affiliate. The Executive Director's reference to an attempted "Alabama CEA" presumably refers (if so, not very accurately) to a wider casting of nets than into a single state, by Earle Labor—always a staunch supporter of my efforts to expand regional CEActivity. In November, 1969, he attended the convention of the South Atlantic Modern Language Association in Atlanta as speaker at a breakfast for English professors sponsored convention-wide by the long-existing Georgia - South Carolina CEA and arranged by its Executive Secretary *pro tem.*, Frank L. Hoskins, Jr. In a style you will recognize, the October *CEA Critic* had said: "A Laborious effort to create a continuing SACEA organization, complete with officers, dues, and a newslettter, is expected." Alas, in the upshot there existed no more SACEA than MWCEA—even less, indeed, for in later times a Northern Plains CEA came into being.

Someone, I believe, sometime said something or other about "best laid schemes." At least I can boast that my efforts at regional development were never Mickey Mouse. During those busy years, as I was to continue to do for several more in the early part of the next decade, I bombarded officers, direc- tors, regionalists, and almost anyone else who I thought might react—with exchange lists, a bulletin of irregular frequency headed NEWS OF THE REGIONALS, rosters of officers, editors, and governing boards, "pastoral letters," speeches at as many meetings as I could afford or find time to attend, and of course invitations to the annual Regional Delegates Breakfast or Regional Delegates Reception. [25] I fear that I may have been a disappointment especially to hard-sellers like Ed Huberman, who stuck a membership form into every left hand while shaking the right. A meetings, I seldom did more than point to a supply of blanks piled on a side table along with sample *Critics* (later *Forums*, also) and other impedimenta of soft-sell.

My budget became five hundred dollars a year. [26] I am by no means certain that there would not have been a net fiscal gain to the Association's treasury if I had never been appointed in the first place, or not given any allowance to squander. The only question is, what the aims should be for a non-profit organization like CEA. With Abraham ibn Ezra, I was inclined to urge those who came to parties at my invitation, or invited me to their provincial gatherings:

> Have fun along with me!
> The best is yet to be,
> The zest of life, from which the dumps are banned ...

—and to say to the hierarchy:

> So take and use my work,
> Amend what flaws may lurk,
> What strain o' the stuff, what warpings past the aim!
> Let youth approve of age, and laughter end the game!

I realize that Browning did not translate the lines quite that way, but he probably was working from a corrupt text.

(Here endeth the reading of LUSTRUM SIX.)

Notae pedales for

LUSTRUM SIX

[1] I still treasure a neat definition provided by the author, Paul E. Dougherty: "The application of linguistic methods to the study of style has come to be called stylistics."

[2] Knowledge is power. From my own direct knowledge as Regional Coordinator, I could not have named a single affiliate of which the same assertion could have been made.

[3] " ... it is the sort of thing that doesn't appear in official histories, and that melts away from probing fingers. This is the sanative function that CEA has performed, through the years and to the profession—by means of what CEA old-timers have come to call, affectionately, our 'Zany Element.' This has been one of CEA's main counterpoises to the deadening solemnity of humorlessness that casts a blight upon so much American organizational and academic life."

Well, Max, beloved Master, it does appear in this seldom solemn History and does not (I hope) melt away from musing minds or probing fingers.

[4] The speech was published in the *Newsletter* of Tennessee CEA, No. 6 (May 10, 1967).

[5] Under the Constitution of 1970-71, the National Coordinator of Affiliates became explicitly designated as a member of the Executive Committee. I wish to say that prior to that elevation I was always treated with courtesy and deference by the unmistakable members of the Committee (consisting of the President, the Vice-Presidents, and so to speak the administrative heads of departments), which handles emergent affairs for the Association between meetings of the Bored—though on one occasion I can recall being asked to step aside from a special conclave, probably of a subcommittee, that was about to take place in the corner of a hotel suite where we had been powwowing. I stepped lively.

I must add that in 1971 as National Coordinator, I also became constitutionally an ex-officio member of the Board of Directors; but the real seat of influence was in the Executive Committee, from which elected directors were excluded.

[6] Because the Book-of-the-Month Club enterprise was roughly coextensive with the whole *lustrum*, it will be discussed as a "package" later in this chapter.

[7] Executive Secretary Sears took the more exalted title of Executive Director upon departure (possibly to impress colleagues and students in Northern Nigeria). He retained it upon his return.

[8] Headed "Prolegomena to a Freshman English Utopia," it attempted to draw up "ground rules" for improvement if not perfection of the basic College English course: "Whatever our Utopia is, it must mediate between the legitimate needs and demands of society, the teacher, and the student. It must provide that dignity which is the need of all three."

[9] It actually reviewed several numbers of the Writers and Critics series, and so perhaps should be called a short review article. It was signed with the initials of Editorial Assistant William Washington.

[10] Please, one and all, not me! I am a late Victorian in my dotage, as more than a few might say I always have been. Incidentally, I do not defend my *jeu d'esprit* on Christmas and criticism, though I will say that some readers seemed to enjoy it. For the May, 1967, issue of the *Critic*, David Russell of Lincoln College wrote a spoofing reproof, to which I made a snorting retort against "animadversions of the Mousquetaire from Mid-Illinois."

[11] Francis L. Utley also performed signal service for the Modern Language Association, especially in a constitutional overhaul that helped to rescue MLA from chaos during the Troubles. That, however, is **his** story, not CEA's history.

[12] The hill of Dala is to Kano what the seven hills of Rome were to Latium. (Oh, what learning is!)

[13] At the Bored meeting on the evening before the main session, Donald Sears gave an account of his stewardship, of the current situation in CEA, and of the proposed new administrative arrangements, which were thereupon formally approved. His report was published in the January, 1968, *CEA Critic*.

[14] The designation "smoker" (apparently associated in some pervasive way with the Loop) was restored for the social hour after the main meeting. Since both were scheduled in the same space, a notice in the November *Critic* reading "SMOKER: Following the open meeting, CEA members and guests are invited to linger in the Skyline Terrace to partake of the cash bar" sounds strangely inhospitable; however, possibly the phrase "and guests" was intended to include at least fuming representatives of the general public who might have dropped by to hear the speeches.

[15] Henry Adams' doubly Presidential address, titled "Mini-Scholarship"— promptly published in the January, 1968, *CEA Critic*—cautioned against "any work of the kind we all may undertake, work done for the sake of a name, a reputation, a pay raise, a promotion," as inhumane: "The work may be small or large . . . It is mini-scholarship when it is undertaken and researched for a lesser goal than illumination of the subject itself."

[16] If you are wondering about Ed Huberman, who once was headlined in the *Critic* (February, 1970) as "A Man for All CEAsons," read on.

[17] Obliquely pertinent is a CEA Chap Book of June, 1968: *Digressions and Indiscretions*, by Richard Leighton Greene. Since at least 1965, through several Editorships including that of Earle Labor, readers of the *CEA Critic* had become familiar with the graceful *vers de société académique* of Greene— who, I might add, was one of the charter "Thirty-Year Members of CEA" named by the Laborite *Critic* in June, 1969.

[18] Not only had a general index been proposed, but an anthology of writings to be selected from the file of CEA journals was originally contemplated. The anthology is still an unfulfilled dream (except for analects on special topics occasionally gleaned for reprinting). I predict that someday someone will wake to its value and find ways and means. A trove of treasures is moldering in what ought not to remain a grave.

[19] Records I have seen do not make sufficiently clear whether there had ever really been a previous RMCEA, apart from a distinct English section when the Rocky Mountain MLA was new. Language about it used by CEA's journal in early post-war years suggests symbiosis rather than parasitism. (I suspect I may have just invented the Eighth Wonder of the Empsonian world.)

[20] The text of Fran Utley's highly **relevant** Presidential address of 1969 can be found in the *CEA Critic* , February, 1970.

[21] The attentive reader is urged to notice my formal usage (not consistently sustained) of the word "Conference" for CEA's New Style yearly meetings beginning in 1970. The term has been in use, though not exclusively, for announcements, programs, and the like, in contradistinction from Old Style "Annual Meeting" or generic "convention." Since the meetings have been renumbered commencing with Notre Dame, reckoned as the first Conference, some (shall we say *conventional?*) means is needed for easy discrimination of previous ones (through 1969) conducted normally though not invariably in December, from the current series still being held each Spring. "Annual Meeting" vs. "Annual Conference" may come to mark the distinction, though accurate *numbering* of the original series is, at best, difficult for several reasons that have previously been explained. Nomenclature is slightly muddied by current use on programs and elsewhere of the phrase "Meeting and Conference" for yearly gatherings under the new dispensation. Meantime, this lax History has taken questionable license to employ "meeting," "convention," "session," "gathering," and so on, virtually (hardly virtuously) ad libitum.

[22] The full quota of fourteen was not always met in subsequent years. The total number of $3,000 awards in four years was fifty.

[23] A 2d. ed., rev., with the same title (including the phrase *Creative Writing*), edited again by Donald A. Sears, was also brought out as a CEA Chap Book in April, 1970. A decade later, Gerald Siegel edited for the College English Association Foundation as its first publication (1980, using the format but not the name of the Chap Books) *The CEA Directory of Writing Programs in the United States and Canada* . Without mention of the 1968 original, he pointed out that his *Directory* differed from that of 1970 in giving "brief listings of programs in various kinds of writing (excluding beginning level composition courses) rather than detailed citations of creative writing curricula alone . . ." Having spent an enormous outlay of my lifetime energies in attempting to teach "technical English" when it was generally deprecated as a mere service course about on a par with surveying and mechanical drawing, I prick up my ears at such signs of new times and regret that I have had but one life to give to the profession.

[24] For the record, they were: Chicago, Florida, Georgia - South Carolina, Greater New York, Indiana, Michigan, Middle Atlantic, New England, North Carolina - Virginia, Ohio, Pennsylvania, Southern Calfornia, South Central, Tennessee, Texas, and Western New York.

[25] I shall defer an account of the Articles of Affiliation that I promulgated for the Association until the next chapter, because though drafted in 1968-69

they were ultimately absorbed into the general constitutional revision of 1970-71.

[26] Maybe it started at that figure (I honestly forget), but I am almost certain it was zero dollars and no cents until December of 1966. I took some pride in never (well, hardly ever) spending the total allotment, in the same way that polite guests do not consume everything on their plate, so as to avoid making the host feel that they have "not had enough to eat."

SAILING TO BYZANTIUM

being

LUSTRUM SEVEN (1970 - 1975)

of

S A N S C U L O T T E

A NONKNICKERBOCKER HISTORY

of the

COLLEGE ENGLISH ASSOCIATION

Donald Everett Morse (1984)

LUSTRUM SEVEN (1970 - 1975)

SAILING TO BYZANTIUM

The College English Association's convention of 1969 at Denver had been something of a triumph in bringing order out of ambient chaos. Nevertheless, from complex, even contrary motives pulling both right and left, many of our elder statespersons were resolved to endure no longer the Troubles that had befallen the host Modern Language Association. Negotiations with the Indiana College English Association (an affiliate several years older than its adoptive parent) had already elicited willingness to co-sponsor a combined national - regional meeting. Both hierarchy and lowerarchy of CEA were consulted, formally and informally. Ah, me of little faith: to my abiding shame, I opposed a split from MLA on the ground that we could not possibly attract sufficient delegates of our own for a worthwhile separated assembly.

Courage, optimism, enthusiasm, and common sense prevailed over such tremors of timidity as mine. As early as its December, 1969, issue, directly below a notice on the front page of the current "Thirtieth CEA Annual Meeting"[1] in Denver, the *Critic* ran an announcement—headed EXTRA! EXTRA!—of a "first Annual Meeting of the National CEA together with one of the CEA regional affiliates," projected four months in the future for April 24-25, 1970, at the University of Notre Dame. Contemporary Relevance and the Teaching of Literature would be the general theme. The March number had as front-page leader "A Letter from the New President" (Edward Huberman) proudly mentioning speakers, topics, and special features, and alerting officers and directors about "an official board meeting extending to portions of both days." The third and fourth pages carried a detailed program of "The College English Association ... Annual Meeting and Conference."[2]

At Notre Dame some two hundred and fifty attendants[3]

gathered on an expansive and handsomely Gothic campus in weather that was universally declared not too hot nor yet too cold, but just right. The delightfully christened University of Notre Dame du Lac had, not long before, become coeducational, and to my intense gratification I observed that numerous young gentlemen and ladies of the Lake were just then engaged on a prolonged kiss-in. (I was reminded of a ukase promulgated many years before at my own university, that "women students shall not sit prone on the campus.") Osculants stretched on greenswards in single or clustered pairs, the four lips of each twosome pressed together under what I apprehended as inviolable rules against parting even for air or refreshments. I tried not to stare rudely, but behind cloister colonnades and magic mullions I peeked and pined. To this moment I kick myself daily for neglecting to ascertain, from a student newspaper or office of information and public relations, the record time of uninterrupted labiation. From direct observation, I know that it smacked more of hours than of minutes.

Besides the dinner speech on Friday night by Darwin Turner (promptly printed in the May, 1970, *CEA Critic*) with its witty exordium followed by a serious inquiry into "The Relevance of College English Today"—at a time when "students declared even the National Students Association to be irrelevant" and when "study of the English language and of literature written in English need not be irrelevant, but some English teachers may make it seem so"—prompt arrivals at the Conference first had been greeted with opening addresses by Harry Barba, Robert Drake, and Terence A. Tobin, and then had gone into divided sections. In the afternoon they had the opportunity (among much else) to listen to Siegfried Mandel's intriguingly titled "Relevance or the Eggs of the Nightingale." On Saturday morning a series of papers by Helen Johnson, Howard Brogan, and others was followed with parallel sessions on "Relevance in Graduate Study" and "Relevance and Vitality in Literature Study in Two-Year Colleges." Clearly, the announced over-all theme of RELEVANCE was never forgotten by program co-chairpersons Edward Huberman (national) and Louis Hasley (regional).[4]

Other more immediate business of the Association was not

forgotten, either. As Regional Coordinator, I was invited to participate in discussion of a proposal that had originated with Managing Editor Earle Labor, to divide the monthly journal (October through June) into two quarterlies. One (October, December, February, April) would emphasize pedagogy, general issues, and in-house including regional news; the other (November, January, March, May) would specialize in "usable criticism" (Labor's own unlabored term): that is, articles that could lead toward penetrating and effective presentation of literature within the classroom. [5]

The consultation was held in a pleasant drawing room behind an Oxford-like façade, where we sat in comfortable furniture and talked to one another freely and easily, without the constraints of a formal conference room. I have neither a memorandum nor a clear memory of all who were present, but the discussants included worthies outside the current administration—among others, Pat Hogan and Sam Workman. Opinion was divided, but for once I was on the right (and winning) side of a debate. I believe everyone agreed that continuance of the name *CEA Critic* would perfectly suit the new literary quarterly. Rival claims, which I shall not attempt to adjudicate, are made for initial suggestion of the name *Forum*; the Earle of Labor remembers lifting the *pat*ent from Hogan. Actually, it had been hovering in the wings since the latter 1940's when, facing the necessity of adopting a new banner for the original *News Letter* in order to establish eligibility for a second-class mailing permit, Executive Secretary - Editor Robert Tyson Fitzhugh called for nominations. Someone sent in "Forum," but in the end "Critic," favored by Editor Emeritus Burges Johnson, was selected. (For a fuller account, review LUSTRUM TWO.)

The now old *CEA Critic* finished out its thirty-second volume (including in that reckoning the first nine years under the name *News Letter*) by issue No. 9 (June, 1970), with Donald A. Sears still listed as Editor and Earle Labor as Managing Editor. Vol. I, No. 1 of the *CEA Forum* appeared in October of that year, and Vol. XXXIII, No. 1 of the new *CEA Critic* in November. Probably because Don Sears was still Executive Director of the Association though never shown on the new masts as Editor, Earle Labor continued to be named in the early issues as Managing Editor. In the *Forum* of December, 1970, and the *Critic* of January, 1971, he at last blossomed out as *de-signo* as well as *de-jure* and *de-facto* Editor of both quarterlies.

It has been argued (by me) that a mistake was made in continuing the numbers of an expired *CEA Critic* for a publication essentially different in both outward form and main editorial content. The format of the CEA Chap Books[6] was borrowed, entailing some difficulty for librarians, and even for common readers, that to a degree could have been obviated by calling the November issue of 1970 *n.s.* Vol. I, No. 1. For the *Forum*, on the other hand, the long-familiar dimensions of nine by twelve inches (now since 1977 somewhat trimmed to "standard letter" size) were continued, though the slightly psychedelic front-page design of the old *Critic's* latter daze was abandoned and the new journal given a more sober facelift. (See illllustrations.)

The most evident innovation in the *CEA Forum* was revival of a practice inaugurated but only briefly continued by Donald A. Sears when he began to edit the *CEA Critic* in January, 1960: the use of photographs. After the elder journal was taken over by Managing Editor Labor at the end of 1967, the paper stock used had grown more and more slickly sized, as if evolving toward a glazed surface better suited than semi-limp quasi-rag paper to photographic reproduction. On the editorial page of the February, 1970, *Critic*, mention was made of President Huberman's new hobby of photography, with the closing admonition: "Bring your camera to Notre Dame, Ed!" Evidently he did, for (without credit lines) two double-column pictures[7] of persons and events there were exhibited, one at the top of the front page, in the first *Forum*. Two more large photos appeared in the next issue, taken by Willa Swanson, who would be named official photographer for the Conferences at Jacksonville (1971) and Boston (1972) and continued to furnish expert pictorial records of later CEA gatherings. The first page of the December *Forum* in 1970 showed an exceedingly smiling Edward Huberman at a meeting of the Greater New York affiliate on November 21, 1970; and page 9, a group of panelists at the same meeting including Donald R. Swanson, who contributed a report of it. Several pictures (both one and two columns in width), taken at Jacksonville by Willa Swanson and by Earle Labor, were given instant exposure in the *Forum* for that same month of April, 1971 (delayed in press "so that members who missed the annual meeting in Jacksonville might learn something about the success of that convention"). Photographs—and, in addition, line drawings and other display matter—continued to be featured in the *CEA Forum* throughout its Laborite period, and beyond. [8] Artwork other than photographs appeared in the new *Critic* occasionally (and for cover decoration), but never so freely as in the *Forum*.

When the bureau of Labor began, in 1968, to reduce the curvaceous front cover of the *Critic* first used in December, 1967 (see illustrations in LUSTRUM SIX), so that the design occupied only the top two-thirds of the two columns at the left instead of the entire front page, use of the lower third of those columns for a leading article or feature had been encouraged (though not compelled). Since the whole left column of the *CEA Forum's* first page normally was preempted for its mast and a list of "Presidents of Regionals," return of the leader to the two right columns, often below a photograph or drawing instead of at the top as in the Sears years, was encouraged (though not compelled). In consequence of the divided editorial intentions of the two new quarterlies, leading articles in the Laborite *Forum* were not primarily literary or critical in tendency, as often in the old *Critic*. Thrice they were accounts of annual Conferences, *ex post facto* or *ex praefacto*; thrice, lists of candidates for elections; once, an Open Letter from the Pennsylvania regional on the question: "What changes would the colleges like to see take place in high school English?"; once, an inquiry into the status of the Ph.D. in two-year colleges.

As a matter of fact, the Earle of Labor treated his first pages with great freedom. Twice, he used the whole right two-thirds of a *Forum* front for a decorated printing of the opening lines of Chaucer's "Prologue," the first time with implicit and the second time with explicit reference to an impending annual convention. The total front page of the October, 1971, issue

CEA FORUM

THE CEA FORUM
An Official Organ of the
College English Assoc., Inc.

Published Bi-Monthly
October through April

founded 1939

THE COLLEGE ENGLISH ASSOCIATION

Editorial Office:
Centenary College of Louisiana
Shreveport, Louisiana 71104

President: Edward Huberman, Rutgers at Newark

Vice Presidents:
William J. Griffin, George Peabody College
Harry M. Campbell, Oklahoma State Univ.

Executive Secretary:
Donald E. Morse, Oakland University
Rochester, Michigan 48063

Treasurer:
James J. Napier,
Newark College of Engineering
Newark, New Jersey 07102

Director of Bureau of Appointments:
Edward Huberman, Rutgers at Newark
38 James St., Newark, N. J. 07102

Editor:
Earle Labor, Centenary College

Regional Coordinator:
Joe D. Thomas, Rice University

Presidents of Regionals

Caribbean: Eugene V. Mohr, University of Puerto
Rico, Rio Piedras Campus

Chicago: Joseph Williams, University of Chicago;
Maurita Willett, University of Illinois at
Chicago Circle, Liaison Officer

Florida: C. P. Lee, Jacksonville University

Georgia-S. C.: Helen A. Johnson, York C., CUNY;
Donald R. Swanson, Upsala College, Liaison
Officer

Greater N. Y.: Helen A. Johnson, York C., CUNY;
Donald R. Swanson, Upsala College, Liaison
Officer

Indiana: Louis Hasley, University of Notre Dame;
Robert A. Miller, Purdue U., Liaison Officer

Michigan: Hugh Schram, Lansing Community C.

Mid-Atlantic: H. Alan Wycherley, U. S. Naval
Academy

New England: Lee E. Holt, American International
College

New York State—Western Branch: Hans Gottschalk,
State University of N. Y., Geneseo

N. C.-Va.: James Davis, Virginia Military Institute

Ohio: Stanley K. Coffman, Jr., Bowling Green
State U.; Robert W. Daniel, Kenyon College, Liaison Officer

Pacific Northwest: Keith Rinehart, Central Washington State College; David H. Stewart,
Idaho State University, Liaison Officer

Penn.: James D. Simmonds, U. of Pittsburgh

Rocky Mountain: Paul T. Bryant, Colorado State
University, Liaison Officer

So. Calif.: Ronald E. Freeman, U.C.L.A.

So. Central: Owen J. Reamer, U. of Southwestern
Louisiana

Tennessee: John W. Warren, Tennessee Tech. U.

Texas: Melvin Mason, Sam Houston State U.

Published at the Saratoga Printing Co., Inc.
Saratoga Springs, New York
Annual subscription $5.00

2nd Class Postage Paid at Saratoga Springs, N.Y.
Copyright © 1971 by the College English Association, Inc.

Whan that Aprille

with his shoures soote
The droghte of March hath perced to the
  roote,
And bathed every veyne in swich licour
Of which vertu engendered is the flour;
Whan Zephirus eek with his sweete breeth
Inspired hath in every holt and heeth
The tendre croppes, and the yonge sonne
Hath in the Ram his halve cours yronne,
And smale foweles maken melodye,
That slepen al the nyght with open ye
(So priketh hem nature in hir corages);
Thanne longen folk to goon on
  pilgrimages . . .

VOL. I – No. 3   **February 1971**

The CEA Forum

THE CEA FORUM
An Official Organ of the
College English Assoc., Inc.

President: William J. Griffin, George Peabody
College for Teachers

Vice Presidents:
Samuel N. Bogorad, University of Vermont
Glenn O. Carey, Eastern Kentucky University

Executive Secretary:
Donald E. Morse, Oakland University
Rochester, Michigan 48063

Treasurer:
Donald R. Swanson, Wright State U.
Dayton, Ohio 45431

Director of Bureau of Appointments:
Edward A. Harris, Lorain County C. C.
1005 N. Abbe Rd., Elyria, Ohio 44035

Coordinator of Regional Affiliates:
Joe D. Thomas, Rice University

Editor:
Earle Labor, Centenary College
Shreveport, Louisiana 71104

PRESIDENTS OF REGIONALS

Caribbean: J. Raban Bilder, U. of Puerto Rico,
Rio Piedras Campus; Eugene V. Mohr, UPR-RP,
Liaison Officer.

Chicago: John E. Price, DePaul U.; Maurita Willett,
U. of Illinois at Chicago Circle, Liaison Officer

CCTE of Texas (Comity Affiliate): James W.
Culp, Texas Tech University

Florida: Ward Hellstrom, University of Florida

Georgia-S. C.: Virginia Meehan, West Georgia C.

Greater N. Y.: Larry Cohen, Middlesex County C.;
Bernard Weinstein, Newark State C., Liaison
Officer

Indiana: William A. Sutton, Ball State U.; Robert
A. Miller, Purdue U., Liaison Officer

Michigan: Edward Sharples, Jr., Wayne State U.;
John H. Metle, Henry Ford Community College,
Liaison Officer

Mid-Atlantic: Nick Aaron Ford, Morgan State C.

New England: Fred E. Steele, Vermont College

N. C.-Va.: Robert Bain, UNC-Chapel Hill

Ohio: Robert W. Daniel, Kenyon College

Pacific Northwest: Paul Allen, Green River C. C.;
Keith Rinehart, Central Washington State C.,
Liaison Officer

Penn.: Roger William Cummins, Bryn Mawr College

Rocky Mt.: Paul T. Bryant, Colorado State U.,
Liaison Officer

South Central: Thomas Meade Harwell, Arkansas
State University

So. Calif.: Samuel I. Bellman, California State
Polytechnic University, Liaison Officer

Tennessee: John B. Tallent, East Tenn. State U.

Texas: John D. Brantley, Trinity University

Upstate New York: T. J. Spencer, Rochester Institute of Technology

West Virginia (Comity Affiliate): Billy Freeland,
Salem College; Margaret P. Goddin, Davis &
Elkins College, Liaison Officer

A New Chapter in *The Book of Snobs*:
The Ph.D. in the Two-Year College

Everyone who has gone through graduate school, and even some who have not, will recognize that there are Ph.D.s and Ph.D.s. There are some like Marjorie Nicolson and Noam Chomsky, and there are some like what's-his-name. Almost everyone who has taught in a two year college will recognize that there are two year colleges and two year colleges—mine and nearly any other, for example. Serious students of snobbery will no doubt recognize that there are snobs and snobs, as well.

Through all the bewildering diversity of Ph.D.s and two year colleges and snobs, however, some constants may be discerned. For example, every snob, as Thackeray observed in his *Book of Snobs*, is someone who "meanly admires mean things." And newly minted Ph.D.s, who do not know—or at least have not shown —whether they are Nicolsons or Chomskys or what's-his-names, face common problems and respond to them in common ways as they begin to teach in two year colleges, both mine and the others.

Take for example one type of the newly minted Ph.D. Call him Crump, after one of Thackeray's University snobs, just to avoid deciding prematurely whether he is to be a Nicolson or a what's-his-name. Crump has taught for a year and a half at Commuter Junior College—long enough to reveal quite a lot about his snobbery, if not his scholarship.

Crump scorns the utilitarian. He doesn't want to teach the regular freshman composition course, although he's experienced as a composition teacher, having worked his way through grad school as a T.A. He's tired of assigning process papers. He's sick of explaining about documentation in research papers. He doesn't think that a Ph.D. should have to face stacks of themes on Saturday morning.

Crump is even less willing to teach sections in technical writing or business writing. The last person he knew who was involved in a business writing course was the brassy blonde who sat in front of him in home room in high school. She went on to secretarial school—Business College, she called it. To do him credit, Crump wouldn't mind taking a section or two of creative writing. He knows of plen-

ty of people who are quite highly regarded in the profession and who teach creative writing. But there's not much demand for creative writing at Commuter Junior College.

So even though as a Ph.D. Crump is somewhat favored in his teaching assignments, he has to teach a lot of freshman composition. Half his course load is devoted to composition classes, almost half his students are composition students, and they take up more than half his time. He lets them know what an imposition this is, though, so that they think twice before taking up any more time than is absolutely necessary.

People who knew Crump in grad school might expect him to be a happier and more effective teacher in his lit. courses than he is in composition. But at Commuter Junior College, at least, he is not.

For his courses, Crump chooses works and writers which interest him—Donne, Blake, and Hopkins, particularly—and in his lectures (he ends up lecturing in almost every class), he tries to explain his interests. But his students, starting so far behind him, cannot follow his explanations of metaphysical imagery and symbolic systems and inscape and instress. They suspect that he chooses confusing works just so that he will have something to explain, and as far as they are concerned, his explanations are nit-picking, arbitrary and irrelevant—really more confusing than the works they are supposed to explain. When his students challenge his choice of texts, Crump answers that they are proper objects of study simply because someone somewhere once thought them worth writing, and someone else then found them worth reading. When his students try to make their own interpretations, based on their own standards of relevance, he insists on the superiority of the views that he favors. After all, he's a Ph.D.

Crump doesn't really understand his problem as a teacher in lit. courses, although some of his students come close to understanding it. The problem is that while Crump pays lip service to the traditional defense of literature—that it is enjoyable and instructive—he really **(Please turn to page 2)**

VOL. III – No. 1

October 1972

between banner and dateline was devoted to a letter from President William J. Griffin pleading for individual action in solicitation of new memberships, the mast and "Presidents of Regionals" being moved to the left-hand column of the second page.

I am fain to mention that "An Open Letter from the PCEA" (April, 1972), alluded to above, was destined to arouse the kind of prolonged thoughtful controversy for which CEA publications had always been known, wherein everyone gains a point and no one really loses. Pennsylvania CEA's Open Letter reflected, albeit rather cautiously, the stance of the New Linguistics and other advanced pedagogical attitudes:

> We wish to see a greater number of students aware that English is a social phenomenon, that it is used by individuals in different ways, that as members of a complex society they must be able to use their language flexibly and creatively....
>
> Likewise, PCEA would like to see more students become aware ... that their use of non-standard English is not a sin or crime ...
>
> ... we would encourage the study of contemporary and popular writers in the high schools, for we are not convinced that the traditional methods of studying traditional writers have been extremely successful in engendering love and understanding of literature in students.
>
> ...Milton, for example, is one of our greatest writers, but we feel that it is possible to live something like a good life without having read Milton....
>
> Thus PCEA believes that the traditional survey courses of English and American literature should be done away with in the high schools.

In a Letter to the Editor dated June 5, 1972, and printed in the October *Forum*, Howard Brogan responded:

> While it is always good to start out where the student is, in his own time and situation, the object must be to

enhance his sense of the significance of his own time and situation by getting him to see it in the perspective of other times and other people, in the light of other ideas than those with which he is already familiar.

. . . .

To me the suggestions of the Pennsylvania Association represent an abnegation of our responsibility as teachers, to our society first of all. But, because humane individuals can be developed only in humane societies, the abnegation will ultimately be stultifying to the development of the individual who is rightly considered to be the center—but would be wrongly considered the circumference—of our concern.

Roger Cummins, who had been President of Pennsylvania CEA when the Open Letter was originally sent to all public and private secondary schools in the state, replied on March 22, 1973 (*Forum*, October, 1973), defending it in even tones against the charge of any intention to "abandon all idea of structure and sense of tradition," but rather pointedly objecting to what he considered an *argumentum ad homines* against "the total membership of PCEA." In a riposte printed in April, 1974, Howard Brogan again supported the importance of traditional studies against "innovation" and "follies . . . largely the spawn of schools of education" which "now have respected scholarly associations encouraging them."

Under Earle Labor, the *Forum* exhibited the kinds of interest and variety—obviously, however, within a somewhat narrowed topical scope—that had characterized the former *Critic* during his Managing Editorship. Minireviews continued along with full reviews, and also short "Book Notes" sometimes grouped under a new heading, *Browsworthy*, over the signature "EL." Former Editor Donald Sears, a late convert to steady use of the journals for reviewing, served as reviewer-in-ordinary. Verse—serious, satirical, light, occasional—was accepted sparingly but with discrimination. Letters to the Editor were used in abundance. National and regional in-house news and announcements were carefully reported to the membership.

One deficiency of the *Forum* was its abandonment of the table-of-contents (afterwards to be revived) that had been added to the old *Critic* in its last year or so, although that useful device was continued in the new *Critic*.

The great variety of substantial articles in Editor Labor's *CEA Forum* can be sampled by title: "Report of the CEA Committee on the Academic Status of Women" and "Recommendations of the National Study of English in the Junior College" (October, 1970); "Professor Scylla and Professor Charybdis" and "A Workshop Approach to Poetry" (December, 1971); [review article] on "The New Texts Dealing with the Structure of Contemporary English" and "They're Ruining My [*scil.*, dirty] Words" (February, 1972); "An Experiment in Grading" and "Kate Millett's Sexless Politics" (April, 1972); "The Teaching of Poetry: A Case for Structure in the Student-Centered Classroom" (December, 1972); "Linguistics and the Literature Major" (April, 1973). Papers and addresses from the annual Conferences were often printed in the *Forum*, and at least as often in the *Critic*.

The *CEA Critic* (New Style) that began to appear in November of 1970 was recognized as a distinguished literary journal from the start, as it has continued to be. If good reporters have a nose for news, Editor Labor had an ear for literary criticism and an unusual sense for its relation to the marketplace of ideas in which teachers of English transact their scholarly business. Members of the Association and other readers learned to open each successive issue with assured anticipation of finding food for thought, meat for meditation, verve in verse, helpful hints, sage suggestions, counsel for the classroom.

My direct connection with the two new quarterlies was limited to support of the karyokinesis of 1970 and to occasional contributions thereafter (much more often to *Forum* than *Critic*). Meantime, of course, I had a whole hand in all regional affairs, as well as a main finger in larger CEActivities through ongoing ex-officio membership, as National Coordinator of Affiliates, on the Executive Committee that steers between conventions and, at them, blends into the larger body of the Bored.

When the College English Association began to gang its own way to a Springtime Conference, the custom of a Regional Reception during MLA at Christmastide, which had been developing for a couple of years as the former Regional Breakfast was being turned into a more general function (see preceding chapter), was continued and regularized. That given at New York eight months after Notre Dame, and also the one at Chicago a twelvemonth later, were announced as Vice-Presidential (1970) or Presidential (1971) parties hosted by William James Griffin.

Let me say that despite differences of temperament and style, I never got on better in any of my endeavors for CEA than with Bill Griffin. He and I harmonized as perfectly as Pat Hogan and I did in other situations. Neither Bill nor certainly I ever felt the slightest competition on or for CEA turf. For the Regional Reception at New York in 1970, I billed myself as "greeter-bouncer" for "Bill Griffin's vicious Vice-Presidential CEA party." (Those who know the verray parfit gentil William James Griffin will smile at that *lucus a non lucendo*, as at the moniker "Wild Bill Griffin" I fixed upon him in other contexts.) At Chicago the next year, through a lucky blunder in the hotel's handling of our preregistration, we were able to obtain (at regular convention rates) adjoining rooms in the posh Tower of the Palmer House, an "exclusive" annex with separate elevator, five-star flunky service, and an arrangement for guests to serve themselves drinks *on the honor system* (!) from well-stocked cabinets in a well-appointed lounge area on each floor.

Announcements of the gathering at Chicago in 1971 indicated that it was not exclusively a Presidential party but was given in cooperation with the Regional Coordinator. In anticipiation of return to New York in 1972, a joint invitation to attendance there was again issued, with a hint that adjoining rooms would once more be sought. Actually, after going back to an efficiency kitchenette of a theatrical hotel on West Fifty-fifth Street, my wife Helen and I found ourselves effectively hosts of the party. Again in 1973, she and I were in charge of the next Regional Reception—with indispensable dispensing of ice by First Veep Glenn Carey, the Kentucky Colonel, who ran it at need to the Palmer House from a hole-in-the-wall dispensary several dark and perilous blocks to the south. (As a recurrent guest of the YMCA Hotel during meetings at Chicago, he knew the route well and was able to traverse it safely by scuttling from one street lamp or lighted store front to another.) Supplies are hard to come by at night in downtown Chicago (unlike Mid-Manhattan) if one does not feel like paying ransom to room service.

An important regional factor was automatically built into the CEA's new Spring conventions as joint undertakings of the national Association with an affiliate (or, in later years, occasionally with more than one). Thus the general Association met with Indiana CEA at Notre Dame (1970), Florida at Jacksonville (1971), New England at Boston (1972), Michigan at Detroit (1973), Pennsylvania at Philadelphia (1974), and Georgia - South Carolina at Atlanta (1975). Normally, part of each annual program is arranged by the host affiliate, which also may conduct a separate business meeting and sometimes other regional activities. The sharing of time has varied considerably in proportions, through the years, and depends partly upon the inclination of the national program chairman (now always the First Vice-President), although some unwritten customs have been gradually developing through experience.

On the afternoon of Friday, April 2, 1971, at Jacksonville, Florida, I tore a leaf out of my own black book and for the sake of delayed April foolery imitated a mock-wedding (reported in the previous chapter) that I had conducted at New York in 1966. By extended correspondence and personal negotiations, meantime, I had persuaded the Conference of College Teachers of English of Texas and the West Virginia Association of College English Teachers to seek—or, at any rate, consent to accept—Comity Affiliation with CEA. In an improbably named Capri-Riviera Room of a sightly outré Thunderbird Motor Inn, which "proved to be an intimate, isolated structure romantically set in the clearing of a grove and bearing the natural appearance of a Green Chapel," not quite solemn nuptials were solemnized. I continue to quote from the society column (nonce edition) of *Texas College English:*

The Business Meeting was [a] blind.... Instead of calling for Old Business, President Edward Huberman stepped forth in sacerdotal robe and intoned: "Up with the bride; let the groom be unconfined!" Beaming Kline A. Nall, of Texas Tech University, and blushing Margaret P. Goddin, of Davis and Elkins College, rose and tripped forward, proxies for their respective regional associations of college English teachers.

"Who giveth these regionals to be joined in Comity Affiliation to the College English Association?" asked the reverend President.

"I do," responded the irreverent National Coordinator of Affiliates. "If anyone knows why for they should not be received, let him keep silent now and forever hold his peace."

Thus, in simple rustic ceremony, the Conference of College Teachers of English of Texas and the West Virginia Association of College English Teachers became the first two Comity Affiliates of CEA, as provided in the new Constitution and Bylaws adopted by a plebiscite of the national membership in early 1971.[9]

I should explain that I helped Bill Griffin in hammering out the "new Constitution and Bylaws" alluded to in the quotation just above, which with subsequent amendments embodied in a recension of 1980 still serves as the Association's fundamental statutes, by protracted exchanges of correspondence mainly during 1970. I can find no documentary evidence that I was formally a member of his committee, though I presume I must have been. In immediately preceding years (with the collaboration of Patrick G. Hogan, Jr.,) I had drawn up formal Articles of Affiliation to define as explicitly as possible the reciprocal relations of the national College English Association and those organizations affiliated, or thereafter to be affiliated, with it. Three relationships were described: Regular Affiliation (the usual regional relation); Special Affiliation (available to groups that "may represent a particular interest or branch of the college-teaching profession not geographically defined");[10] Comity Affiliation ("mutually extended with organizations having aims and interests that complement those of the College English Association"). Throughout, the emphasis in this document was on mutuality and assurance that no affiliate could ever be treated as a captive. The Articles, after repeated redrafting and submission to the existing affiliates and to the national officers and directors, were published in the February, 1969, *CEA Critic* and then, by a two-thirds vote of the membership, became part of the (old) By-Laws. In the new Constitution and Bylaws of 1970-71, with slight further changes, they were officially incorporated as an appendix of the Constitution. *Si monumentum regionale expetis, aspice.*

During this *lustrum*, I continued my practice of not only attending national conventions (CEA and MLA) and regional meetings of CCTE, Texas CEA, and SCCEA (with SCMLA) in my own area, but visiting more distant affiliates as often as time and funds permitted—sometimes offering a "Mark Onest" presentation as well as uttering more inspirational commentary on the state of the Association. I attended the Georgia - South Carolina meeting early in March, 1971, at Georgia Southern College (Statesboro) as dinner speaker. Twenty-five months thereafter, I returned to the always gracious biennial assembly of the Tennessee College English Association, which I had first addressed at Lambuth College on San Jacinto Day six years before. On April 27-28, 1973, at Cumberland College, not far from a Cedars of Lebanon Park and surrounded by lovable Lebanese who seemed all to regard me as a long-lost family friend, I was billed for both "Mark Twain's Wit and Wisdom" and a speech titled "A Long Way, Baby" as my contributions to the general convention theme: Crisis in the Profession.

A serio-comic episode, in which I was involved as National Coordinator early in 1970, erupted first as a sour note at the last CEA convention with MLA, in December of 1969. By-Laws then in force, like all such proper documents, contained a clause providing an orderly procedure in the remote contingency of dissolution of the organization. In the Bored meeting at Denver, one of the directors, Vern Wagner, though not corporeally present, spiritually invoked by proxy that very Article XIII, declaring that the national CEA served no useful purpose:

In the fifteen years that I have been closely associated
with the Michigan College English Association, I have
noted that the national CEA has had no value at all for
us. And it is only in the local (state and regional) organizations that College English Associations do have a
function.

When a new Editor of the South Central College English
Association's *Round Table* invited me to comment on the
Denver convention in the February, 1970, issue, I saw fit to
do so, under the by-line of "An Imperfect Wagnerite," in "An
Argument to Prove that / THE ABOLISHING OF THE
NATIONAL CEA / May, as Things now stand, be attended
with some Inconveniences and perhaps not produce those
many good Effects proposed thereby":

> I am very sensible what a weakness and presumption
> it is to reason against a Vernal humor. It may perhaps
> be neither sane nor prudent to argue against the
> abolishing of our Association; however, whether from the
> affectation of singularity or the perverseness of human
> nature, it so unhappily falls out that I cannot be quite
> of this opinion. I have heard it affirmed for certain, by
> some old CEA-dogs, that the abounding CEA can never
> be drained.
>
> One great advantage proposed by the abolishing of the
> Association is the clear gain of one day in the year, which
> is now entirely lost in meetings, and consequently our
> holidays made the less enjoyable. I hope I shall be
> forgiven a hard word, if I call this a perfect cavil. What
> if we scholars are forced, one day in the year, to travel
> abroad? Where are more appointments and rendezvous
> of gallantry, where so may enticements to pleasure? Are
> not the taverns and coffee-houses open in Chicago or
> New York? Has the vice-squad burnt the topless joints
> of Denver?

From that swift sample, you perceive the tone and intent. The
compelling Argument went on for some three columns, concluding with a (not especially pertinent) Latin quotation from

St. Augustine on the Two Cities, followed by the (not especially pious) exclamation: *Ach, du lieber Augustin!* No more has been heard of any proposed dissolution of the College English Association, Inc.

As has previously been passingly mentioned, the Presidential term of Edward Huberman, instead of being allowed to expire at the close of 1970 (just when the end of calendar years was in process of becoming rather a meaningless date for CEActivities), was—by improvisation, quickly confirmed by constitutional change—extended to the next (Second) Annual Meeting and Conference in the following Spring. Thus, although his actual term in office ran only a little more than three months beyond the normal year, he presided twice, as Refounding Father, over the Association entering its New Era: at both Notre Dame (1970) and Jacksonville (1971). His successor, William James Griffin, was also to serve an extended term in the office of President, actually two successive full-year terms (permissible under both the old By-Laws and the new Constitution). What happened was that Second Vice-President Harry Modean Campbell, who would automatically have risen to First Vice-President in April of 1971, suffered a breakdown of health, necessitating his resignation from office. On recommendation of incoming President Griffin, CEA's directors appointed Howard Oakley Brogan to the First Vice-Presidency for 1971-72. Although Howard Brogan was an eminently suitable potential candidate for the Presidency (which he was later to occupy with distinction), it did not seem to some of us on the Executive Committee that anyone should inherit the highest office of the Association by way of appointment. On that constitutional principle, Bill Griffin was persuaded to accept nomination (leading to assured election) for a second term as President in 1972-73. Consequently, like Ed Huberman before him, he presided at two successive Annual Meetings and Conferences: Boston (1972) and Detroit (1973). Samuel Nathaniel Bogorad, President for 1973-74, presided in Philadelphia (1974); and his successor, Glenn Owaroff Carey, in Atlanta (1975)—with George Mills Harper President-Elect for the coming activity year (1975-76) that would open a new *lustrum* of the College English Association beyond the scope of this self-limiting History.

Not only were there some irregularities during this period in Presidential sequences; there also were frequent (and sometimes disrupting) changes in executive and editorial offices. In 1970 (by the familiar pattern of a "round-numbered" year), after a decade or really eleven years of heavy service in varied functions, Donald Albert Sears asked to be relieved as Executive Director of the Association. Tribute was paid to his achievements in an editorial written by Earle Labor for the December *Forum*:

> Under the capable leadership of Donald Sears, the CEA has achieved a remarkable growth during the Sixties ("The Sears Years," as that decade has been called), more than doubling the national membership and developing a nation-wide cadre of executive officers while at the same time . . . expanding the independent activities of autonomous regional affiliates in keeping with the tru[e] principles of federation. In an age when bureaucracy was accepted as necessary if not always evil, CEA managed somehow to promote successfully the concept of academic personalism: of individual responsibleness and diversity within the larger unity of professional fellowship.
>
> The same decade witnessed corresponding gains in the prestige of CEA publications: e.g., *The CEA Critic* achieved wide recognition as not only a lively organizational newsletter and forum but also as an important journal of usable literary criticism; the CEA chap book series was revitalized with publications on linguistics, myth, folklore, and such vital professional concerns as articulation, the Ph.D., and the future of the humanities; and the complete indexing of the CEA's first thirty years of publications. Perhaps the most outstanding single accomplishment, however, was the establishment and successful management of the CEA - BOMC Writing Fellowship Program . . .
>
> Well done, Don!

The editorial went on to salute the second of a "brace of Dons," who was appearing for the first time in the mast of that December issue:

> Those of us who met Donald Morse at Notre Dame last April were impressed by his vigor and his clear-eyed enthusiasm for CEA's future.... Don Morse epitomizes the fusion of versatility and virtuosity which traditionally distinguished the leadership of CEA.
> Welcome, Don!

With an unaffected effort of effective variation, in place of the style of Executive Director assumed by the retiring Don during the latter part of his tenure, the name of Donald E. Morse was run up on the mast under the off-again-on-again title of Executive Secretary.

When Donald Morse received a sabbatical leave to study once more in Ireland during the academic year 1973-74, as he had done in the Summer preceding his CEAppointment, a colleague at Oakland University, Robert Thomas Eberwein (pronounced with a short initial "ebb" and a long terminal "wean") became Acting Executive Secretary for the interim. Then, when Don Hidalgo Morse duly returned and resumed office in the Fall of 1974, shortly after I in my turn had gone on leave and retired as National Coordinator of Affiliates, Robert Eberwein was appointed in my place.

Jim Napier, who had begun to "understudy" Ed Huberman as Treasurer in 1967 and had succeeded him in that office at the beginning of 1968, resigned at the end of the academic year 1970-71 and was replaced by Donald R. Swanson. After two years of what the *Forum* rightly called "yeoman service" during heavy political, economic, and organizational weather, this other Don (of CEAccounts) submitted his resignation effective July 1, 1973, and was succeeded by Herbert V. Fackler. The new Treasurer was resolved to computerize everything that could be trustingly translated into a cabalistic COBOL. In February, 1974, he rather ominously reported that "dues took three months to get out, not the three weeks of the past ..." By that time I was practically packing for a leave in London, and freeing as fast as feasible my cerebrum of CEA concerns, but I have heard hints that the called-for corrections of the computer came a cropper. The next year, Paula J. Barthel was appointed Treasurer.

Edward Huberman had discontinued his long service as director of the Bureau of Appointments at the end of the academic year 1971-72. In keeping with the Don-for-Don practice in replacement of the chief executive officer, another Ed, Edward A. Harris of Lorain County Community College of Ohio, undertook to direct placement beginning in mid-1972. After less than a year, however, Harris threw up his portfolio at the national meeting in Detroit, persuading the Bored not only to accept his personal resignation but to draft amendments to the Bylaws (accepted at the business meeting on April 13, 1973) that abandoned the whole enterprise, after twenty-eight years of continuous and generally successful operation. I never asked Edward I, but I have wondered whether he was not impelled by this action of a succeeding, and yet not succeeding, Edward II to discontinue his minireviewing for the two journals—as he promptly did, allowing that activity to pass into the hands of a willing John R. Willingham beginning in the Autumn of 1973. None of the protean sometime activities of our Huberman for all CEAsons, who had virtually renewed the Association's life at the turn of the '60's to '70's and virtuously served it in innumerable ways previously and thereafter, now remained his responsibility. [11]

A major editorial change occurred during this period when Earle Labor, who had become Managing Editor of CEA publications about the time when Jim Napier was becoming Treasurer and had risen after three years to Editor (in-chief), carrying out with great imagination and energy the division of the Association's former journal into two different quarterlies, received a Fulbright Lectureship for teaching in Denmark during the academic year 1973-74 (the same period in which Don Morse would be in Ireland). Labor's department head at Centenary College of Louisiana, (Ira) Lee Morgan, accepted the title of Interim Editor. Shortly before, the function of Managing Editor had been revived by the Bored at the

Detroit convention in mid-April of 1973, with appointment of
Steven T. Dhondt of the New York State University College
at Buffalo. [12] The Earle of Labor followed his Fulbright Lectureship of 1973-74 with a Senior Fellowship of the National
Endowment for the Humanities, to work on a biography of
Jack London's ranching years, and though he had intended to
return to his CEA Editorship never actually did so. [13] Steve
Dhondt, who might have been expected to succeed him (since
Lee Morgan clearly desired no permanent appointment) in
the same way Earle Labor had succeeded Don Sears in 1970,
unfortunately ran afoul of the up-or-out academic syndrome,
and withdrew in mid-1974 to an administrative post *in partibus
veneficarum* (Salem, Massachusetts), whence he bade CEA
farewell with assurances that he had received no sinecure at
the Custom-House. Morgan, with the help of his departmental
staff, carried on publications through another academic year,
but at the end of 1974 both he and Labor (who of course was
not then in technically active editorial service, though he had
been helping to guide publication by air mail) tendered their
resignations to Association President Glenn Carey. In mid-1975,
as Paula Barthel was becoming Treasurer, Robert A. Miller,
a former director of the College English Association and President of the Indiana CEA at the time of the Notre Dame convention, was appointed Editor, with Thomas L. Kent as
Managing Editor. John Willingham, who had been writing
minireviews for the past two years, receiving a title revived
for him from the old *CEA Critic* of many *lustra* before, was
entered on the mast of Lee Morgan's last *Critic* (May, 1975)
as Book Review Editor. As the final *lustrum* to be traversed
by this true and faithful History of the years 1938 to 1975 drew
to an end, no member of the old guard remained in executive
or editorial charge of CEA; of the middle guard, only—but
most fortunately—the stalwart Executive Secretary Donald
Everett Morse, who on April 18, 1974, had been appointed
to a second three-year term by the directors at Philadelphia;
and of the recent guard, only National Coordinator of Affiliates
Robert Eberwein. [14]

Although no formal or informal division of duties was publicly
stated, I think it is safe to conclude from internal evidence

that during Earle Labor's absence Lee Morgan took close (not total) supervision of the *Critic*, allowing Steven Dhondt (until Steve himself departed) pretty much a free hand in the *Forum*. Editorial policy was not changed greatly in either quarterly. The *Critic* maintained a steady, one might almost say staid, balance of articles, poems, and reviews (including but of assurance not limited to minireviews). The custom of an occasional Special Number was continued. Shortly before his leave-of-absence, for instance, Earle Labor had published in May, 1973, what amounted to a Shakespeare issue (though not explicitly so designated); in January, 1974, the Interim Editor published a SPECIAL ISSUE—Fitzgerald Hemingway Faulkner; and in May, 1975 (his final *Critic*), another SPECIAL ISSUE: Women in Literature and Criticism.

Content in the *Forum* was not greatly different from what it presumably would have remained under an actively continuing bureau of Labor. Just the same, the journal now had a new look and "feel." Verse, mainly light and almost always delightful, became more abundant. Although Steven Dhondt somewhat sparingly continued use of photographs, he showed a penchant for line drawings. [15] He commissioned individual front covers for the four *CEA Forums* I attribute to him (October and December, 1973; February and April, 1974), three of them drawn in ink or in one instance charcoal, signed by Suzanne (Alexander). The fourth is an unusual, foreshortened photograph (from above) credited to Marcia Yules of seven academic types, with clasped hands, ringing a British dartboard (see illustration). Dhondt's most ambitious drawing was a centerfold in the December, 1973, *Forum*, also by Suzanne Alexander, labeled *une génération perdue*—a montage of "notable writers" along with "a few CEA stalwarts" and Father Christmas. Apparently no one claimed the offered prize of free 1974 convention registration and one night at the official Philadelphia hostelry, since the key printed in the April issue gave no hint that it had been discovered by any reader. I suspect that the difficulty was that a strange figure, cheek-by-jowl with an easily recognizable Donald Morse, was preposterously identified in the key to be "Joe Thomas (CEA Coordinator of Affiliates)." The imputed likeness was a libel.

the
cea
fORUM

of the college english association

news & views

volume 4 number 1　　　october 1973

the
CEA
FORUM

English
For All Americans:
College Teaching
Today and Tomorrow

volume 4 number 3   february 1974

CEA Board of Directors Meeting
Atlanta, 1975
Clockwise from top: H. Alan
Wycherley; Robert Eberwein;
George Harper; Samuel Bogorad;
Lee Morgan; Alan Youel.

CEA Conventions

Clockwise from below: Joe D. Thomas as "Mark Onest" and Darwin Turner—*Notre Dame, 1970*; Keynote Address audience—*Atlanta, 1975*; John Willingham, Richard Loughlin, Gerald Garmon, and Edward Huberman—*Altanta, 1975*; Helen A. Johnson and Richard Loughlin—*Florida, 1971*.

A notable innovation that I credit to Dhondt, among other reasons because the accompanying drawing of a rope-bound, prone scholar precariously balancing a typewriter on his head looked a good deal less like Lee Morgan than Steven Dhondt, was headed (*sic*): **"OUT OF MY HEAD** / Edsel Littlefaith." Although for some of us it roused *déjà-vu* reverberations of the stillborn **Gazetteer** column attempted by Allan Lefcowitz in the preceding decade (see LUSTRUM SIX), it was very different from his farrago, for "Out of My Head" consisted in each issue of a single personal literary essay. Another hopeful innovation that came to nothing because of Steve's departure from editorial service, or Lee's if the idea actually originated with Morgan, was a column headed **CEA Bookies**—consisting of brief notices of books by Association members—that appeared in a few of their later *Forums* and then was no more CEAn.

One of the casualties of the cabined, cribbed, confined programs of the College English Association's last years with MLA had been discontinuance of a formally stated theme or topic for each meeting. That custom was revived when CEA instituted its separate two-day (later to be even more extended) Spring convention, and continues to the present. As has been remarked, the theme at Notre Dame (April 24-25, 1970) was Contemporary Relevance and the Teaching of Literature. At Jacksonville (April 2-3, 1971) it was Cultural Contexts of English Studies; at Boston (April 28-29, 1972), A Look into the Future of College English; at Detroit (April 13-14, 1973), Teaching College English: The Uses of the Past, Present, and Future; at Philadelphia (April 19-20, 1974), English for *All* Americans: College Teaching Today and Tomorrow; at Atlanta (April 10[*sic*]-12, 1975), "The Past Instructs . . . the Future Invites": Teaching English 1975.[16] Through early custom, with somewhat contingent confirmation in the Bylaws, the Conference programs came to be developed by the national First Vice-President, normally in association with a regional program chairman designated by the sponsoring affiliate.[17] Although the specified themes always are treated more like a caravansary then a procrustean bed, the meetings have been generally characterized by a sense of intention and direction. Perhaps I can suggest this quality by quoting from the opening paragraphs of the last of Quidnunc Passim's occasional reports of CEA's conclaves:

> If the College English Association has ever owed a debt to the minority users of the English language in America, that debt was satisfied in full and with interest in the fifth annual [Meeting] and Conference (n.s.) held . . . at Philadelphia on April 19-20, 1974, with the theme of English for *All* Americans. Although one session was teasingly titled "English and the Majority," more than half were devoted to topics ranging from "English and Ethnic Writing" to "English and the Convict." If the report of the CEA Commission on "Racist and Sexist Abuses in Language" and a separate session on "English and Sexism" are included, the balance was even more heavily tipped.
>
> Almost no minority constituency was forgotten. Vigorous at eighty-six, the distinguished Emeritus Professor of Duke University, Allan H. Gilbert, came to the podium to deplore such patronizing epithets as Senior Citizen . . . Some particular topics from various sessions will give an idea of the range of interests in this 1974 Conference of CEA: "Now That We're Liberated, What Do We Do?". . .; "College English and Native Alaskans" . . .; "What Every English Teacher Should Know about Black Studies" . . .; "Teaching Narrative Skills to Drug Addicts" . . .; "Creative Writing in Prison" . . .; "Literature and the Gay Student" . . .

Another general quality of the new CEA Conferences— one that has become a leitmotif making them especially stimulative—can also be suggested by Quidnunc Passim's report on the Detroit convention:

> The keynote of the meeting on its intellectual side was planned controversy, with respondents set against (or upon) the principal speakers and panelists. The note was

sounded instantly when Norman Holland's opening address on "The Literary Experience, Teaching, and Curriculum Reform" was subjected to anti-Freudian analysis by Ann Berthoff, with lively riposte by the speaker and sustained discussion back and forth at head table and from the floor. On Saturday morning, Joyce Carol Oates, as designated Panel Discussant, made a sincere effort to steal the show from panelists Daniel Marder and Paul Bryant on "The Interdisciplinary Programs." . . . So searching were the debates, and so loud the sound of revelry by day, that at closing time delegates were observed sneaking into—rather than, as customary, out of—the three rooms in session.

Sometimes whimsy took over. In planning the Detroit meeting, Sam Bogorad inserted catchy rhetorical questions into the headings for most sessions: "Language and Composition: We Still Speak and Write, Don't We?"; "Literature: We Still Read, Don't We?"; "Media: We Still Look and Listen, Don't We?"; "Collective Bargaining: We Did (Didn't) Do It and We're Glad (Sorry), Aren't We?"; and so on. In his Presidential address at the convention banquet, Bill Griffin wittily trumped the trick, devoting his "brief valedictory remarks" to "The College English Association: We Still Need It, Don't We?"

By general consensus, during CEA's first *lustrum* of independent Meetings and Conferences, the most successful was that at Boston[18] in 1972, presided over by President Griffin in his first term and planned almost wholly by Howard Brogan of the University of Massachusetts (Amherst) for both the national and the regional sponsorship. It was specially commemorated by a CEA Chap Book distributed in November, 1972, *The Future of College English: Selected Papers from the Thirty-Third Annual Meeting of The College English Association, Inc.*, for which William Griffin was able to arrange cooperative publication with the *Peabody Journal of Education* under copyright of his George Peabody College for Teachers. Eleven excellent presentations were chosen to show how the Boston program had looked into such aspects of the future of college English as collective bargaining, "grammaticality," psychoanalytic criticism, African literature in English, "Accountability in the Two-Year College," and proposals for a teaching doctorate and for "greening the undergraduate curriculum in English."

As the *lustrum* of 1970-75 drew toward its close, an important action was taken in 1975 at Atlanta [19] in connection with a hefty increase of dues from eight to twelve dollars. An idea that had long been skulking about (though repeatedly chased away by officers and directors fearful it might gobble national income) for combined, but non-obligatory, national and regional membership was finally adopted in the form of reduced dues for persons holding membership in one of the CEAffiliates. The advantage of this plan, mistakenly suspected of being costly to the central treasury, is that it is the best single method, by far, of recruiting new members for the College English Association. The moment when regional CEAers (whose large aggregate number is a true legend, if not quite legion) have their wallet or checkbook out to pay local dues is the time when they are most open to act upon any half-resolve they may have been meditating to become national communicants. Membership committees always find themselves frustrated by the low rate of return from solicitations by mail. An enthusiastic and well-informed representative in attendance at every regional meeting (someone belonging to the affiliate can be drafted to act) will do more of promotion and of persuasion than all your junk mail can.

At Philadelphia on April 19, 1974, looking forward to a semester's leave-of-absence from academic duty and to four blissful months in the fairyland of London, I uttered my farewells to the national College English Association in convention assembled:

> ... I spoke just now with affection and admiration for Max Goldberg ... I cannot name all the others whose example and support have meant much to me at [my] lowerarchy end of the CEA hierarchy. I will mention only the late lamented Fran Utley ...; Ed Huberman, whose faith in a separate annual convention carried us in one giant leap from unhealthy parasitism upon MLA to our

own flourishing condition of today; and Wild Bill Griffin of Tennessee, who like Ed Huberman accepted the burden of the Presidency for a double term, and among many other services gave us our new Constitution and Bylaws. Those here present whom I do not name know what our relationship has been, and have my assurance that it shall not be forgotten.

And, now, I mount my horse and gallop off in two directions: toward the Western sunset in Texas; and then, after ... Commencement ... of Rice University, eastward-ho! to the still sceptered isle of Great Britain.

I was encouraged to speak of the Association's "flourishing condition" by the proximate return of our doughty Don Hidalgo Morse of La Mancha mustachios to the bridge of the Executive Secretaryship *CEA* , where he had kept a steady course beginning late in 1970 and where he now agreed to continue for another three years. If I had known that both the absent Earle Labor and his surrogate Lee Morgan would presently tender their resignations, and that the young, vigorous, personable, imaginative, innovative Steve Dhondt was about to depart our company, I might have been more hesitant. It gives furiously to think when one speculates what the future of our CEA publications might have been if Steve could have become heir, as he apparently was, to his former teacher and noble patron, the Earle of Labor. The next Editor after the Interim period carried, unknown, the seeds of a fatal malady that would soon cut short his career, forcing a willing but overburdened Donald Morse, approaching the end of his final term as Executive Secretary, to take on also a temporary Editorship. Well, that is the way of CEA: we survive to thrive.

Notwithstanding that preaching is not my wont, I wish to conclude with a kind of lay sermon. I could name dozens of persons yet living who once served the College English Association almost with their heart's blood, but of whom today it would be near euphemism to say that they are forgotten. Their names have been drowned at CEA: no one asks whether they are still alive, for almost no one remains aware that they once lived, and breathed, and had a presence among us. Yet they were faithful bearers of our standard, vexillaries ofttimes left vexed by our very unawareness. What happened? Some were defeated for election to Second Vice-President, though presumptively then among the very best of our company. Some passed through a term as director and afterward were never tapped for any other office or special service. Some worked long and valiantly as authors for our periodicals, or as members of our committees, or as attendant lords and ladies and occasional readers of papers at our meetings. Some loyally spread the national gospel and proselyted in the provinces, yet never were called from outer darkness to the inner light. I know that everyone cannot be a winner, but just the same to allow spoilage in our storage bins of talent seems appalling. It is not the individual who may lose, for such dedicated academicians more often than not go on to other rewarding, useful endeavor in parts less faithless.

I will tell you an inside story. When CEA arranged to meet at Houston in 1982, I was, first, officially instructed to plan a meeting and self-perpetuating organization of Old Timers; and, afterwards, officially notified that the commitment had been canceled. That is symptomatic of the casual way in which our Association has neglected the bonds of continuity—but, I hopefully add, need not continue to do so. [20] Gentles, as my last word I say unto you: Go ye hereafter and act otherwise! If not, the deCEAsed life lost might be your own.

(Here endeth the reading of LUSTRUM SEVEN—
and of *Sansculotte*.)

Notae pedales for

LUSTRUM SEVEN

[1] There were meetings in 1938, 1939, 1940, 1941, 1943, 1945, and yearly thereafter—a total of thirty through 1969, to be sure, if not altogether annual.

[2] As was mentioned in a footnote of the preceding chapter, the term "Conference," employed generally though not with complete consistency, is a useful device for instantly discriminating conventions of the new series beginning at Notre Dame (1970) from the original series beginning at New York (1938), followed by New Orleans (1939), and terminating at Denver (1969).

[3] Registrations showed approximately equal division between regional and visiting national delegates. Astoundingly, nearly all attendants swamped the dining room assigned for the official banquet and overflowed into another room that was opened at the last minute. After dinner they regrouped in the first, for a full program consisting of Darwin T. Turner's salso-serious address, a re-screening by Charles Linck of the Waugh film *The Scarlet Woman* that he had shown at the Denver convention in December, 1969, and "A Visit from Saint Mark [Onest]."

[4] In the May, 1970, *CEA Critic*, Paul Schlueter, then of the Indiana as well as the national Association, gave an excellent account—both informative and critical—of this First Annual Meeting and Conference that could serve as a model for yearly reports in the *Forum*. As Historian, I have wished that I could lay my hands on a regular such report in the old *Critic* and *News Letter* before it going far back beyond 1970—to the closing years of the 1930's. I will quote, not quite but almost at random, two successive paragraphs from Schlueter's "Thoughts on CEA's Notre Dame Meeting":

> Perhaps the chief reason for the conference's success was the presence on the program of both traditionally-minded, established scholars concerned primarily with the exchange of ideas, and radically-minded, usually younger, teachers concerned primarily with arousing the study of literature from its torpor and into the fray for ethnic studies, women's rights, and political dedication. Certainly among the foremost addresses by the former category were those by Siegfried Mandel and Howard Brogan; Mandel demonstrated brilliantly the perpetual merit of a tradition in his address "Relevance or the Eggs of the Nightingale," and Brogan, with wry humor, showed the parallel between the youthful Romantics and today's radicals in his paper.
>
> Two addresses by black scholars were among the most exciting and well-received in the conference. Darwin Turner ranged freely and eloquently over the entire discipline of English in his banquet address, concluding with some eminently practical questions for improvement of the English curriculum; and Helen Johnson, by extensive quotation and frequent citation of author and title, provided a rich exposure to the themes and values found in Afro-American literature.

[5] If anyone asks how quarterlies (technically trimestrial publications) can be issued every second month, I answer that it was part of the thaumaturgy of Notre Dame du Lac, as Excalibur was of another magic lake.

[6] Although CEA Chap Books were to become less frequent, they were by no means extinct. Besides Don Sears' revised *Directory of Creative Writing Programs in the United States and Canada* (April, 1970) that was virtually simultaneous with the Great Mitosis of Journals, a Chap Book containing Kathleen Raine's *On the Mythological* and a *Selected Bibliography of Myth in Literature* by James A. S. McPeek had been issued six months before (October, 1969). An impressive twelve were published in the whole 1960's, but radically fewer thereafter.

[7] Don Sears had used only one-column pictures, or smaller, in 1960 and 1961.

[8] Also, I must mention a remarkable triptych, occupying pages 6, 7, and 8 of the final *CEA Critic* (Old Style) in June, 1970: "Shakespeare's English History Plays Genealogical Table," put together with infinite care by Donald V. Mehus, accompanied with a full explanation by the compiler on page 9. The chart deserves to be kept perpetually in print as a "separate," as it was for a while (at 50¢ and then 75¢) after the original publication. It exemplifies the kind of imaginative and valuable ancillary service that can be, and ought to be, performed from time to time by journals like ours.

[9] As historical note, I will add that CCTE remains faithful to CEA, and was a main sponsor for the Thirteenth Meeting and Conference, at Houston, in April of 1982. On the other hand, as Regional Coordinator I had some difficulty from the start in maintaining good contact with the West Virginia Association. My successors have long since dropped it from their listings, as the *Forum* finally did after continuing the name of the same President for several years. I seem to remember that someone once remarked you can't win 'em all; I also hear (with dism a y) that upwards of a third of all American marriages nowadays become je-June and end in divorce.

[10] The Society for the Study of Multi-Ethnic Literatures of the United States (MELUS), admitted to Comity Affiliation in 1983, perhaps could have joined the fold as a Special Affiliate. . . . *Ouaestio difficilis.*

No society has ever yet applied for Special Affiliation. Still, CEA's reach should exceed her grasp: *Manus longa* . . .

[11] In the October, 1973, *CEA Forum* all stations on the masthead between the listings of national President and Vice-Presidents and of the regional Presidents were filled by new names: Eberwein, Fackler, Morgan, and Dhondt. (See text immediately following for the latter two.) For some reason, no Coordinator of Affiliates was named, and of course no director

of the defunct Bureau of Appointments. President Samuel Bogorad's situation does not, in retrospect, strike me as entirely enviable, yet he carried his responsibilites with panache and without disaster.

[12] Beginning with the second issue of the new *CEA Critic*, Joan Girlinghouse at Centenary College had been shown on its mast as Editorial Assistant, but her name disappeared after the May issue of 1972, perhaps creating the vacuum into which Steven Dhondt was drawn as Managing Editor a year later. However, in a valedictory "From the Editor" at the end of his last *Critic* (May, 1975), Lee Morgan thanked "Mrs. Ruby George, our editorial assistant, without whose expert work we could not have carried out our duties." Since Mrs. George's name had never appeared on the mast, I cannot estimate how early her service began. She was given explicit credit for compiling the annual index for both the *Forum* in April, 1974, and the *Critic* of the next month.

[13] Earle Gene Labor was not lost at CEA, for he was elected to a two-year term as Vice-President in 1976, became President for 1978-79, and presided at the Tenth Annual Meeting and Conference of 1979 at Savannah, Georgia, where a prolegomenon for this tardy History (which M'Lud of Labor has encouraged at all stages) was presented on the evening of Thursday, March 22.

[14] For the record, I ought to mention that the publications office remained at Saratoga Springs, New York (where Don Sears had taken it when he migrated to Skidmore College in 1962), to the end of the academic year 1971-72, and then was rather belatedly removed to Shreveport, Louisiana. In 1975, Editors Miller and Kent took it to their Department of English at Purdue University in West Lafayette, Indiana.

[15] The *CEA Forum* for October, 1974, after Dhondt's name had been lowered from the mast and Lee Morgan was totally in charge, included a double page of photographs taken by Willa Swanson of personages at the Philadelphia convention in the preceding Spring—including Steven Dhondt himself dapper in turtleneck sweater, blazer, and striped trousers reading a book under a formal hotel plant. (Morgan also used drawings for two full front covers in *Forums* of his sole editing.)

Although I am attributing editorial charge of the *CEA Critic* in the Interim period largely to Morgan, Dhondt evidently was by no means excluded. I detected his hand, for instance, on the cover of the January and March, 1974, issues. The *Critic* had been using a squarish reproduction of an old woodcut showing four scribes at work in a medieval scriptorium (the pre-Gutenberg equivalent of the printshop). Some sly artist imitated the picture in close detail, but with substitution of portraits above the collar of four current CEA-worthies, among them incumbent President Sam Bogorad, Steve Dhondt, and Lee Morgan, with a fourth figure possibly intended for either Robert Eberwein or Herbert Fackler. (See illustrations at end of chapter.)

[16] For the convention in Atlanta, First Veep George M. Harper, while involved in a Florida State University program abroad, was assisted as national planner by Fred L. Standley, his colleague at FSU.

[17] As was indicated earlier in the chapter, the amount of involvement of the affiliates in planning the program, and consequently the division of time between national and regional participation, has varied considerably. The necessary rigidities of larger organizations have, happily, been evitable: CEArrangements are negotiable.

[18] The meeting originally was planned for a storied Wentworth-by-the-Sea, to take place in early May just before the hotel staff normally arrived for the late Spring and Summer "season." Apparently, as things turned out, the idea of receiving academic guests in numbers without staff taxed the ingenuity of the proprietors. Under the rubric MARK YOUR CALENDAR! the October, 1971, *Forum* reported: "Thanks to the resourcefulness of Executive Secretary Don Morse, the Spring 1972 National Meeting of CEA has been moved from Portsmouth, N.H., to the famous Parker House in Boston. . . . The dates are April 28-29." The Parker House proved to be a trifle short of linens, but—as I took occasion to remark with pleasure—in the hotel's venerable restaurants delicious Parker House rolls were served without the din of rock.

[19] No longer an officer of CEA, or even present for the Atlanta convention, I played no part in an action that I would have supported wholeheartedly. I had felt that my urging of some method for offering combined national and regional dues had been falling on stony ground, but somehow the seeds seemed to sprout in Dixie land.

An unplanned event of the formal dinner on April 11 that I also regret missing was the loss of his platform manuscript by the announced main speaker (a former ambassador to the United Nations), who by report was able to think of so little to say *ex tempore* that, in effect, Glenn Carey's Presidential address served as *pièce de résistance* of the banquet.

[20] A development in very recent years does give me hope. The College English Association, having designated Honorary Life Memberships very sparingly in the past, has devised a wider range of honors with which to award kudos to those who have deserved her thanks by signal service of various kinds and degrees.

Less cheerily, I have to confirm that a pet project of mine for a consultative *witenagemot* of elder if not wiser statespersons has been repeatedly spurned and, I fear, kicked clean off the premises. The nearest approach has been an occasional social hour for veterans during the annual Conference, or one unsucccessfully attempted gatherum-somnium of former Presidents.

The
CEA
Critic

An Official Journal of the College English Association
founded 1939

VOL. XXXV - No. 3   **March 1973**

The CEA Critic

An Official Journal of the College English Association
founded 1939

— SPECIAL ISSUE —
Fitzgerald Hemingway Faulkner

featuring
Carlos Baker
Edwin Moses
Glenn O. Carey

VOL. XXXVI - No. 2   **January 1974**

APPENDIX A

Yearly Meetings (well, almost) *of College English Association, 1938 - 1975*
(held in December unless otherwise indicated in parentheses)

YEAR	CITY	YEAR	CITY
1938:	New York	1958:	New York
1939:	New Orleans	1959:	Chicago
1940:	Boston	1960:	Philadelphia
1941:	Indianapolis	1961:	Chicago
1943 (January):	New York	1962:	Washington (DC)
		1963:	Chicago
1945:	Chicago	1964:	New York
1946:	Washington (DC)	1965:	Chicago
1947:	Detroit	1966:	New York
1948:	New York	1967:	Chicago
1949 (September):	(Leland) Stanford (CA)	1968:	New York
		1969:	Denver
1950:	New York		
1951:	Detroit	1970 (April):	Notre Dame
1952:	Boston	1971 (April):	Jacksonville (FL)
1953:	Chicago	1972 (April):	Boston
1954:	New York	1973 (April):	Detroit
1955:	Chicago	1974 (April):	Philadelphia
1956:	Washington (DC)	1975 (April):	Atlanta
1957 (September):	Madison (WI)		

LE   Organizational meeting: 1938.
GE   Ancien régime: 1939 - 1969.
ND   Nouveau régime: 1970 ad infinitum.

APPENDIX B

Presidents of College English Association, 1938 - 1975

For the system used to designate year or years of tenure,
see LUSTRUM TWO, fn. 22.

1938-39:	Robert Malcolm Gay (President *pro tem.*)
1940:	William Clyde DeVane
1941:	Norman Foerster
1942(-43):	Howard Foster Lowry
1943:	Henry Seidel Canby
1944:	Henry Seidel Canby
1945:	Mark Van Doren
1946:	Mark Van Doren
1947:	Odell Shepard
1948:	Theodore Spencer
1949:	Gordon Keith Chalmers
1950:	Robert Tyson Fitzhugh
1951:	Robert Tyson Fitzhugh
1952:	Ernest Erwin Leisy
1953:	William Louser Werner
1954:	William Louser Werner
1955:	Kathrine Koller
1956:	(George) Bruce Dearing
1957:	Harry Redcay Warfel

1958:	Henry Whittington Sams
1959:	John Ciardi
1960:	Donald Jacob Lloyd
1961:	Harry Thorton Moore
1962:	John Waldron Ball
1963:	Charles Marston Clark
1964:	Elisabeth Wintersteen Schneider
1965:	Muriel Joy Hughes
1966:	Allan Hugh MacLaine
1967:	Henry Hitch Adams
1968:	Henry Hitch Adams
1969:	Francis Lee Utley

1969-70:	Edward Huberman
1970-71:	Edward Huberman
1971-72:	William James Griffin
1972-73:	William James Griffin
1973-74:	Samuel Nathaniel Bogorad
1974-75:	Glenn Owaroff Carey
(1975-76:	George Mills Harper)